W9-DCX-091

Literacy as Snake Oil

Colin Lankshear, Michele Knobel,
Chris Bigum, and Michael Peters
General Editors

Vol. 1

PETER LANG
New York • Washington, D.C./Baltimore • Bern
Frankfurt am Main • Berlin • Brussels • Vienna • Oxford

Literacy as Snake Oil

Beyond the Quick Fix

REVISED EDITION

EDITED BY
Joanne Larson

PETER LANG
New York • Washington, D.C./Baltimore • Bern
Frankfurt am Main • Berlin • Brussels • Vienna • Oxford

The **Library of Congress has catalogued the first edition as follows:**

Literacy as snake oil: beyond the quick fix /
edited by Joanne Larson—revised edition.
p. cm. — (New literacies and digital epistemologies; vol. 1)
Includes bibliographical references and index.
1. Literacy programs—United States. I. Larson, Joanne. II. Series.
LC151 .L4815   372.6'0973—dc21   00-067151
ISBN 978-0-8204-5021-6 (first edition)
ISBN 978-0-8204-9543-9 (revised edition)
ISSN 1523-9543

Die Deutsche Bibliothek-CIP-Einheitsaufnahme

Literacy as snake oil: beyond the quick fix / ed. by: Joanne Larson.
–New York; Washington, D.C./Baltimore; Bern;
Frankfurt am Main; Berlin; Brussels; Vienna; Oxford: Lang.
(New literacies and digital epistemologies; Vol. 1)
ISBN 0978-0-8204-9543-9

Cover art courtesy of Strong Museum, Rochester, New York © 2001
Cover design by Lisa Dillon

The paper in this book meets the guidelines for permanence and durability
of the Committee on Production Guidelines for Book Longevity
of the Council of Library Resources.

© 2007 Peter Lang Publishing, Inc., New York
29 Broadway, 18th floor, New York, NY 10006
www.peterlang.com

All rights reserved.
Reprint or reproduction, even partially, in all forms such as microfilm,
xerography, microfiche, microcard, and offset strictly prohibited.

Printed in the United States of America

Table OF Contents

Series Editors' Foreword

COLIN LANKSHEAR, MICHELE KNOBEL, AND MICHAEL PETERS

Educators around the world are struggling to understand and develop effective and principled responses to deep and far-reaching social, economic, cultural, political, and technological changes that have been developing since the 1950s. This series hopes to contribute to this struggle by addressing two manifestations of these changes that go to the very heart of educational work.

The first is the emergence of diverse new literacies embedded in evolving and emerging social practices associated with contemporary change. Many, but by no means *all* of these new literacies, are mediated by new electronic information and communications technologies. Others—such as those addressed in the present volume—are responses to media-fueled public perceptions that schools are finding it increasingly difficult to ensure literacy for all at the precise historical moment when the information revolution, a diminished welfare state, and an emerging knowledge economy are upping the ante for literacy. Within this context innumerable commodified and packaged "literacies" have appeared on the educational quick-fix market.

The second focus of the series is on digital epistemologies. This is the idea that contemporary changes are generating new kinds of phenomena to be known and understood, as well as calling for new conceptions of knowledge, new approaches to knowing, and a new balance between different kinds of knowledge. Schools and other formal education institutions often seem out of step with trends occurring beyond schools. This does not mean that formal institutions are educating inappropriately.

It does, however, mean that there are issues to be identified, clarified, scrutinized and responded to by parties involved in educational endeavor.

The series aims to promote awareness of such issues associated with contemporary change within mainstream educational thinking and to help encourage appropriate and principled responses in educational theory and practice. The series seeks to challenge familiar ways of thinking and acting in education, and provide a forum for exploring innovative, unusual, and risky ideas and perspectives in the areas of new literacies and digital epistemologies.

Literacy as Snake Oil was the first book published in the series. Fittingly, it is also the first book in the series to be republished as a second edition. This new edition has been substantially revised and enlarged, not merely updated. Three new chapters have been added to strengthen the book's response to current literacy policy directions and emphases. Chapters brought forward from the original edition have been substantially revamped in accordance with the working premise of the volume that since the first edition was published "things have gotten much worse" in literacy education, notably within the United States.

The original edition explored the contemporary fetish for packaged literacy materials as a strategy for pursuing acceptable levels of learning outcomes in a milieu of standards-based accountability. This new edition does likewise, but also responds critically to new circumstances associated with the *No Child Left Behind Act* and with associated initiatives like "Reading First." These include policies that mandate documentation of "annual yearly progress" relative to mandated standardized testing at all grade levels, with schools being liable to loss of funding if a stipulated rise in scores is not met. They also include the emergence of a more aggressive approach on the part of education administrations and businesses toward packaged "fixes" for student performance problems on standardized tests.

As with the first edition, this book assembles a powerful team of literacy scholars ideally placed to develop an active, critical stance in exposing the consequences of commodified literacy on educational practice. One of the book's key strengths is that it moves beyond critique as merely a form of oppositional practice to intensified commodification of literacy. It also advances a wide range of constructive and useful ideas and experiences that will be of much interest to teacher educators' concerns with teaching what is known about literacy as socio cultural practice within contexts of intensifying standardization, surveillance and systems-defined accountability.

Acknowledgments

This book would not have been possible without the help of several dedicated people. I am indebted to Colin Lankshear and Michele Knobel for entrusting me with this project and for considering it worth a second edition, and to Christopher Myers at Lang for asking me to do it. I want to thank the distinguished scholars who contributed their insights to this volume and for taking the time to update their chapters. I am grateful to the new authors who were willing to add to the conversation begun in the first edition. All of the work in this volume helps to keep us mindful of the problems we face and of battles ahead. I owe a great deal of gratitude to the many students and colleagues who gave me wonderful feedback about the first edition; it all helped me to think about what we needed to say in this volume. Finally and always, I want to thank my husband, Morris Smith, for his enduring love and support and my three children, Anna, Eric, and Marcus, for always reminding me why this work is important.

CHAPTER ONE

In Sheep's Clothing

Uncovering the Wolf

JOANNE LARSON

When we published the first edition of *Literacy as Snake Oil: Beyond the Quick Fix* teachers were under increasing pressure to implement packaged literacy curricula and reform, but did have some space for dissent and resistance. Since the first publication, however, things have gotten worse, much worse. The government policies in the US, for example, now mandate documentation of annual yearly progress (AYP) with the consequence of loss of funding if the rise in scores is not met. George W. Bush succeeded in passing legislation that mandates standardized testing at all grade levels (NCLB), the scores on these tests being what AYP is based upon. Furthermore, the "stakes" attached to these scores have risen: students cannot graduate from high school until they pass them in all foundational content areas (e.g., math, English, science, and social studies). I argue that the autonomous model of literacy that we critiqued in the first edition has risen to the forefront of public discourses of accountability and deficit ideologies of non-dominant children in high poverty areas are once again guiding curriculum and pedagogy in increasingly disciplinary ways.

This highly charged feared-based context makes a second edition of this book timely indeed. I hope this second edition will remind us of our political commitments to resist oppression and unethical practice and find ways to subvert teacher- (and student-) proof packages. The promises they make are as false as those made by the 19th century snake-oil salesman who claimed on the cover of the first edition:

"My bilious friend," said Sturdy Brown, "it would not be amiss, if you'd regain your health, to take a dose or two of this."

A full dose of NCLB is operating in the US and has had extraordinary consequences on classroom practice, from early childhood to higher education (witness the recent calls for standards and testing in higher education institutions in the US). In one sense we have lost teacher education to this movement already. In New York State, for example, schools of education were required to be nationally accredited or lose their ability to certify teachers at any level. Given the extent to which colleges and universities rely on teacher education monies, no school opted out of this requirement. New packaged teaching software is being marketed aggressively to schools of education (see www.completeteacher.com) and reactionary opinion pieces are appearing in respected publications that decry the woes of higher education (Fogg, 2006; Levine, 2006). As Street, Lefstein, and Pahl argue in a new chapter to this book, the situation may not be as dire in the UK, given recent shifts in the National Literacy Strategy toward more contextualized literacy practices.

In the US, however, NCLB has brought with it deeper, more reductionist calls for "fixes" to the problem of student performance on standardized tests as measured by AYP. The lower performing the school, the more aggressive the attempted fixes. As Irvine & Larson and Gatto discuss in this volume, the packaged reforms mandated in the urban school district they discuss have increased in number and intensity since the first edition. The list includes Americas Choice®, Success for All, Gates-funded small school initiatives, and the highly restrictive federally funded Reading First. The lower performing schools in the US are overwhelmingly located in high-poverty areas in which non-dominant families struggle. The targets of these fixes, then, are pathologized as deficit and in need of repair. Schools are forced to accept these packages to demonstrate AYP in particular ways or lose their funding. Those ways are highly scripted and coincide with textbook and test packages, packages that have been inappropriately authorized by the government (*Education Week*, February 23, 2007; Gutiérrez, this volume). The recent release of the Inspector General's audit of Reading First that reveals some of the inappropriate contracts and serious flaws in the research base for the program that literacy researchers, many of whom are represented in this volume, have been pointing out since its inception may offer some tools for future resistance (http://www.ed.gov/about/offices/list/oig/aireports/i13f0017.pdf, Accessed October 28, 2006).

Along with an aggressive focus on the fix comes an oppressive surveillance system designed to eliminate dissent or innovation through the examination (Foucault, 1977; Gutiérrez, this volume). Reading First comes with a top-down model of professional development in which teachers are targeted as pawns of reductionist reforms. Testing packages abound. One such test, the Dynamic Indicators of Basic Early Literacy Skills or DIBELS® (http://www.dibels.org, Accessed October 28, 2006), requires students to read a text in 60 seconds. The teacher marks errors on an adjoining sheet and scores the students according to a rubric; these sheets are then inputted into a monitored website that teachers access using their employee identification number. Gatto (this volume) was forced to implement such tests upon beginning a new 2–4-grade loop (Reading First is a K-3 reform package). After she discussed her problems with the test at a professional development meeting, rumors began to circulate that she was refusing to implement the tests; all in spite of the fact that she had completed all tests early and documented her students' scores online. Central office officials came to her school to "observe" her giving the tests. At the beginning of the 2006 academic year, central office officials and NYS Department of Education representatives held a meeting with the Reading First teachers to let them know their school was the worst Reading First school in the state. They offered a state report as evidence, a report in which Gatto was specifically named. After starting to think about early retirement for the first time, she recommitted to her students for the remainder of the looping experience after seeing them on the first day of school. She talked at length to the new principal about what she does and learned what she needed to do to meet the requirements. After all, she didn't want to be blamed for the school notoriety as a failure; no one would. As a result, her classroom "looks" quite different than it did before, but her tactics for resistance are even more powerful (Larson & Gatto, 2004).[1] These disciplinary practices to quell dissent have serious consequences on teachers who know that these packaged fixes are damaging children and increasing the educational debt (Ladson-Billings, 2006) we owe children. Morale is lower than ever before.

The original purpose of this book was to critically examine quick-fix literacy programs peddled by corporate publishers and governments seeking to solve what they are calling the current reading crisis. As I mentioned earlier, the problem not only remains but also has worsened, at least in the US. Literacy scholars in the US and the UK who are researching and writing about these issues come together in this second edition to offer analyses of the problem of commodified literacies and the consequences of these packages on practices of educational communities. The book is intended for anyone who is struggling with how to advocate for what we know about authentic literacy learning in the context of standardization and accountability. We hope that teacher educators, new and practicing teachers, and researchers find our work useful.

This introductory chapter reviews the issues in literacy education described in the first edition, focusing briefly on the larger context within which packaged literacy programs emerged, and then closes with an overview of the book. Accountability and standardization movements feed the market for packaged literacies and inflame the public fears of falling behind in a complex global marketplace. Educational researchers, policymakers, administrators, and teachers struggling to deal with increasingly powerful external pressure for proof of effectiveness focus primarily on improving achievement rather than critically examining the larger context that is motivating the drive for standardization. In literacy education, the obsession with a normalized, competitive product has polarized public discourse into antagonistic arguments over which method works best in spite of calls to the contrary (Coles, 1998, 2000; Luke, 1998). Profit-oriented publishing houses have seized the moment and produced "research-based" methods and associated packaged material that they promise will fix the problem.

Teachers tend to fall back on their existing beliefs and practices, citing the oft-heard "pendulum swing" excuse as their reason for ignoring district mandates or simply following the directions in new packaged literacy materials. It is hard to blame them given the pressure to hold them accountable for student achievement. Their jobs are at stake. They are bombarded by their district administrators and by advertising in professional literature with commercially produced materials that promise new and improved literacy outcomes. By relying on commercially produced materials, teachers and administrators can shift responsibility to the materials and the reason for continued underachievement to students and families.

As relevant now as it was in the first edition, the survival of teaching as a profession requires us to get beyond quick-fix solutions. To assume a quick fix is possible is to assume that teaching itself is simply a matter of technique and that the "problem" lies in children. The nearer teaching gets to machine-like behavior the more readily it can be displaced; the more deskilled it becomes, the less bargaining power teachers have as professionals (Lankshear, personal communication). This book does not argue for new and improved methods, or quick fixes, but presents carefully reasoned discussions that will help researchers, teacher educators, classroom teachers, and school administrators understand the consequences of commercially produced literacy packages, or commodified literacy, on the teaching and learning of literacy.

OVERVIEW OF THE BOOK

Each chapter author from the first edition significantly revised his/her chapter, updating the arguments, often in response to published reviews of the first edition. Several new authors have been added: Brian Street, Adam Lefstein, and Kate Pahl; Nancy Ares and Ed Buendía; and classroom teacher Dan Osborn.

In chapter two, James Paul Gee updates his original analysis of the 1998 National Research Council report called *Preventing Reading Difficulties in Young Children* by bringing his recent scholarship on language, literacy, and learning to the conversation. He argues that the narrow focus on phonics and phonemic awareness in the report and in subsequent literacy packages evades the more central issue of language development in specialist discourses. He outlines how the narrowness of the neoliberal political agenda contributes to the growing disparities in wealth, access, and equity in a "new capitalist" global world, grounding his discussion in his current research on video game practices.

Building on his discussion of the National Reading Council's report in *Misreading Reading: The Bad Science That Hurts Children* (2000) and from *Reading the Naked Truth: Literacy, Legislation, and Lies* (2003) Gerald Coles unpacks the "distorted facts and suppressed truth" in reading research contained in and surrounding the National Reading Panel Report (NICHD, 2000) in chapter three. Building on the arguments made in his first edition chapter, Coles moves to discuss how facts have been distorted to promote a particular ideological stance, and discusses the consequences of this agenda on children's ability to understand themselves and the world.

In chapter four, Patricia Irvine and Joanne Larson update their exploration of how elementary teachers in an urban district serving predominantly low-income African American and Latino students use basal reading series in their instructional practices. They describe how teachers used the materials selectively, choosing activities that reflected deficit ideologies about students' language and abilities. They describe a study of a basal reading series pilot and present data to show that the "autonomous" definition of literacy (Street, 1995) that underlies the materials, in combination with a deficit model of students' abilities, resulted in pedagogical practices that academically disadvantaged students.

Chapter five describes how veteran classroom teacher Lynn Astarita Gatto struggles with the ferocity of the literacy packages mandated in her district while trying to construct authentic learning contexts in her urban classroom. Gatto is a teacher in the same district described by Irvine and Larson and continues to be bombarded with commercially produced materials and marginalized by her peers for her vocal resistance. This chapter outlines what she does and how she avoids using these materials.

Patrick Shannon revisits the commodification of both virtue and literacy embedded in the efforts of William Bennett's attempts to civilize Americans in chapter six. As a "moral entrepreneur", Bennett has written, edited, or collaborated on four books, five anthologies for adults and children, six collections for children, a PBS cartoon series, and a popular Internet Website in order "to overcome the consequences of the 1960s." Shannon explores the transformations of virtue and literacy pedagogy into commodities through his analysis of Bennett's work. His chapter positions us well to understand potential consequences of unchecked capitalism and how we have come to be a susceptible market.

In chapter seven, Kris D. Gutiérrez examines what she terms the "perfect storm of national curricula, xenophobia, and a thick morality" that positions difference as deviance that needs to be remedied. She presents two cases of learning settings where this storm is resisted in spite of some dramatic external pressures.

In chapter eight, Brian Street, Adam Lefstein, and Kate Pahl challenge us to see how teachers and students are enacting literacy curricula in specific ways in spite of the way they are packaged. In a three-part organization, they discuss: (1) the underlying conceptual issues in addressing literacy in this way (i.e., why they need snake oil); (2) the background debates and conflicts, including public representations (e.g., the synthetic phonics issue as snake oil); and (3) what does and could go on in schools (i.e., alternatives to snake oil).

Nancy Ares and Edward Buendía explore schools' choices of literacy programs in relation to the sociohistorical and political social space within which those choices were operating in chapter nine. Through analyses of interview and document data, they explore the complicated ways in which both spatialized and spatializing technologies and practices in these schools were influential in their varied choices in literacy programs and schools with which to collaborate based on program choice.

In the last chapter, Dan Osborn investigates the packaging of literacy in America's Choice® from his position as a veteran classroom teacher in elementary school. He traces the program's historical development from a not-for-profit organization to a for-profit program linked to corporate publishing and NCLB legislation in the US. Furthermore, he explicates the complex relationship between the National Reading Panel report, the Snow et al. book (1998), and McGraw-Hill's Reading First/Direct Instruction program using the metaphor of the family tree.

NOTE

1. Since this book went to the publisher, Gatto has taken significant action. After learning that the district was going to add another 30 minutes of phonics instruction to the already 90 minutes required by Reading First, she couldn't take it anymore. She wrote a letter to her principal, copying the superintendent, the school board, and the union president expressing her outrage. She received an immediate phone call from the superintendent and a daylong classroom visit by a school board member. This action served as the catalyst for the teachers to form a coalition that succeeded in voting out Reading First. Sometimes one person really can make a difference.

REFERENCES

Coles, G. (1998). *Reading Lessons: The Debate Over Literacy.* New York: Hill and Wang.
Coles, G. (2000). *Misreading Reading: The Bad Science That Hurts Children.* Portsmouth, NH: Heinemann.
Coles, G. (2003). *Reading the Naked Truth: Literacy, Legislation and Lies.* Portsmouth, NH: Heinemann.
Complete Teacher™, www.completeteacher.com. Accessed August 15, 2006.
Dynamic Indicators of Basic Early Literacy Skills or DIBELS®, http://www.dibels.org, Accessed October 28, 2006.

Fogg, P. (September 19, 2006). Report Blasts Teacher-Education Programs as Outdated and Low-Quality. *The Chronicle of Higher Education.*

Foucault, M. (1977). *Discipline and Punish: The Birth of the Prison.* Harmondsworth: Penguin.

Klein, A. (2007). Critics of NCLB ask Congress to overhaul it. *Education Week,* 26(25), 1–26.

Ladson-Billings, G. (2006). From the achievement gap to the educational debt: Understanding achievement in U.S. schools. *Educational Researcher,* 35(7), 3–12.

Larson, J., & Gatto, L. (2004). Tactical underlife: Understanding students' perspectives. *Journal of Early Childhood Literacy,* 4(1), 11–41.

Levine, A. (2006). *Educating School Teachers.* http://edschools.org/pdf/Educating_Teachers_Report.pdf, Accessed October 30, 2006.

Luke, A. (1998). Getting over method: Literacy teaching as work in "New Times." *Language Arts,* 75(4), 305–313.

National Institute of Child Health and Human Development. (2000). *Report of the National Reading Panel. Teaching Children to Read: An Evidence-based Assessment of the Scientific Research Literature on Reading and its Implications for Reading Instruction* (NIH Publication No. 00–4769). Washington, DC: U.S. Government Printing Office.

Snow, C.E., Burns, M.S., & Griffin, P. (Eds.). (1998). *Preventing Reading Difficulties in Young Children.* Washington, DC: National Academy Press.

Street, B. (1995). *Social Literacies: Critical Approaches to Literacy in Development, Ethnography and Education.* London: Longman.

U.S. Department of Education Office of Inspector General (2006). *The Reading First Program's Grant Application Process Final Inspection Report.* http://www.ed.gov/about/offices/list/oig/aireports/i13f0017.pdf. Accessed October 28, 2006.

CHAPTER TWO

Reading AND Language Development

Beyond Limited Perspectives

JAMES PAUL GEE

INTRODUCTION

In this chapter I want to argue that the national debate we have had over phonics—a debate about how best to deliver early decoding instruction—often evades a more important and central issue. The phonics debate takes reading—in the narrow sense of decoding skills with literal comprehension—to be the basis of school success. I will argue here that it is language development, in a quite specific sense to be specified below, that is the real basis of school success. The narrow focus of the phonics debate, in my view, fits with the current neoliberal political agenda in the United States (and most of the developed world) and reinforces the growing disparities in wealth, access, and equity in our "new capitalist" global world. It does so by concentrating on an important basic early resource (i.e., decoding) while evading a richer, more central, and necessary early resource (i.e., language development). The richer resource is, thus, left to those from more privileged homes and schools.

Let me start my argument with a brief consideration of one of the best of the now many official reports on early reading, the National Research Council's *Preventing Reading Difficulties in Young Children* (Snow, Burns, & Griffin, 1998), hereafter referred to as "PRD." This report appeared amidst much applause and approval from the public, politicians, and educational organizations like AERA, IRA, and NCTE, organizations that, by and large, with some dissenting voices, celebrated the report in newsletters and sessions. I discuss PRD as a way to point out the narrow perspective taken on reading in recent public discussion and the evasions such a narrow perspective enacts (Gee, 1999). After my discussion of PRD, I will turn to a broader view of early reading in the context of language development. In fact, my discussion of PRD will show that the document itself points in this direction without actually going there. We will, however, have to be careful in specifying exactly what we mean by "language development." I will not be referring to anyone's vernacular native language development (that takes care of itself), but rather to what we might call "school-based language development," or what is better called "specialist language development" (where academic varieties of language are one type of specialist language).

Let me hasten to say, however, before I start in earnest, that I am not "anti-phonics." All children need to learn to decode, effortlessly and fluently, no later than the end of first grade. But they need to learn to do so in a rich language development context that does not render them victims of the so-called "fourth-grade slump" (discussed below). There are a variety of good ways to teach phonics—in some cases different ways work better or worse for different children—though the ideal is to have phonics teaching integrated with rich language development that underlies, supports, and eventually eclipses phonics instruction as children become full members of a literate "culture" (Gee, 2004). Children who do not get such rich language development often need more and more overt phonics instruction—a necessary evil caused by their lack of access to the sort of rich language development we will discuss below.

WHAT'S THE CRISIS?

PRD is part of a long line of reports written in the now familiar "we have a crisis in our schools" genre. Unfortunately, the report has a hard time naming the crisis to which it is directed. Its authors are well aware that there is, in fact, no general "reading crisis" in the United States:

> . . . average reading achievement has not changed markedly over the last 20 years (NAEP, 1997). And following a gain by black children from 1970 to 1980, the white-black gap has remained roughly constant for the last 16 years.

> . . . Americans do very well in international comparisons of reading—much better, comparatively speaking, than they do on math or science. In a 1992 study comparing reading skill levels among 9-year-olds in 18 Western nations, U.S. students scored among the highest levels and were second only to students in Finland . . . (Elley, 1992, pp. 97–98)

There is, of course, the hint of paradox here. The report does not take note of how odd it is that a country could do very well in reading, but poorly in content areas like math and science. For the writers of the report, it is as if content (things like math and science) has nothing to do with reading and vice versa.

However, this paradox is endemic to the report as a whole. Note the report's remarks on the much-discussed issue of the "fourth-grade slump":

> The "fourth-grade slump" is a term used to describe a widely encountered disappointment when examining scores of fourth graders in comparison to younger children (Chall et al., 1990). . . . It is not clear what the explanation is or even that there is a unitary explanation. (p. 78)

The fourth-grade slump is the problem that lots of children learn to read in the early grades, but then cannot read to learn content (e.g., social studies or science) in the later grades (*American Educator*, 2003; Chall, Jacobs, & Baldwin, 1990). The fourth-grade slump would, on the face of it, lead one to worry about what we mean by "learning to read" in the early grades and how and why this idea can become so detached from "reading to learn." No such worries plague the Academy's report. It assumes throughout that if children learn to engage in what the report calls "real reading" (decoding plus literal comprehension), they will thereafter be able to learn and succeed in school. But the fourth-grade slump amply demonstrates that this assumption is false.

READING, RACISM, AND POVERTY

PRD is well aware that, in the United States, poor readers are concentrated "in certain ethnic groups and in poor, urban neighborhoods and rural towns" (p. 98). In fact, this is the true "crisis" in reading in the United States, though one the report never focuses on. Here, too, we are faced with paradoxes. Let us return to the quote from the report with which we started:

> . . . average reading achievement has not changed markedly over the last 20 years (NAEP, 1997). And following a gain by black children from 1970 to 1980, the white-black gap has remained roughly constant for the last 16 years.
>
> . . . Americans do very well in international comparisons of reading—much better, comparatively speaking, than they do on math or science. In a 1992 study comparing reading skill levels among 9-year-olds in 18 Western nations, U.S. students scored among the highest levels and were second only to students in Finland . . . (Elley, 1992, pp. 97–98)

Here the report mentions the now well-known and much studied issue that from the late 1960s to the early 1980s, the Black-White gap, in IQ test scores and other sorts of test scores, including reading tests, was fast closing (Neisser, 1998; Jencks & Phillips, 1998). This heartening progress, especially in regard to achievement tests, ceased in the 1980s. One certainly would have thought that a reading report would care deeply about the factors that had been closing the Black-White gap in reading scores. Clearly, whatever else they were, these factors were powerful "reading interventions," since they significantly increased the reading scores of "at risk" children. But the report shows no such interest, presumably because these factors were social and cultural and not factors only narrowly germane to classroom instructional methods.

Though the matter is controversial (Neisser, 1998; Jencks & Phillips, 1998), these factors were, in all likelihood, closely connected to the sorts of social programs (stemming originally from Johnson's "War on Poverty") that were dismantled in the 1980s and 1990s (Grissmer, Flanagan, & Williamson, 1998, pp. 221–223). An approach like PRD's that sees the key issue as "real reading" (i.e., decoding plus literal comprehension) is not liable to see such social programs as central to a report on reading. Ironically, though, the progress made on reading tests during the time the Black-White gap was closing was far greater, in quantitative terms (Hedges & Nowell, 1998), than the results of any of the interventions (e.g., early phonemic awareness training) that the PRD discusses and advocates.

The following remarks from the report are typical of the sense of paradox bordering on outright contradiction that pervades the report on the issue of poor and minority children:

> . . . for students in schools in which more than 75 percent of all students received free or reduced-price lunches (a measure of high poverty), the mean score for students in the fall semester of first grade was at approximately the 44th percentile. By the spring of third grade, this difference had expanded significantly. Children living in high-poverty areas tend to fall further behind, regardless of their initial reading skill level. (p. 98)

If these children fall further and further behind "regardless of their initial reading skill level," how, then, can we help them by increasing their initial skill level at "real reading" through things like early phonemic awareness and overt instruction on decoding, as the report recommends? Obviously the real issue goes well beyond early decoding instruction, and early decoding instruction will only speak to these real issues when it is embedded in a larger context (I will claim that this larger necessary context is early language development).

Finally, we reach the issues of racism and power. It is widely believed that such issues are "merely political," not directly relevant to reading and reading research. PRD is certainly written in such a spirit. But the fact of the matter is that racism and power are just as much cognitive issues as they are political ones. Children will not identify with—they will even disidentify with—teachers and schools that they perceive as hostile, alien, or oppressive to their home-based identities (Holland & Quinn, 1987; Holland, Lachicotte, Skinner, & Cain, 1998).

Claude Steele's (Steele, 1992; Steele & Aronson, 1995, 1998) groundbreaking work clearly demonstrates that in assessment contexts where issues of race, racism, and stereotypes are triggered, the performance of even quite adept learners seriously deteriorates (see Ferguson, 1998, for an important extension of Steele's work). Steele shows clearly that how people *read* when they are taking tests changes as their fear of falling victim to cultural stereotypes increases. To ignore these wider issues, while stressing such things as phonemic awareness built on controlled texts, is to ignore, not merely "politics," but what we know about learning and literacy, as well.

In fact, one can go further. Given Steele's work, it is simply wrong to discuss reading assessment, intervention, and instruction, as the Academy's report does, without discussing the pervasive *culture of inequality* that deskills poor and minority children and its implications for different types of assessments, interventions, and instruction. This is an empirical point, not (only) a political one.

LANGUAGE ABILITIES

It is a deep irony that a report that spends most of its time recommending early phonemic awareness and early sustained and overt instruction on phonics is replete with comments that appear to undermine its recommendations. For example, consider the following remarks from the report:

> . . . studies indicate that training in phonological awareness, particularly in association with instruction in letters and letter-sound relationships, make a contribution to assisting at risk children in learning to read. The effects of training, although quite consistent, are only moderate in strength, and have so far not been shown to extend to comprehension. Typically a majority of the trained children narrow the gap between themselves and initially more advanced students in phonological awareness and word reading skills, but few are brought completely up to speed through training, and a few fail to show any gains at all. (p. 251)

When classificatory analyses are conducted, phonological awareness in kindergarten appears to have the tendency to be a more successful predictor of future superior reading than of future reading problems (Wagner, 1997; Scarborough, 1998). That is, among children who have recently begun or will soon begin kindergarten, few of those with strong phonological awareness skills will stumble in learning to read, but many of those with weak phonological sensitivity will go on to become adequate readers.

In sum, despite the theoretical importance of phonological awareness for learning to read, its predictive power is somewhat muted, because, at about the time of the onset of schooling, so many children who will go on to become normally achieving readers have not yet attained much, if any, appreciation of the phonological structure of oral language, making them nearly indistinguishable in this regard from children who will indeed encounter reading difficulties down the road (p. 112).

There would seem to be an important theme here, one to which PRD might have paid a bit more heed. Tests of early phonological awareness (or lack thereof) do not fruitfully select those students who will later have problems in learning to read. Furthermore, while a stress on phonological awareness and overt phonics instruction does initially help "at risk" students, it does not bring them up to par with more advantaged students, and they tend to eventually fall back, fueling a fourth-grade or later "slump" (this fact is amply documented in the report, see pp. 216, 228, 232, 248–249, 251, 257).

From remarks like those above, it would certainly seem that the problems children (particularly poor and minority children) have with reading must lay, for the most part, someplace else than on a lack of early phonemic awareness. The fourth-grade slump tells us this much, as well. Though much of PRD is driven by the correlation between early phonological awareness and later success in learning to read, the report does readily acknowledge that such a correlation does not prove that phonological awareness causes success in reading. And, indeed, remarks from the report like those cited above, and the fourth-grade slump problem itself, would seem to indicate that something else causes *both* reading success (or failure) and early phonemic awareness (or lack of it).

The report is, ironically, aware of what this something else might be. It readily acknowledges, but ignores the fact, that another correlation is just as significant (if not more so) as that between early phonological awareness and learning to read. This is the correlation between *early language abilities* (what I have been referring to as early language development) and later success in reading. And, as one might suspect, early language abilities and early phonological awareness are themselves correlated:

> Chaney (1992) also observed that performance on phonological awareness tasks by preschoolers was highly correlated with general language ability. Moreover it was measures of semantic and syntactic skills, rather than speech discrimination and articulation, that predicted phonological awareness differences. (p. 53)
>
> What is most striking about the results of the preceding studies is the power of early preschool language to predict reading three to five years later. (pp. 107–108)
>
> On average, phonological awareness (r = .46) has been about as strong a predictor of future reading as memory for sentences and stories, confrontation naming, and general language measures. (p. 112)

It is something of a mystery—at least to me—why PRD stresses throughout the correlation between early phonemic awareness and learning to read, while giving such short shrift to early language abilities, a factor that seems to have so much more relevance to both becoming literate and being able to use literacy to learn. One can only suspect that it was the urge to make the report a "report on reading," and to speak within the frame of current public debates about reading.

So what are these early language abilities that seem so important for later success in school? According to the report, they are things like vocabulary—receptive vocabulary, but more especially expressive vocabulary (p. 107)—the ability to recall and comprehend sentences and stories, and the ability to engage in verbal interactions. Furthermore, I think that research has made it fairly clear what causes such verbal abilities. What appears to cause enhanced verbal abilities are family, community, and school language environments in which children interact intensively with adults and more advanced peers and experience cognitively challenging talk and texts on sustained topics and in different genres of oral and written language (see pp. 106–108).

However, the correlation between language abilities and success in learning to read (and in school generally) hides an important reality. Almost all children—including poor children—have impressive language abilities. The vast majority of children enter school with large vocabularies, complex grammar, and deep understandings of experiences and stories. It has been decades since anyone believed that poor and minority children entered school with "no language" (Labov, 1972; Gee, 1996).

The verbal abilities that children who fail in school fail to have are not just some general set of such abilities, but rather specific verbal abilities tied to specific school-based practices and school-based genres of oral and written language. The children whose vocabularies are larger in ways that enhance their early school success, for instance, are children who know, and especially can use, more words tied to the specific forms of language that school-based practices use. A stress on language abilities would have required an emphasis on learning, content, and the relationships between home-based cultures and school-based practices (i.e., social, cultural, and, yes, "political" issues).

READING: A TRAJECTORY APPROACH

So let's now move on beyond PRD. Consider anew the situation of a child learning to read. What should our goal for this child be? On the face of it, the goal would seem to be that the child learns to decode print and assign basic or literal meanings to that print. But the situation is not that simple. We know from the phenomenon of the "fourth-grade slump" that the goal of early reading instruction has to be more forward-looking than simple decoding and literal comprehension (*American Educator*, 2003; Chall, Jacobs, & Baldwin, 1990). The goal has to be that children learn to read early on in such a way that this learning creates a successful trajectory throughout the school years and beyond. Such a trajectory is based, more than anything else, on the child's being able to handle ever increasingly complex language, especially in the content areas (e.g., science and math), as school progresses. Children need to get ready for these increasing language demands as early as possible. It is as if school were conducted in Greek more and more as the grades increased: surely it would be better to be exposed to Greek as early as possible and not wait until school becomes the equivalent of advanced Greek.

Let's call this a "trajectory approach" to early reading. Such an approach has to look not only forwards, but backwards as well. Early phonemic awareness and home-based practice with literacy are the most important correlates with success in first grade, especially success in learning to read in the "decode and literally comprehend" sense (Dickinson & Neuman, 2006). However, the child's early home-based oral vocabulary and early skills with complex oral language are the most important correlates for school success—not just in reading, but in the content areas—past the first grade, essentially for the rest of schooling (Dickinson & Neuman, 2006; Senechal, Ouellette, & Rodney, 2006). Thus, a child's oral language development is key to a successful trajectory approach to reading; that is, an approach that seeks to make a long-term school-based reader of academic content (and that's what's in the high school biology textbook, for example). It is the key to avoiding, even eradicating, the fourth-grade slump.

However, we must pause here, for two reasons. First, I am aware that some people consider the sort of academic language used in biology or sociology simply to be exclusionary jargon attempting to colonize people's everyday cultural identities in the name of a rationalist positivism. I am as interested as anyone in the politics of schooling and science (Gee, 1996, 2004), but in this chapter my concern is with the fate of children who get to high school and cannot cope with that textbook and related language practices. In my view, it does no good to rail against the language of the textbook while leaving the textbook and other instances of academic language behind as the litmus test of school success—the "revolution" had better be total or children will suffer for adults' politics.

For the record, while I fully concede that aspects of academic language have been used historically for little more than exclusion and the creation of status—and that textbooks should be replaced with texts more specially tied to activities and practices—by and large I believe that specialist varieties of language, when used appropriately, are critically and integrally tied to the functioning (workings) of specialist domains, and access to these domains is severely limited without such language and related representational systems.

Second, I must pause because we are on the brink of what could be a major misunderstanding. Decades of research in linguistics have shown that every normal child's early language and language development are just fine (Chomsky, 1986; Labov, 1972, 1979; Pinker, 1994). Every child, under normal conditions, develops a perfectly complex and adequate oral language: the child's "native language" (and, of course, sometimes children develop more than one native language). It never happens, under normal conditions—and normal here covers a very wide array of variation— that, in acquiring English, say, little Janie develops relative clauses, but little Johnnie just can't master them. That is, of course, in a way a surprising fact, showing that the acquisition of one's native language is not particularly a matter of ability or skill.

But when I say that children's early oral language—vocabulary and skills with complex language—are crucial correlates of success in school, correlates that show up especially after the child has learned to decode in first grade (one hopes)—I am not talking about children's everyday language, the sort of language that is equal for everyone. I am talking about their early preparation for language that is not "everyday," for language that is "technical" or "specialist" or "academic" (Gee, 2004; Martin, 1989; Schleppegrell, 2004). I will refer to people's "everyday" language—the way they speak when they are not speaking technically or as specialists of some sort—as their "vernacular style." I will refer to their language when they are speaking technically or as a specialist as a "specialist style" (people eventually can have a number of different specialist styles, connected to different technical, specialist, or academic concerns).

AN EXAMPLE

Let me give an example of what I am talking about, both in terms of specialist language and in terms of getting ready for later complex specialist language demands early on in life. Kevin Crowley has talked insightfully about quite young children developing what he calls "islands of expertise." Crowley and Jacobs (2002) define an island of expertise as "any topic in which children happen to become interested and in which they develop relatively deep and rich knowledge" (p. 333). They provide several examples of such islands, including a boy who develops relatively deep content knowledge and a "sophisticated conversational space" (p. 335) about trains and related topics after he is given a Thomas the Tank Engine book.

Now consider a mother talking to her four-year-old son, who has an island of expertise around dinosaurs (the transcript below is adapted from Crowley & Jacobs, 2002, pp. 343–344). The mother and child are looking at replica fossil dinosaur and a replica fossil dinosaur egg. The mother has a little card in front of it that says:

- Replica of a Dinosaur **Egg**
- From the Oviraptor
- Cretaceous Period
- Approximately 65 to 135 million years ago
- The actual fossil, of which this is a replica, was found in the Gobi desert of Mongolia

In the transcript below, "M" stands for the mother's turns and "C" for the child's:

C: This looks like this is an **egg**.

M: Okay, well this . . . That's exactly what it is! How did you know?

C: Because it looks like it.

M: That's what it says; see, look, *egg*, *egg* . . . Replica of a dinosaur *egg*. From the oviraptor.

M: Do you have a . . . You have an oviraptor on your game! You know the **egg** game on your computer? That's what it is, an oviraptor.

M: And that's from the Cretaceous period. And that was a really, really long time ago.

M: And this is . . . the hind claw. What's a hind claw? [pause] A claw from the back leg from a velociraptor. And you know what—

C: Hey! Hey! A velociraptor!! I had that one my [inaudible] dinosaur.

M: I know, I know, and that was the little one. And remember they have those, remember in your book, it said something about the claws . . .

C: No, I know, they, they . . .

M: Your dinosaur book, what they use them . . .

C: Have so great claws so they can eat and kill . . .

M: They use their claws to cut open their prey, right.

C: Yeah.

This is a language lesson, but not primarily a lesson on vernacular language, though, of course, it thoroughly mixes vernacular and specialist language. It is a lesson on specialist language. It is early preparation for the sorts of academic (school-based) language children see ever more increasingly, in talk and in texts, as they move on in school. It is also replete with "moves" that are successful language-teaching strategies, though the mother is no expert on language development.

Let's look at some of the features this interaction has as an informal language lesson. First, it contains elements of non-vernacular, specialist language; for example: "**replica** of a dinosaur egg"; "from the **oviraptor**"; "from the **Cretaceous period**"; "the **hind claw**"; "their **prey**." The specialist elements here are largely vocabulary, though such interactions soon come to involve elements of syntax and discourse associated with specialist ways with words as well.

Second, the mother asks the child the basis of his knowledge: Mother: "How did you know?" Child: "Because it looks like it." Specialist domains are almost always "expert" domains that involve claims to know and evidence for such claims. They are in, Shaffer's (2007) sense, "epistemic games."

Third, the mother publicly displays reading of the technical text, even though the child cannot yet read: "That's what it says, see, look, *egg*, *egg*. . . . Replica of a dinosaur *egg*. From the oviraptor." This reading also uses print to confirm the child's claim to know, showing one way this type of print (descriptive information on the card) can be used in an epistemic game of confirmation.

Fourth, the mother relates the current talk and text to other texts the child is familiar with: "You have an oviraptor on your game! You know the **egg** game on your computer? That's what it is, an oviraptor"; "And remember they have those, remember in your book, it said something about the claws." This sort of intertextuality creates a network of texts and modalities (books, games, and computers), situating the child's new knowledge not just in a known background, but in a system the child is building in his head.

Fifth, the mother offers something like a technical definition: "And this is . . . the hind claw. What's a hind claw? [pause] A claw from the back leg from a velociraptor." This demonstrates a common language move in specialist domains, that is, giving relatively formal and explicit definitions (not just examples of use).

Sixth, the mother points to and explicates hard concepts: "And that's from the Cretaceous period. And that was a really, really long time ago." This signals to the child that "Cretaceous period" is a technical term and displays how to explicate such terms in the vernacular (this is a different move than offering a more formal definition).

Seventh, she offers technical vocabulary for a slot the child has left open: Child: "Have so great claws so they can eat and kill . . ." Mother: "They use their claws to cut open their **prey**, right." This slot and filler move co-constructs language with the child, allowing the child to use language "above his head" in ways in line with Vygotsky's concept of a "zone of proximal development" (Vygotsky, 1978).

INFORMAL SPECIALIST-LANGUAGE LESSONS

So, let's be clear about two things. This is an informal language lesson. And such lessons involve more than language and language learning. They involve teaching and learning cognitive (knowledge) and interactional moves in specialist domains. Finally, they involve teaching and learning identities, the identity of being the sort of person who is comfortable with specialist, technical knowing, learning, and language. Of course, even formal language lessons—in learning a second language, for instance, in school—should involve language, knowledge, interaction, and identity. But this is not formal teaching; it is informal teaching, the teaching equivalent of informal learning. Let's call such informal language lessons, with the sorts of features I have just discussed, "informal specialist-language lessons" (ironically, they are informal formal-language lessons!).

Along with all we know about "emergent literacy" at home (Dickinson & Neuman, 2006; Emergent Literacy Project, n.d.; Gee, 2004), informal specialist language lessons are crucial if one wants to take a trajectory view of reading development. They are pre-school pre-reading activities that lead to early reading instruction that avoids the fourth-grade slump. Of course, the reading instruction the child receives at school must continue these language lessons, informally and formally. It must place reading from the get-go in the context of learning specialist styles of language, just as this mother has done. This, however, raises the issue of what happens for children who come to school without such informal specialist language teaching, and often without other important aspects of emergent literacy, too. My view is that this cannot be ignored. We cannot just move on to reading instruction of the "decode and literally comprehend" sort as if it just doesn't matter that these children have missed out on early specialist language learning. For these children language teaching needs to start, start with a vengeance, and sustain itself throughout the course of reading instruction. And, again, remember, this claim has nothing to do with teaching "standard" English or ESL, *per se*; it is a claim that even native speakers of vernacular standard English need language learning to prepare for specialist varieties of language.

SPECIALIST LANGUAGE IN POPULAR CULTURE

There are other things beyond such informal specialist-language lessons that can prepare children for the increasing language demands of school in the content areas. And we can see one of these if we look, oddly enough, at young people's popular culture today. Something very interesting has happened in children's popular culture. It has gotten very complex, and it contains a great many practices that involve highly specialized styles of language (Gee, 2003, 2004). Young children often engage with these practices socially with each other in informal peer learning groups. And some parents recruit these practices to accelerate their children's specialist language skills (with their concomitant thinking and interactional skills).

For example, consider the text below, which appears on a *Yu-Gi-Oh* card. *Yu-Gi-Oh* is a card game involving quite complex rules. It is often played face-to-face with one or more other players, sometimes in formal competitions, more often informally, though it can be played as a video game as well.

Armed Ninja
Card-Type: Effect Monster
Attribute: Earth **Level:** 1
Type: Warrior
ATK: 300 **DEF:** 300
Description: FLIP: Destroys 1 Magic Card on the field. If this card's target is facedown, flip it face-up. If the card is a Magic Card, it is destroyed. If not, it is returned to its facedown position. The flipped card is not activated.
Rarity: Rare

The "description" is really a rule. It states what moves in the game the card allows. This text has little specialist vocabulary (though it has some: e.g., "activated"), unlike the interaction we saw between mother and child above, but it contains complex specialist syntax. It contains, for instance, three straight conditional clauses (the "if" clauses). Note how complex this meaning is: First, if the target is face down, flip it over. Now check to see if it is a magic card. If it is, destroy it. If it isn't, return it to its face-down position. Finally, you are told that even though you flipped over your opponent's card, which in some circumstances would activate its powers, in this case, the card's powers are not activated. This is "logic talk"; a matter, really, of multiple related "either-or," "if-then" propositions.

Note, too, that the card contains a bunch of classificatory information (e.g., type, attack power, defense power, rarity). All of these linguistic indicators lead the child to place the card in the whole network or system of *Yu-Gi-Oh* cards—and there are over 10,000 of them—and the rule system of the game itself. This is complex system thinking with a vengeance.

I have watched seven-year-old children play *Yu-Gi-Oh* with great expertise. They must read each of the cards. They endlessly debate the powers of each card by constant contrast and comparison with other cards when they are trading them. They discuss and argue over the rules and, in doing so, use lots of specialist vocabulary, syntactic structures, and discourse features. They can go to web sites to learn more or to settle their disputes. If and when they do so, here is the sort of thing they will see:

> **8-CLAWS SCORPION:** Even if "8-Claws Scorpion" is equipped with an Equip Spell Card, its ATK is 2400 when it attacks a facedown Defense Position monster. The effect of "8-Claws Scorpion" is a Trigger Effect that is applied if the condition is correct on activation ("8-Claws Scorpion" declared an attack against a face-down Defense Position monster). The target monster does not have to be in facedown Defense Position when the effect of "8-Claws Scorpion" is resolved. So if "Final Attack Orders" is active, or "Ceasefire" flips the monster face-up, "8-Claws Scorpion" still gets its 2400 ATK. The ATK of "8-Claws Scorpion" becomes 2400 during damage calculation. You cannot chain "Rush Recklessly" or "Blast with Chain" to this effect. If these cards were activated before damage calculation, then the ATK of "8-Claws Scorpion" becomes 2400 during damage calculation so those cards have no effect on its ATK. http://www.upperdeckentertainment.com/yugioh/en/

I don't really think I have to say much about this text. It is, in every way, a specialist text. In fact, in complexity, it is far above the language many young children will see in their school books, until they get to middle school at best and, perhaps, even high school. But seven-year-old children deal and deal well with this language (though *Yu-Gi-Oh* cards—and, thus, their language—are often banned at school).

Let's consider, for a moment, what *Yu-Gi-Oh* involves. First and foremost it involves what I will call "lucidly functional language." What do I mean by this? The language on *Yu-Gi-Oh* cards, web sites, and in children's discussions and debates is quite complex, as we have seen, but it relates piece by piece to the rules of the game, to the specific moves or actions one takes in the domain. Here, language—complex specialist language—is married closely to specific and connected actions. The relationship between language and meaning (where meaning here is the rules and the actions connected to them) is clear and lucid. The *Yu-Gi-Oh* company has designed such lucid functionality because it allows them to sell 10,000 cards connected to a fully esoteric language and practice. It directly banks on children's love of mastery and expertise. Would that schools did the same. Would that the language of science in the early years of school was taught in this lucidly functional way. It rarely is.

So we can add "lucidly functional language" to our informal specialist-language lessons as another foundation for specialist language learning, one currently better represented in popular culture than in school. And note here that such lucidly functional language is practiced socially in groups of kids as they discuss, debate, and trade, with more advanced peers often playing a major educative role. They learn to relate oral and written language of a specialist sort, a key skill for specialist domains, including academic ones at school. At the same time, many parents (usually, but not always, more privileged parents) have come to know how to use such lucidly functional language practices—like *Yu-Gi-Oh* or *Pokémon*, and, as well as we will see below, digital technologies like video games—to engage their children in informal specialist-language lessons.

Of course, the sorts of lucidly functional language practices and informal specialist-language lessons that exist around *Yu-Gi-Oh* or *Pokémon* could exist in school—even as early as first grade—to teach school-valued content. But they often don't. Here the creativity of capitalism has outrun that of educators. Furthermore, what *Yu-Gi-Oh* and other such practices show us is that learning specialist languages is not "hard" for young people. It only becomes hard in school—remember, this is what fuels the fourth-grade slump. It is hard there because we ignore it as a process and expect it to show up all by itself thanks to good decoding instruction.

Let me point out what other important lesson we can learn from *Yu-Gi-Oh*. The lucidly functional of language of *Yu-Gi-Oh* cannot be separated from *Yu-Gi-Oh*'s content (*Yu-Gi-Oh* as a domain of knowledge). If such content was school content—part of the school curriculum—then a language gap in regard to *Yu-Gi-Oh* would be equivalent to a knowledge gap. Like all content, *Yu-Gi-Oh* content is structured by its representations (the language) and access to that knowledge is through those representations. It makes no sense to say that full access could be had to *Yu-Gi-Oh* only through the vernacular—though, of course, vernacular mixes with *Yu-Gi-Oh* language all the time—precisely because *Yu-Gi-Oh* language has been invented to allow the game to be created and played as a new sort of human enterprise. Precisely the same is true of biology, algebra, or physics.

CONCLUSION

School is carried out more and more in specialist (in this case, academic) varieties of language as children progress through the grades toward high school and college. Children's success in school ultimately depends on their abilities to talk, listen, read, and write in these varieties, just as does their success in *Yu-Gi-Oh*. Early preparation for these specialist varieties is essential. Otherwise, for many children it is as if the language of school has changed from English to Greek in the middle years and they have never taken any Greek. Better to start early—as early as three, as we saw from our example of the mother and child talking about dinosaurs above.

Reading instruction that takes part as part and parcel of this larger language development process is done in the midst of children becoming enculturated to school-based forms of literacy and "native speakers" of school-based varieties of language. Phonics instruction here—even overt systematic phonics instruction—becomes a supplement and guiding device for a process already well supported and well underway. Reading instruction that evades this process—pretends it doesn't really matter—requires, of course, lots more overt and direct instruction, but instruction that, in the end, doesn't make a "Greek speaker," let alone a member of that school-based "Greek culture." The fourth-grade slump is inevitable.

We know much less about how to deliver such language-development-based instruction for children who have not had a lot of it at home before school. No reports have been written about this. No legislation passed in regard to it. The folks who made *Yu-Gi-Oh* got a lot of it right. Hopefully, if we quit evading the issue, we will catch up with them for the good of all children.

REFERENCES

American Educator (2003, Spring). "The Fourth-Grade Plunge: The Cause. The Cure."

Cain, K. (1996). "Story Knowledge and Comprehension Skills." In C. Cornoldi & J. Oakhill (eds.), *Reading Comprehension Difficulties: Processes and Intervention* (pp. 167–192). Mahwah, NJ: Lawrence Erlbaum.

Chall, J. S., Jacobs, V., & Baldwin, L. (1990). *The Reading Crisis: Why Poor Children Fall Behind.* Cambridge, MA: Harvard University Press.

Chaney, C. (1992). "Language Development, Metalinguistic Skills, and Print Awareness in 3-Year-Old Children." *Applied Psycholinguistics* 13(3), (pp. 485–499).

Chomsky, N. (1986). *Knowledge of Language.* New York: Praeger.

Crowley, K., & Jacobs, M. (2002). "Islands of Expertise and the Development of Family Scientific Literacy." In G. Leinhardt, K. Crowley, & K. Knutson (eds.), *Learning Conversations in Museums* (pp. 333–356). Mahwah, NJ: Lawrence Erlbaum.

Dickinson, D. K., & Neuman, S. B. (eds.). (2006). *Handbook of Early Literacy Research: Volume 2.* New York: Guilford Press.

Elley, R. (1992). *How in the World do Students Read?* Hamburg: The Hague International Association for the Evaluation of Educational Achievement.

Emergent Literacy Project. (n.d.). *What is Emergent Literacy?* [Online]. Available: http://idahocdhd. org/cdhd/emerlit/facts.asp.

Ferguson, R. F. (1998). "Teacher's Perceptions and Expectations and the Black-White Test Score Gap." In C. Jencks & M. Phillips (eds.), *The Black-White Test Score Gap.* Washington, DC: Brookings Institution Press, (pp. 273–317).

Gee, J. P. (1996). *Social Linguistics and Literacies: Ideology in Discourses.* Second Edition. London: Taylor & Francis.

Gee, J. P. (1999). "Reading and the New Literacy Studies: Reframing the National Academy of Sciences Report on Reading," *Journal of Literacy Research* 31.3, (pp. 355–374).

Gee, J. P. (2003). *What Video Games Have to Teach Us About Learning and Literacy.* New York: Palgrave/Macmillian.

Gee, J. P. (2004). *Situated Language and Learning: A Critique of Traditional Schooling.* London: Routledge.

Grissmer, D., Flanagan, A., & Williamson, S. (1998). "Why Did the Black-White Score Gap Narrow in the 1970s and 1980s?" In C. Jencks & M. Phillips (eds.), *The Black-White Test Score Gap.* Washington, DC: Brookings Institution Press, (pp. 182–226).

Hedges, L. V., & Nowell, A. (1998). "Black-White Test Score Convergence Since 1965." In C. Jencks & M. Phillips (eds.), *The Black-White Test Score Gap.* Washington, DC: Brookings Institution Press, (pp. 149–181).

Holland, D., Lachicotte, Jr., W., Skinner, D., & Cain, C. (1998). *Identity and Agency in Cultural Worlds.* Cambridge, MA: Harvard University Press.

Holland, D., & Quinn, N. (eds.). (1987). *Cultural Models in Language and Thought.* Cambridge: Cambridge University Press.

Jencks, C., & Phillips, M. (eds.). (1998). *The Black-White Test Score Gap.* Washington, DC: Brookings Institution Press, (pp. 401–427).

Labov, W. (1972). *Language in the Inner City.* Philadelphia, PA: University of Pennsylvania Press.

Labov, W. (1979). "The Logic of Nonstandard English." In Giglioli, P. (ed.), *Language and Social Context.* Middlesex, U.K.: Penguin Books, (pp. 179–215).

Martin, J. R. (1989). *Factual Writing: Exploring and Challenging Social Reality.* Oxford: Oxford University Press.

National Assessment of Educational Progress. (1997). *NAEP 1996 Trends in Academic Progress.* Washington, DC: U.S. Government Printing Office.

Neisser, U. (ed.). (1998). *The Rising Curve: Long-Term Gains in IQ and Related Measures.* Washington, DC: American Psychological Association.

Pinker, S. (1994). *The Language Instinct: How the Mind Creates Language.* New York: William Morrow.

Scarborough, H. S. (1998). "Early Identification of Children at Risk for Reading Disabilities: Phonological Awareness and Some Other Promising Predictors." In B. K. Shapiro, P. J. Accardo, & A. J. Capute (eds.), *Specific Reading Disability: A View of the Spectrum.* Timonium, MD: York Press, (pp. 77–121).

Shaffer, D. W. (2007). *How Computer Games Help Children Learn.* New York: Palgrave/Macmillan.

Schleppegrell, M. (2004). *Language of Schooling: A Functional Linguistics Perspective.* Mahwah, NJ: Lawrence Erlbaum.

Senechal, M., Ouellette, G., and Rodney D. (2006). "The Misunderstood Giant: Predictive Role of Early Vocabulary to Future Reading." In D.K. Dickinson & S.B. Neuman (eds.), *Handbook of Early Literacy Research: Volume 2.* New York: Guilford Press, (pp. 173–182).

Snow, C. E., Burns, M. S., & Griffin, P. (eds.). (1998). *Preventing Reading Difficulties in Young Children.* Washington, DC: National Academy Press.

Steele, C. M. (1992, April). "Race and the Schooling of Black America," *Atlantic Monthly,* (pp. 68–78).

Steele, C. M. & Aronson, J. (1995). "A Threat in the Air: How Stereotypes Shape the Intellectual Identities and Performance of Women and African Americans," *Journal of Personality and Social Psychology* 69(5), (pp. 797–811).

Steele, C. M. & Aronson, J. (1998). "Stereotype Threat and the Test Performance of Academically Successful African Americans." In C. Jencks & M. Phillips (eds.), *The Black-White Test Score Gap.* Washington, DC: Brookings Institution Press, (pp. 401–427).

Vygotsky, L. S. (1978). *Mind in Society: The Development of Higher Psychological Processes.* Cambridge, MA: Harvard University Press.

Wagner, R. K. (1997, March). "Phonological Awareness Training and Reading." Paper presented at American Educational Research Association Conference, Chicago, IL.

CHAPTER THREE

Forging "Facts" to Fit an Explanation

How to make Reading Research Support Skills-Emphasis Instruction

GERALD COLES

Forging facts to "prove" a predetermined "scientific" explanation is an enduring strata-gem. Contriving economic and social data at the beginning of the 19th century, Thomas Malthus opposed the English Poor Law Act, arguing that the evidence revealed that the legislation was ill-conceived because the poor had no right to even the smallest portion of food, and their early deaths simply accorded with the political-economic "Laws of Nature." (Chase, 1975, pp. 77–83). Later in the century, mismea-sures of brain sizes were employed to prove the mental superiority of Caucasians; mismeasures of head shapes to reveal the superiority of Northern Europeans; and mismeasures of body shapes to uncover innate criminality. In the 20th century, IQ tests were widely employed on behalf of numerous conceptions of social and racial hierarchies that emphasized the mental inferiority of certain groups. In his book *The Mismeasure of Man*, Stephen Jay Gould wryly observes that a "moral" in this work is that "numbers do not guarantee truth" (1981, p. 77).

Criticisms of the George W. Bush administration's misuse of science illustrate that there continues to be no shortage of similar manipulations, with varieties added. As the Union of Concerned Scientists (UCS) has observed, "When scientific knowledge has been found to be in conflict with its political goals, political sup-porters in various Federal departments have been censored and scientific Federal reports whose findings run contrary to the Bush administration policies have been suppressed." Scientific advisory committees whose views contradict Bush admin-istration policy have been disbanded. Highly qualified scientists who did not share the Bush agenda "have been dropped from [scientific] advisory committees." Insistent on effecting policies even when they "are not scientifically sound," the Bush administration has ignored independent scientific advice. A UCS statement, signed by thousands of scientists, including Nobel laureates, stressed that, "The distortion of scientific knowledge for partisan political ends must cease if the public is to be properly informed about issues central to its well being." There needs to be an end to "distorted facts and suppressed truth" that serve an "ideological agenda" in numerous areas from drug safety to air pollution to reproductive health to global warming (2006).

The UCS critique applies equally to ideologically driven reading research that has been used to push an agenda aimed at dominating classroom teaching and learning. Like other areas of concern to the UCS, this agenda, formulated in the "Reading First" claims and mandates in Bush's "No Child Left Behind" legislation, is deeply enmeshed in federal policy and influence. Its aim is to create a top-down, narrow, highly controlled instruction resting heavily on prepackaged reading programs. This instruction minimizes thinking, especially critical thinking, by emphasizing preordained right answers to preordained questions. It eschews children's participation in the creation of the reading curriculum. Promoting superficial reading, it is instruction hostile to using reading to understand oneself and the world. It pretends to be a "magic bullet" answer to poor children's educational needs by concentrating on skills that supposedly will bootstrap them to future academic success. A supposedly "teacher-proof" curriculum, it undercuts the opportunity for teachers to be creative agents who formulate a curriculum based on children's various needs. It is the perfect education for creating unthinking, conformist students who will grow up to be unthinking, conformist citizens, the citizens desired by those who increasingly promote authoritarian social rule. It is beyond the scope of this chapter to amply discuss these educational and ideological ends, but fuller discussions of them can be found in this book and elsewhere (Altwerger, 2005; Edelsky, 1999).

Here I will focus on "distorted facts and suppressed truth" in reading research contained in and surrounding the National Reading Panel Report (National Reading Panel, 2000a), the document cited in Reading First/No Child Left Behind and elsewhere as the gold standard evidence for the superiority of the instruction the legislation mandates. I will discuss the report from the perspective of how facts about reading are forged in various ways to promote an "ideological agenda" similar to that identified by the UCS in other policy areas. In using the term "forged," I rarely mean that the facts are simply faked, as, for example, when psychologist Cyril Burt published I.Q. data in twin studies for twins who did not exist (Kamin, 1974, pp. 35–47). Rather, "forged" usually means "contrived," as when facts, true within themselves, are arranged in various ways to fit and arrive at a foregone conclusion.

CONCLUSIONS FROM THE FORGED FACTS

The National Reading Panel (NRP) concludes that skills-heavy instruction, rigidly sequential, tightly administered, and moving from small parts of language to larger ones is the most effective kind of teaching, especially for poor children. More precisely, according to the NRP Report the research shows this kind of instruction (which afterward became the instruction mandated in Reading First) to be superior:

- To instruction that teaches skills as needed: "Systematic phonics instruction produces significant benefits for students in kindergarten through 6th grade and for children having difficulty learning to read" (NRP Summary, 2000, p. 9).
- For teaching comprehension: "Growth in reading comprehension is also boosted by systematic instruction for younger students and reading disabled students" (NRP Report, 2000a, p. 2–134); phonemic skills training (the ability to hear, distinguish and manipulate word sounds) "did improve students' reading comprehension" (Ehri et al., 2001, p. 276).[1]
- To literature-based teaching in which skills are taught as their need arises: The report concludes there was "better reading growth" in skills-emphasis over whole language classrooms.
- For "at risk" children: "Large effects sizes were produced and maintained in the 2nd and 3rd years of instruction for children who were at-risk for future reading problems and who began receiving systematic phonics instruction in kindergarten or 1st grade" (NRP Report, 2000a, p. 2–137).
- For poor children: "Systematic phonics instruction was significantly more effective in improving low socioeconomic status children's alphabetic knowledge and word reading skills than instructional approaches that were less focused on these initial skills" (NRP Summary, 2000, p. 9).

FORGERS OF FACTS

As underscored by the Union of Concerned Scientists, forging facts requires starting with the right fact-pickers. Foremost among those working on behalf of Reading First facts has been G. Reid Lyon. Dubbed Bush's "reading czar" by the *Wall Street Journal*, Lyon had been the president's chief adviser on reading, going back to Bush's years as governor of Texas. Before going to work for Best Associates, an education corporation, in 2005, Lyon had been chief of the Child Development and Behavior branch of the National Institute of Child Health and Human Development of the

National Institutes of Health. As chief of the branch (hereafter called NICHD, as it is commonly referred to in discussions of reading policy and research) Lyon administered an annual budget of $60 million, most of it going to 44 research sites across the nation. Researchers at these sites share similar conceptions of what counts as scientific reading instruction and what facts contribute to making the case for this instruction. The researchers also uniformly ignore all facts that undercut arguments for this instruction. Lyon's role in transforming this "evidence" into political policy was recognized in a reading conference's description of him as the key person "responsible for translating scientific discoveries relevant to the health and education of children to the White House, the U.S. Congress, and other governmental agencies" (International Dyslexia Association, 2006). When Lyon joined Best Associates, the press release announcing his employment noted that he was "a primary architect of 'Reading First' " (Best Associates, 2005).

This is not to say the embodiment of these "scientific discoveries" into legislation was readily achieved. Although the NICHD research sites continued to grind out studies favoring skill-heavy instruction teaching, something more was needed for policy-mandating it; something seemingly objective, something that would appear to stand outside of NICHD's work and political influence. The answer was a national panel that would look at reading instruction, a panel that would be heavily laden with researchers and appears to be objective. Behind this appearance, however, would be a sufficient number of the right kind of fact-forging panelists to ensure the desired result of creating a document that served as an imprimatur to NICHD-type research and conclusions. With such a document, legislation mandating this instruction could easily be the next step. Enter the National Reading Panel, whose composition was essentially created by the NICHD.

This creation commenced when NICHD, an organization with considerable congressional support for its views on reading, especially among conservative Republicans, obtained a congressional "request" to organize a study of "the effectiveness of various approaches to teaching children how to read" and report the "best ways to apply these findings in classrooms and at home" (NICHD, 1998). Describing this invitation as a "request" is like saying that Boeing got a "request" from the Pentagon to build bombers. That is, that the company chair and board, by merely overseeing the manufacturing work—and without ever lobbying, making campaign contributions, and sitting in chairs that revolve between the company board and the Pentagon— received the request in the mail one fine day.

Although the Department of Education was formally included as a consulting organization in this undertaking, the NICHD's primary role in heading the selection, organization, and administrative processes of the panel for this study was clear. All information releases about the panel flowed from the NICHD; when the panel finished its work, the NICHD announced the results. It was no accident that the panel was slanted toward the NICHD's view that reading skills were central in understanding the reading process, that reading skills deficiencies best explained the cause of reading problems, that skills-heavy instruction was the best way to teach reading, and that reading skills should be the primary focus of reading researchers.

Foremost among the panelists slanted toward this view was Sally Shaywitz, a physician, reading researcher, and recipient of considerable NICHD funding through a NICHD-supported research site at Yale University. There was no question what "review of the literature" she would encourage and conclusions she would reach. A critic of the panel might have had little objection to her participation had she been part of a genuinely broad representation of views if, for example, a researcher with an opposing position had also been on the panel, one who might have publicly and consistently criticized the NICHD perspective commensurate with Shaywitz's support of that perspective. But there was no such person. A pure scientist, Shaywitz served on the national steering committee of "Educators for Bush" in the president's 2004 campaign, following publication of the report and its use in creating Reading First. Afterward, she was appointed to the National Board for Education Sciences, a panel charged with advising the U.S. Department of Education on research and what counts as "scientific evidence" (Institute of Educational Sciences, 2006).

Another panelist was active in various literacy groups at the state and local levels in Texas, and in Governor George W. Bush's Reading Initiative Task Force. One of these groups strongly promoted skills-emphasis direct instruction in beginning reading and had, in fact, invited NICHD-supported researchers to speak to local teachers.

The research and publications of a third panelist contained an interpretation of reading development fully in accord with that in the NICHD research. For him, sight reading of words and knowing the connections between spelling and sounds were what primarily mattered in beginning reading instruction.

A fourth panelist was editor of a journal that had devoted an entire issue to NICHD reading research. Guest editors of the special issue were two NICHD-supported reading researchers. With respect to "diversity," we can again ask, "Did the panel include an editor of an educational journal with an alternative viewpoint?" Once more, the answer is "no."

In addition to the instructional direction in which the reading researchers learned, most, if not all, of their research was quantitative and empirical, exactly the kind that the NICHD advocated and funded. There was no representation of qualitative research, ethnographic research, critical literacy research, research on influences "external" to the classroom that shape teaching and learning, whole language research, sociohistorical research, social process research, or other kinds of research approaches and assumptions about the nature of reading and learning to read.

Only one panelist, Joanne Yatvin, a principal and former teacher, had a clear affiliation with an alternative reading instruction approach: whole language, teaching considered by NICHD reading researchers to be the devil's work. Yatvin had written a guide for developing a whole language program in schools and several articles on literacy improvement generally sympathetic to a whole language orientation, but had no background in quantitative reading research.

The rest of the panel ranged from researchers whose views on reading were similar to the NICHD's to educators who had no background in reading instruction. The chair of the panel was the chancellor of the University System of Maryland, and a physicist by profession. (For a full description of the panelists, see Coles, 2003).

With this diverse panel in place, the right forging of facts was ensured, a forging that employed several methods.

METHOD ONE: BUILD A PROCRUSTEAN PEN

Before the panel reviewed a single piece of research, it established its conclusions about what instruction is best! Although Congress asked the Panel "to assess the status of research-based knowledge, including the effectiveness of various approaches to teaching children to read" (NRP Report, p. 1), the skills-heavy, building-blocks model of reading instruction that the majority of the panel brought to the task was also the only one examined. At the panel's first meeting, in April 1998, the minutes reveal that they identified five areas of reading to be evaluated—phonemic awareness, phonics, fluency, comprehension, and computer technology—and formed a subcommittee for each. Not only was any other model of reading ignored; the panel chose to focus on "reading," not "literacy," thereby excluding the extensive work done showing that writing and reading build upon one another. Besides "writing," Joanne Yatvin wrote in her dissenting "minority view" that the panel also ignored other topics such as "how children's knowledge of oral language, literature and its conventions, and the world apart from print affects their ability to learn to read" and how the "types, quality, or amounts of material children read" affect reading. The panel does deserve credit for choosing a report title that perfectly describes the panel's predictably narrow focus, a predictably not surprising to Yatvin, who observed, "With no powerful voices from other philosophical camps on the panel, it was easy for this majority to believe that [the predetermined dominant view] was the only legitimate view" (Yatvin, 2002, p. 366).

Following the first meeting, the panel had several regional meetings around the country, presumably to listen to and learn from "many voices and perspectives." One such voice came from a representative of the International Reading Association, who urged considering "that no single approach to reading instruction will work equally well for all children." After hearing this and similar kinds of testimony, the panel had a second meeting, at which it spent little time discussing the hearings. Neither did the panel consider surveying the research literature and first identifying a spectrum of areas of reading acquisition that appeared to have promising impacts, such as the aforementioned issues or the size of classroom libraries and children's access to them (NRP, 2000b).

As the NRP Report states, "following the regional meetings," the panel "settled" on the same "topics for intensive study" that they had selected prior to the regional meetings (NRP Report, 2000a, p. 1–2). Putting this more precisely, the report's conclusions were not derived from an appraisal of a spectrum of educational research or opinion. Rather, the panel merely reaffirmed at the end of its research review process that reading instruction—which it had initially identified as the single best instruction worth investigating—was, in fact, the best instruction.

METHOD TWO: INFLATE FACTS

Following publication of the report came an often-repeated claim, exemplified in the Department of Education's announcement on the launching of Reading First. Citing the report's findings, the announcement noted that the National Reading Panel's findings were issued following a review of "100,000 studies on how students learn to read" (U.S. Department of Education, April 2, 2002). A formidable number! However, reality reveals otherwise. Because of the panel's predetermined conclusions about what counts as valid reading instruction, research, and facts, only a small number of the "100,000 studies" with which it began its database were applicable to the panel's predetermined standards. Consequently, the numbers actually reviewed were: 52 studies on phonemic awareness; 38 studies for phonics; 14 for fluency; and 203 for 16 categories of comprehension instruction. That is about 12 or 13 studies, on average, in each category; a long distance from the inflated "100,000." While these numbers might be sufficient for drawing some reasonable conclusions, they would not likely be sufficient for establishing restrictive national policy. Given the actual facts in these studies, the latter possibility is even more unreasonable. Nonetheless, "100,000 studies" surely gives the impression of a huge amount of digging, sifting, and examining to get to the truth.

METHOD THREE: MAKE THE MEANING
OF FACTS ACQUIRE A NEW MEANING

What is "reading"? Throughout the report the term is used liberally, but its definition is ever changing. Reading in one place might mean reading real or nonsense words;

somewhere else it might mean reading aloud smoothly and rapidly. Seldom does it mean comprehending text, a process most people would define as key in reading.

The report's predominant definition of reading is reading at the word level, with a special stress on decoding skills. Nonetheless, all definitions of reading are transformed into the cryptic term "reading." For example, the report states that an eleven-week training program for poor kindergarteners, focusing on phonemic awareness activities and games that included learning to read real words, "transferred to reading" (NRP Report, 2000a, pp. 2–34 to 2–35). The report makes no mention of the inconvenient fact that the measures of "reading" success did not include reading of sentences or tests of comprehension. "Reading" boiled down to the results of phonemic awareness and word-list tests. Nevertheless, the report includes this study as one demonstrating that "training boosts children's *reading*."

Another study supposedly showing that phonemic training boosts *reading* was done in Sweden with kindergartners. Unreported in the report are the following facts noted by the original researchers at the conclusion of their study: in a follow-up of the children at the end of first grade, although the students in the phonemic training program did better on phonemic awareness tests, *there were no group differences for silent reading*, spelling, and reading nonsense words (Olofsson & Lundberg, 1985). "Boosts" of this kind are abundant in the studies the panel reviewed.

As for the real definition of "reading," that is, reading and comprehending sentences and paragraphs, remarkably, the panel used only *ten* studies, a fact omitted in the report! And what did the facts in these studies reveal about the effect of skills-heavy reading instruction? From these ten studies, twenty correlations were derived, among which only *six* showed a large effect. Of the rest, six showed a moderate effect, and eight showed either *a small or a negative effect*. Furthermore, within this small number of overall studies on comprehension, of the six "large" effects, three came from a single study, not three different studies. This is another fact the report fails to mention.

Determining the power of the studies showing "large" effects is difficult because of the control groups used in these studies. In one study the researchers reveal almost nothing about the instruction that was an alternative to skills teaching. In another study, the skills-training group was pitted against controls only doing "coloring, cutting and sticking." A third study compared skills training against sight-word recognition (or "look-say") teaching, a method that has been criticized and rejected by all reading experts, especially those advocating a whole language approach. The final study showing a "large effect" on comprehension compared children who had two years of instruction that included an additional skills training program with children who had only one year of instruction. I leave it to the reader to deduce which group had the higher reading comprehension scores: the group with one year of instruction or two? None of these facts is discussed in the report.

Most critically, for these and similar skills-training studies that, according to the report, included significant effects on comprehension, these studies did not demonstrate a sustained effect on comprehension where follow-up testing was done one or two years after training. As one researcher who did attempt to achieve such an effect concluded, "As in other studies, this amount of [skills training] did not lead to unique benefits for growth in reading comprehension," an outcome "similar to the findings of most controlled studies of explicit training even with somewhat longer training times" (Wise, 2000, pp. 230–231). Not surprisingly, this appraisal of the research facts on comprehension outcomes does not appear in any of the report's discussion of "reading" (see Coles, 2003, pp. 63–67 for a full discussion of these ten studies on comprehension benefits).

METHOD FOUR: REFASHION NO COMPARISON
INTO AN INFORMATIVE COMPARISON

Running through the report is the "compared with what" problem, which uses two kinds of fact fashioning. One, as I noted above, compares various kinds of skills-training with no other kind of beginning reading instruction—e.g., "coloring, cutting and sticking"—and finds that the first group obtains better test results, especially when the tests are related to the skills that were taught.

A second kind of refashioning no comparison into an informative comparison uses a control group whose reading instruction is never clearly defined. An example is a study by Joanna Williams (1980). The experimental group, composed of students ages seven to twelve, had a skills training program (e.g., segmenting and blending phonemes, phonics exercises, spelling word sounds) added to their regular classroom teaching. At the end of the training period, the report states, the training group had significantly superior outcomes in decoding words and nonwords compared to "the untreated controls," thereby demonstrating that the program "was highly effective at teaching decoding skills to disabled readers" (NRP Report, 2000a, p. 2–36).

Omitted from the report is any information about the students and the instructional curriculum. The Williams' paper itself explains that the children were identified as "learning disabled" and in special education classrooms in New York City (in schools in Harlem and the Lower East Side) in 1975. She states that "the regular reading instruction provided in these classrooms might best be described as eclectic. Teachers used a different basal reading program in almost every classroom; three teachers used only one series, and two teachers each used two other series. About 75% of the teachers also used phonics materials. (Sometimes the phonics component of the basal series and sometimes a separate phonics program was used.)" (p. 8). Worksheets were part of the curriculum as well.

What we had, in other words, were special education classes that appeared to be doing nothing "special" with the students. No doubt the classes were going through the basal readers at a slower pace, but there was no indication that the classrooms used anything other than the traditional, conventional reading programs used in the regular classes, reading programs that perhaps were those that contributed to the students' reading failure in the first place.

Therefore, we could say that the training program was helpful as an adjunct to a conventional basal reading program used in conventional special education classes in 1975, classes that duplicated, at a slower pace, the literacy program that the children used before being placed in special education. This is hardly a persuasive demonstration of the reading benefits of phonemic awareness training or the need for such training over alternative substantive reading education approaches.

METHOD FIVE: MISREPRESENT CAUSATION

The third method configures accurate research facts to support foregone conclusions about causation that do not follow from these facts. Here is an example. The report states that a study by David Share and colleagues (1984) "showed that phonemic awareness was the top predictor along with letter knowledge" (knowing the names of letters) of later reading achievement. This description suggests that because there was a high correlation between phonemic awareness and "reading achievement scores" in kindergarten and first grade, phonemic awareness could "play a causal role in learning to read" (NRP Report, 2000a, p. 2–11). The fact that phonemic awareness was a "top predictor" is true, but the panel finessed the facts for its own predetermined ends by not discussing the meaning of the term "predictor," especially with respect to the study's third strongest predictor of reading achievement.

That predictor was the degree of success on a "finger localization" test, in which a child whose vision is blocked identifies which of his or her fingers an adult has touched. Despite its predictive correlation with future reading achievement, finger localization skill in itself could not be considered causal to learning to read, and no educator would suggest finger localization training as a beginning reading method.

Then there's the matter of the second predictor, letter knowledge, and what the researchers themselves made of their facts. In addition to not mentioning the third predictor, the report also fails to mention that the researchers offered an explicit caveat about confusing correlation with causation, particularly with respect to this second predictor. Yes, they did find that letter knowledge was a strong predictor of future reading, but they emphasized its predictive strength did not mean that beginning readers needed to know letter names in order to get off to a fast, secure start in reading.

Although "knowledge of letter names has been traditionally considered the single best predictor of reading achievement," they observed, "there appears to be no evidence that letter-name knowledge facilitates reading acquisition" (p. 1313).

Letter-name knowledge is likely to be part of and represent early experience with and accomplishment in written language activities, and is knowledge, like that of various beginning reading skills, that can be considered to be a marker of these experiences and accomplishments (Coles, 1998). One can readily suggest the same is true for phonemic awareness: being a "top predictor" does not necessarily equal causation. Like many other investigations of phonemic awareness, this one identifies predictors that are in fact "products" related to a variety of experiences with written language (Coles, 2000) None of these issues is captured in the report's manipulation of facts that enable it to produce the simplistic summary; the study "showed that phonemic awareness was the top predictor along with letter knowledge."

Another example is the report's discussion of a 1997 study by Brennan and Ireson (1997). The report states that a "phonemic awareness treatment group" was "compared to one no-treatment group" and the "effect size was impressive." This provides evidence, says the panel, that the skills training program "can be used effectively" in classrooms (NRP Report, 2000a, p. 2–35).

The comparison that the report made was correct as far as it went, but it omitted one large set of facts that came from a second control group that the report does not mention. Besides the one described—the no-treatment group—another control group learned phonemic awareness skills in an informal, "as needed" way similar to the way skills are taught in a whole language approach. In other words, what we have in this study is an opportunity to obtain facts about causation by comparing children learning phonemic awareness either through a training program or an implicit, "as needed" method. Although this comparison would have provided the panel with an opportunity to delve into the question of how phonemic awareness should be taught and learned, it chose not to take advantage of this opportunity.

Let us do so. At the end of the school year the phonemic awareness training group did significantly better on phonemic tests, but there were "no significant differences between the [training and implicit teaching] groups on the rhyme and syllable synthesis tests or *on the tests of word reading and spelling*" (p. 251, my emphasis). What facts did the panel include in the report? Only the phonemic test results; not the others, which showed no significant differences. In contrast, the researchers who did the study were well-aware of implications of these facts with respect to causation, noting that "the significantly superior scores achieved by the training group in this study on tasks of phonemic awareness suggest that this group should also achieve higher scores on the reading tasks, but this was not in fact the case" (p. 257). This too does not appear in the report.

The researchers went on to propose that the "writing experiences" of the informal learning group might have accounted for their reading success. On average they "wrote longer stories than either" the training group or the normal kindergarten group (p. 258). These conclusions about causation also are omitted from the report.

In other words, the study showed that in order for children to learn rhyme, syllable synthesis, word reading, and spelling, they do not require such a skills-training program. Furthermore, extensive writing activities are likely to be effective for attaining the literacy knowledge for which the researchers tested. This study lends some support to a holistic written language approach insofar as it indicates that phonemic skills can be readily learned within a rich array of reading and writing activities. It also demonstrates that not only is there no need for a stepwise approach to literacy learning; such an approach can reduce time spent on essential and causally productive literacy activities, such as "writing experiences."

METHOD SIX: KEEP UNWELCOMED OUTCOMES
FAR AWAY FROM THE PROCRUSTEAN PEN

One concern that should be central in reading education is children's conception of "reading" and of themselves as "readers." To a reader, does "reading" mean word identification or does it include comprehension and, if so, what kinds? Is "reading" seen as an activity that has applications beyond the immediate process itself? Does instruction produce competent but apathetic "readers," those who become "aliterate," that is, able to read but unmotivated to do so? These and similar questions are critical to the overarching question: what are the purposes of reading education and education in general? Not only are none of these concerns included in the panel's focus on a narrow, mechanical definition of reading training and outcomes; when facts shed light on these concerns, they are kept at bay.

A graphic example is a study by Penny Freppon (1991) comparing reading outcomes for first-grade children taught with either skills-based or literature-based/whole language instruction. Because only narrow horse race outcomes interested the panel, they merely report that the study found similar results on conventional reading tests for both groups, thereby excluding what the study revealed about how students conceptualized "reading" and being a "reader."

In the literature-based instruction, decoding skills were focused on as needed, but more of the students' attention was drawn to meaning, with the teacher encouraging the children to think about what was going on in the story. The implicit definition of "reading" in whole language instruction made decoding "a" key, not "the" key, in orchestrating the thought processes. For the skills group, the grapheme-phoneme task loomed larger both as a strategy and as the meaning of "reading" and was more "the" key than "a" key. In the skills classroom, reading for meaning was included but it was "incidental" to word skills instruction (p. 144).

Almost all of the children in the literature group "said that understanding the story or both understanding and getting words right is more important in reading." In contrast, only half the children in the skills group chose these explanations; nearly all of the remaining half chose "getting words right as most important" (p. 153). Asked about the "characteristics of good readers," skill-emphasis readers stressed "knowing and learning words and sounding out words," while the literature-based group discussed factors such as "reading a lot" and "understanding the story." The skill group included "paying attention to the teacher" and "knowing their place in the book," characteristics that were not mentioned by the literature group. These latter findings suggest that skills-emphasis teaching tends to encourage conformity and dependence, whereas literature emphasis teaching tends to encourage independence and self-confidence. Presumably, these would be critical facts in considering the ends of reading education and in formulating national policy. Not so for the panel, who ignore these facts not simply because they do not fit into the narrow functionalist criteria it established at the beginning. More significantly, these facts would begin to raise questions about the kind of people we want children to become, questions now eschewed in "scientific" reading education research and policy.

METHOD SEVEN: ASK THE WRONG QUESTION AND THEREBY AVOID NECESSARY FACTS

The report frames questions about reading education around identifying the ingredients of an effective reading program, a framing that serves as another forging device by posing the wrong question. Rather than, "What's the best instruction for teaching reading?" the question should be, "What needs to be done to ensure that all children learn to read?" By asking the first question, we are constrained to stick solely to "the ingredients," but with the second question, we include attention not only to instruction but to all other influences on children's reading outcomes, such as nutrition, health, housing, toxic environments, stress, and similar "non-instructional" influences that directly affect learning. By avoiding that second question, we also avoid a full examination of governmental policies that harm children's learning.

A look back at Texas under then-governor Bush offers insights into the consequences of using these alternative questions to frame school and reading education policy. While Governor Bush bemoaned the reading test failures of Texas school children and insisted that the state get "back to the basics," Texas ranked second among states in the percentage of people, particularly children, who went hungry and ranked third in the percentage of malnourished citizens. After Bush vetoed a bill to coordinate Texas hunger programs, reporters asked him about hunger in the state. "Where?" was his reply. Under Bush, Texas was tied for third place in the state percentage of children in poverty. Just three states provided lower welfare help. Under Bush, the state's food stamps payments, an essential program for poor children, were slashed by $1 billion. Also under Bush, Texas ranked second in the percentage of poor children who lacked health insurance. When Texas had a large budget surplus, Bush fought against providing affordable health care for 250,000 children and instead pushed through a $45 million tax break for oil-well owners. Having the opportunity to invest some of the surplus in education, he instead pursued tax cuts. Although there are ample empirical facts demonstrating the direct benefits of health, hunger, housing, family income, and numerous similar non-instructional influences on academic success, Bush and the reading researchers who supported him chose instead to keep their lens on "the basics," the ingredients of the heavily prescriptive, prepackaged, "teacher-proof," skills-heavy instruction.

All of the social policy neglect, coupled with "back to the basics," contributed to making the "Texas education miracle" a sham. Students showed test progress on the state-created tests, but not on independent national tests. During the Bush years, the gap in Texas reading scores between minority and white students actually increased! (See Coles, 2003 for a full discussion of Texas under Bush).

Neglect of the critical non-instructional influences on reading success continued into the Bush presidency, despite the substantial data compelling anyone serious about reading education to ask the question, "What needs to be done to ensure that all children learn to read?" For example, research has established a "link between children's nutrition and academic performance." Hungry children are more likely to repeat a grade, have more academic problems, exhibit slower memory recall, and to be absent from school. Conversely "hunger reduction and improved nutrition" improves children's learning (Child Nutrition Policy Brief, 2006).

Similar documentation links children's health and learning success. For example, asthma problems are associated with lost school days and lower academic achievement, a connection that especially affects poor children, whose academic success is already under pressure in numerous other ways. As the Children's Defense Fund notes, "Although the prevalence of asthma is increasing for all children, black and low-income children are disproportionately affected. Black children and children from poor families are not only more likely to have had asthma than white or Latino children and children from higher-income families, they also are more likely to have suffered asthma attacks." (Improving Children's Health, 2006).

The environmental toxin lead continues to affect millions of children—particularly poor children—despite the 1978 U.S. national ban on lead in paint and gasoline. A continuing problem is deteriorating lead paint in older housing, which is the chief source of lead exposure in young children, occurring when they ingest, especially from hand-to-mouth activity, lead-laden paint chips, house dust, or soil. Lead is more dangerous to children than adults because children's growing bodies absorb more of it and their brains and nervous systems are more sensitive to lead's damaging effect. Children with high levels of lead "can suffer damage to the brain and nervous system" which in turn contributes to learning and behavior problems, slowed growth, hearing problems, and headaches (U.S. Environmental Protection Agency, 2006). Researchers have found a strong correlation between low blood lead concentrations and scores on reading and arithmetic tests (Canfield et al., 2003). These associations have been found even with very low amounts of lead levels in children, confirming the view that there is no low level of lead that is without adverse consequences.

Toxic stress should also concern policy makers committed to children's reading success. Caused by various combinations of poverty factors, such as housing insecurity, homelessness, or excessive noise, toxic stress has been shown to have dire affects on children's cognition and academic achievement (see reports of The National Scientific Council on the Developing Child, 2006).

Summarizing much of the research on childhood poverty and social class influences on academic outcomes, grade attainment, special education placement, and so forth, Richard Rothstein concluded that "the influence of social class characteristics is probably so powerful that schools cannot overcome it, no matter how well trained are their teachers and no matter how well designed are their instructional programs and climates" (Rothstein, 2004, p. 5). Yet all of this is ignored by the panel's framing of its key question as, "What is the best instruction?" By doing so, its analysis perfectly deflected attention away from the Bush administration's callous indifference to children's well-being, as expressed in policies that affect academic success. For example, every Bush administration budget, except for the one crafted when he was campaigning for a second term, has included substantial cuts in funding for Children and Family Services; Low Income Home Energy Assistance; Head Start; Special Supplemental Nutrition Programs for Women, Infants, and Children; Child Care and Development Block Grant; Medicaid (a chief source of health care for poor children); food stamps; Section 8 Housing vouchers (rent support program); and lead prevention and abatement programs. In education areas, cuts were proposed for K-12 education for the disadvantaged, teacher training, before- and after-school learning programs in high-poverty areas, and education for homeless children (Center on Budget and Policy Priorities, 2006). The panel handily excludes policies such as these from view!

CONCLUSION

Forging the facts enabled the National Reading Panel to conceal that its very own research, without including a single study outside of its own database, which really shows that:

1. Skills-emphasis instruction is not superior to teaching skills as needed.
2. Students learn skills as well in literature-based instruction, where they are taught as needed, as in skills-focused instruction.
3. Skills-emphasis instruction has no greater benefits, compared with other instruction, in comprehension beyond first or second grade.
4. Skills-emphasis instruction is not superior to whole language teaching.
5. On conventional reading tests that include skills tests, whole language classes do as well as skills-emphasis classes.
6. Skills-emphasis instruction does not help "disabled" readers overcome their problems and become normal readers.
7. Skills-emphasis instruction is not superior for poor, "at-risk" children.

Moreover, the research used in the report shows that:

1. Whole language promotes comprehension without diminishing the use of word skills to obtain meaning.
2. Whole language encourages a more positive attitude and more enthusiasm toward reading than does skills-emphasis teaching.
3. Whole language is more likely to include extensive writing, which helps children learn not only written expression, but word skills and vocabulary.[2]

Regrettably, these facts remain largely hidden from teachers and the public, in large part because of the dominant control the Bush administration has had in orchestrating what is identified as "science" for public policy. The Union of Concerned Scientists' persistent condemnation of the administration's ideological grip on science, one that produces "devastating human impacts" and puts "people in harm's way," continues to apply to reading education.

Another influence contributing to cloaking the facts is the support that skills-heavy, lock-step teaching receives from well-funded conservative think tanks. At the time I was finishing this chapter, for example, the National Council on Teacher Quality (NCTQ)—a joint project of the ultra-conservative Fordham Foundation and Education Leaders Council, and the recipient of millions of dollars from the Bush administration—issued a report, *What Education Schools Aren't Teaching About Reading—and What Elementary Teachers Aren't Learning* (2006). No wonder the NRP report "became the foundation for federal legislation," the NCTQ report observed;

the NRP report's evidence for skills-heavy instruction is "especially strong," and its conclusions are "conclusive." (2000a, p. 8). Not surprisingly, Reid Lyon served as a key adviser to the study. Yes, the NCTQ report acknowledged, there had been some initial criticism of the report, "with some findings by the panel" initially meeting with resistance through "many educators expressing skepticism over its methodology and findings." But this resistance has not held up, the NCTQ report assured the public, because "no subsequent work of serious scholarship has challenged its findings" (p. 8).

As reading expert Richard Allington noted, one would not know from the NCTQ report that at least two dozen professional articles critiquing the report have appeared in peer-reviewed journals such as *Harvard Educational Review, Reading Research Quarterly*, and *Elementary School Journal*. There have also been book-length critiques, including my *Reading the Naked Truth*, which have examined the report's research in considerable *scholarly* detail (Allington, personal communication). (One personal note regarding the "no serious scholarship" assertion: *Reading the Naked Truth* won a District Administration's Choice Award, which identifies "outstanding" books recommended for school administrators.)

The NCTQ report uses a not-so-clever ploy initiated by NICHD several years ago. By dismissing all contrary evaluations as works devoid of "serious scholarship," defenders of skills-heavy, lock-step teaching do not have to engage critics and thereby include them in a public debate. The ploy also allows the defenders to bolster an assumption that science has won the day and the only objections have come from grousers whose feeble scholarship is not worth the time to address it.

The facts also remain hidden from the public because of the gross imbalance between viewpoints in the media: articles and opinion pieces continue to reaffirm the report's "findings," while alternative views seldom appear and when they do, they usually are no more than a brief letter responding to a major piece that lauds the report. For example, right after the NCTQ report was published, an opinion piece on "our illiteracy crisis" appeared in *USA Today*. Why the illiteracy "malady," William Moloney, Colorado's commissioner of education asked? Simple, he explained; "Schools across the nation" are not teaching the "five common tenets of reading research" identified by the NRP report. A mere "15% employ all," demonstrating that NICHD was right in insisting that reading teachers have not been "properly trained" in scientific reading. Responsible for the nation's "literacy deficits" were the professors of reading education: "When those who teach our teachers are clueless about or even outright hostile to reading research, is it any wonder that our children become the victims of a monumental literacy deficit?"(Moloney, 2006).

Besides *USA Today*, other media reported approvingly on the NCTQ study. For instance, the *Baltimore Times*, an African American newspaper, began an article on the study with this paragraph, "At the National Press Club in Washington, D.C., Kate Walsh, president of the National Council on Teacher Quality (NCTQ) unveiled a report" showing that "most teacher prep institutions either teach no reading approach or cling to outdated approaches that years of scientific study have found to be ineffective with at least a third of all children." Concerned about the educational achievement of African American children and hearing no debate over this "scientific study," no wonder the newspaper reported only Walsh's comments (Herring, 2006).

On National Public Radio, the story on the NCTQ report included a sound clip by Kate Walsh and stressed, "A new report has some rather disturbing news. The functional illiteracy rate in this country is 25 percent—same as it's been for decades. Teachers aren't being taught how to teach reading. Turns out they're not learning about the science behind reading, despite decades of research" (NPR, 2006).

Also cloaking the facts is, unfortunately, the support of the leaders of teachers unions, particularly the leaders of the American Federation of Teachers (AFT). Discussing the NCTQ report under the title, "Teaching Reading Is a Science," the AFT assured teachers that "research indicates that the percentage of struggling readers could drop by two-thirds—and possibly by as much as 95 percent—by implementing a scientifically based approach to reading instruction. Unfortunately, that message is only slowly spreading across the country, and apparently has not made its way into most teacher preparation programs." Reiterating a view contained in its earlier AFT publications on reading—such as its 1998 report, *Teaching Reading Is Rocket Science*, authored by NICHD-supported Louisa Moats—the AFT told its members that the NCTQ study found "that the key components of a scientifically based approach to reading are rarely taught in a way that conveys their solid research foundation" (American Federation of Teachers, 2006).

A few professional organizations, such as the National Council of Teachers of English, have opposed this form of instruction, but the major professional reading organization, the International Reading Association (IRA), has not. Although IRA has provided some publication space for alternative views of what comprises "scientific" reading education, its organizational policy has been mostly supportive of the findings of the report and has included collaborative meetings with NICHD.

A lack of broad public consciousness about the actual facts of "scientific" reading instruction has, in turn, guaranteed an absence of any broad opposition. In Chris Mooney's book, *The Republican War on Science*, he observes that "in the end," to beat back the attack on science and the political use of pseudoscience, we must confront "the reality that we face a political problem, one that requires explicitly political solutions"(Mooney, 2005, p. 255). Unfortunately, with respect to reading "snake oil," we are a long way from enacting Mooney's recommendation. The years accumulate and the assault of Reading First-type instruction on classrooms continues, wrapped in the illusion that it offers a literacy cure.

Above the *USA Today* opinion piece by William Moloney was one on the U.S. war in Iraq, a war that has parallels to the reading snake oil insofar as the evidence justifying the invasion was as threadbare as the evidence for Reading First teaching. Unfortunately, public opinion did not turn against the war until the number of its casualties increased and the barren answers for starting and "winning" the war became evident time and time again. I fear that, barring some teacher and public opposition that is unforeseeable at this time, a substantial opposition to "scientific" reading might have to await similar public recognition of its student casualties. Of course what are missing in this parallel are the anti-war activists who relentlessly continued to expose the fabrications justifying the Iraq war. Although they were in the minority for several years, they persisted, sustained in part by a commitment to stop its ever-growing number of victims. I wish I could end this chapter on a more optimistic note, but the best I can offer right now is this: in the absence of a movement against Reading First snake oil, a commitment to end its casualties remains reason enough for a minority to keep fighting.

NOTES

1. For consistency, "phonemic awareness" is used throughout the chapter. The studies discussed here use either this term or "phonological awareness," with both terms generally referring to the ability to hear, distinguish, and manipulate word sounds.
2. Full documentation for these conclusions is beyond the scope of this chapter, but can be found in my book, *Reading the Naked Truth*.

REFERENCES

Allington, R. (2006). Personal communication. June 16, 2006.

Altwerger, B. (2005). *Reading for Profit: How the Bottom Line Leaves Kids Behind*. Portsmouth, NH: Heinemann.

American Federation of Teachers. (2006). *Teaching Reading Is a Science*. (http://www.aft.org/pubs-reports/american_educator/issues/summer06/notebook.htm). Accessed August 31, 2006.

Best Associates. (2005). *National Reading Expert Joins Best Associates*. (http://www.bestassociates.com/reading.html). Accessed August 31, 2006.

Brennan, F., & Ireson, J. (1997). Training Phonological Awareness: A Study to Evaluate the Effects of a Program of Metalinguistic Games in Kindergarten, *Reading and Writing* 9: pp. 241–263.

Canfield, R., Henderson Jr., C. R., Cory-Slechta, D. A., Cox, C., Jusko, T. A., & Lanphear, B. P. (2003). Intellectual Impairment in Children with Blood Lead Concentrations Below 10 μg per Deciliter. *New England Journal of Medicine* 348(16): pp. 1517–1526.

Center on Budget and Policy Priorities. (2006). *Federal Budget Publication Library*. (http://www.cbpp.org/pubs/fedbud.htm). Accessed August 31, 2006.

Chase, A. (1975). *The Legacy of Malthus: The Social Costs of the New Scientific Racism*. New York: Alfred A. Knopf.

Child Nutrition Policy Brief. (2006). *Nutrition for Learning*. Food Research & Action Center, Washington, D.C. (http://www.frac.org/pdf/cnnl.pdf). Accessed August 31, 2006.

Coles, G. (1998). *Reading Lessons: The Debate Over Literacy*. New York: Hill & Wang.

Coles, G. (2000). *Misreading Reading: The Bad Science That Hurts Children*. Portsmouth, NH: Heinemann.

Coles, G. (2003). *Reading the Naked Truth: Literacy, Legislation and Lies*. Portsmouth, NH: Heinemann.

Edelsky, C. (2006). *With Literacy and Justice for All: Rethinking the Social in Language and Education* (Language, Culture, and Teaching). Mahwah, NJ: Lawrence Erlbaum Associates.

Ehri, L.C., Nunes, S.R., Willows, D.M., Schuster, B.V., Yaghoub-Zadeh, Z., & Shanahan, T. (2001). Phonemic Awareness Instruction Helps Children Learn to Read: Evidence from the National Reading Panel's Meta-Analysis. *Reading Research Quarterly* 36(3): pp. 250–287.

Freppon, P. (1991). Children's Concepts of the Nature and Purpose of Reading in Different Instructional Settings. *Journal of Reading Behavior* 23(2): pp. 139–163.

Gould, S.J. (1981). *The Mismeasure of Man*. New York: W.W. Norton.

Herring, N. (2006). New study sheds light on reading levels. *Baltimore Times*. July 9 (http://www.btimes.com/News/article/.asp?NewsID=70181&sID=4). Accessed August 31, 2006.

Improving Children's Health: Understanding Children's Health Disparities and Promising Approaches to Address Them. (2006). Children's Defense Fund, Washington, D.C. (www.childrensdefense.org) Accessed August 31, 2006.

Institute of Educational Sciences. (2006) Members of the National Board for Education Sciences. U.S. Department of Education. (http://ies.ed.gov/director/board/members.asp). Accessed August 31, 2006.

International Dyslexia Association (2006). Events: Research to Practice. (http://www.dyslexia-ca.org/events.html). Accessed August 31, 2006.

Kamin, L. (1974). *The Science and Politics of I.Q.* New York: John Wiley & Sons.

Maloney, W.J. (2006). To Find the Answer to Our Illiteracy Crisis, Americans Must Look Within. *USA Today*. August 17 (p. 11A).

Mooney, C. (2005). *The Republican War on Science*. New York: Basic Books.

National Council on Teacher Quality (2006). What Education Schools Aren't Teaching About Reading—and What Elementary Teachers Aren't Learning. Washington, D.C. (http://www.nctq.org/nctq/). Accessed August 31, 2006.

National Institute of Child Health and Human Development (NICHD). (March 27, 1998). Panel to Assess New Readiness of Reading Research for Use in Nation's Classrooms. Press Release (http://www.nichd.nih.gov/new/releases/re4Panel.cfm). Accessed August 31, 2006.

National Public Radio (2006). Why Johnny can't keep US competitive. May 23. (http://marketplace.publicradio.org/shows/2006/05/23/AM200605236.html). Accessed August 31, 2006.

National Reading Panel. (2000a). *Teaching Children to Read: An Evidence-Based Assessment of the Scientific Research Literature on Reading and Its Implications for Reading Instruction*. Washington, D.C.: NICHD.

National Reading Panel (2000b). NRP Meetings Archives (http://www.nationalreadingPanel.org/NRPAbout/Meetings_Archive.htm). Accessed August 31, 2006.

National Reading Panel Summary. (2000). *Teaching Children to Read: An Evidence-Based Assessment of the Scientific Research Literature on Reading and Its Implications for Reading Instruction*. Washington, D.C.: NICHD.

National Scientific Council on the Developing Child (2006). Reports and Research. Working Papers (http://www.developingchild.net/reports.html). Accessed August 31, 2006.

Olofsson, A. & Lundberg, I. (1985). Evaluation of Long-Term Effects on Phonemic Awareness Training in Kindergarten: Illustrations of some Methodological Problems in Evaluation Research. *Scandinavian Journal of Psychology* 26(2): pp. 21–34.

Rothstein, R. (2004). *Class and Schools: Using Social, Economic, and Educational Reform to Close the Black-White Achievement Gap.* Washington, D.C.: Economic Policy Institute.

Share, D., Jorm, A.F., Maclean, R. and Matthews, R. (1984). Sources of Individual Differences in Reading Acquisition. *Journal of Educational Psychology* 76(3): pp. 1309–1324.

Union of Concerned Scientists (2006). Restoring Scientific Integrity in Policy Making. (http://www.ucsusa.org/scientific_integrity/interference/scientists-signon-statement.html). Accessed August 31, 2006.

U.S. Department of Education (April 2, 2002). Paige Announces "Unprecedented Reading Reform" For U.S. (http://www.ed.gov/news/pressreleases/2002/04/04022002.html). Accessed August 31, 2006.

U.S. Environmental Protection Agency (2006). Lead in Paint, Dust, and Soil. Washington, D.C. (http://www.epa.gov/lead/pubs/leadinfo). Accessed August 31, 2006.

Williams, J.P. (1980). Teaching Decoding With an Emphasis on Phoneme Analysis and Phoneme Blending." *Journal of Educational Psychology* 72(1): pp. 1–15.

Wise, B., King, J., & Olson, R. (2000). Individual differences in gains from computer-assisted remedial reading. *Journal of Experimental Child Psychology* 77(3): pp. 197–235.

Yatvin, J. (2002). Babes in the Woods: The Wanderings of the National Reading Panel. *Phi Delta Kappan* 83(5): pp. 364–369.

CHAPTER FOUR

Literacy Packages
IN Practice

Constructing Academic Disadvantage

PATRICIA D. IRVINE AND JOANNE LARSON

In this chapter, we describe our study of elementary teachers piloting a commodified literacy package in an urban district serving predominantly low-income African American and Latino students. In this district, the central administration had piloted several new literacy packages to choose one for the entire district. The administration believed that adopting a single series would improve students' low reading achievement scores by standardizing instruction and retraining those teachers suspected of having marginal skills. However, interviews with teachers participating in the pilot and observations of their classroom practices showed that teachers used the materials selectively, choosing activities to remedy what they perceived as students' deficits in oral language and academic abilities. We present data to show that the autonomous definition of literacy (Street, 1995) that underlies the materials, in combination with a deficit model of students and their linguistic and cultural resources, resulted in pedagogical practices that we believe academically disadvantage the students whom the district is trying to serve.

Since the 2001 edition of this book, the Bush administration enacted No Child Left (NCLB) legislation. Through the Reading First initiative, NCLB provides competitive funding to states that apply to raise reading achievement through implementing "scientifically-based" literacy packages (http://www.ed.gov/programs/readingfirst). The district we describe in this chapter has since implemented Success for All, America's Choice, and a Reading First curriculum, among others, as quick fixes. The district has received a substantial grant from the Gates Foundation to implement small schools reform in several high schools. It has also created an International Baccalaureate program with an associated middle-school "feeder" program. All of these efforts are based on reductionist views of literacy and of learning associated with commodification. The release of an internal audit that reveals the inappropriate research base of Reading First has so far done nothing to deter the mandated use of grant practices, procedures, and materials (US Dept of Education, 2006).

In California, where Irvine now teaches, Open Court is one of the scripted reading programs adopted by the California State Board of Education in 2002 and again in 2005 (http://www.cde.ca.gov/ci/rl/im/rlaadoptedlist.asp). Despite research evidence that these programs do not raise reading achievement on the state-mandated SAT 9 tests (Moustafa & Land, 2002), California school districts demand teachers use this program or incur negative sanctions. Jaeger (2006), for example, describes being pushed out of her job for resisting Open Court in a Bay Area district. With NCLB tying commodified literacy packages to funding, the stakes are high for all players. We define commodified literacy materials as those materials produced by profit-oriented publishing corporations. Shannon (this volume) describes the fetishism of commodities associated with capitalism as a process that masks the social relations that go into producing a "thing" (literacy curriculum or package). Moreover, values accrue to these commodities in terms of use value, or what someone gets out of it, and exchange value, or what someone can get for it.

Packaged literacy materials have long been criticized for the limited view of literacy they promote and because they attempt to script teachers' behaviors, deskilling them in the process (Apple, 1990; Beyer, 1988; Goodman, Shannon, Freeman, & Murphy, 1988; Luke, 1988; Shannon, 1992). Our study adds to the literature critical of commodified materials by suggesting that it is not just the content of the materials themselves, but how they are used in practice that affects literacy learning and the values attributed to them. Moreover, we suggest that commercial materials, as key components in literacy events (Heath, 1983) and literacy practices (Street, 1995), are imbricated in a nexus of social practices in local contexts that are linked to broader cultural and political practices (Barton, Hamilton, & Ivanic, 2000). In this study, we observed how commercial materials were used to reinforce teachers' beliefs about deficit views of students and, in effect, to construct student disadvantage in the classroom use of the materials (Larson, 2002; Larson & Irvine, 1999).

In the first part of the chapter, we describe the autonomous model of literacy (Street, 1995) that underlies commercial reading programs we studied in use and that informs the practices of the teachers we observed. We contrast it with Street's ideological, or social practice, approach to literacy that we use to interpret the data. Then, we describe the qualitative study we conducted of a specific literacy package used in one urban district. In our discussion of the findings, we argue for more empirical research on the use of commercial materials in local contexts that also accounts for the social, political, and historical factors affecting their use (see Street, Lefstein, & Pahl, this volume). We close the chapter with suggestions for educators who must prepare preservice teachers to enter schools mandating the use of commercial materials.

AUTONOMOUS AND IDEOLOGICAL
MODELS OF LITERACY

The commercial materials we observed in use are based on an approach to literacy that can be characterized as autonomous (Street, 1995; 2005). Street contrasts autonomous approaches to literacy with ideological ones to focus attention on the role of social context in reading, writing, teaching, and learning literacy and in researching these practices.

In the autonomous model, literacy is represented as the sum of the parts of written language, such as letter-sound correspondence and phonemic awareness, and learning to read is a matter of acquiring technical decoding skills that are presumed to operate independently of context (cf., Snow, Burns, & Griffin, 1998). Autonomous approaches to literacy have warranted the description of "scientific" literacy universals, or decontextualized skills that are assumed to govern the processes of reading and writing across contexts (Shannon, 1992). However, as Edelsky (1994) writes, "The activity of performing divisible sub-skills may have little or no relation to the indivisible activity we call reading" (p. 115). Although it is possible to break written language down into a structuralist system of interrelated linguistic subparts, the analysis into parts does not provide a blueprint for how people learn to read; learning to read entails more than acquiring these so-called building blocks of text in sequential order (Gee, this volume; 2003). Street (1995) contrasts an autonomous approach to literacy with an ideological one, in which the cognitive processing of linguistic parts is wholly dependent on context because it takes place "within cultural wholes and within structures of power" (Street, 1995, p. 161).

An ideological view of literacy assumes that literacy is a set of social practices that are historically situated, highly dependent on shared cultural understandings, and inextricably linked to power relations in any setting. In this social practice framework, social and linguistic practices are mutually constituted within past and present power relations among people who write and read to accomplish social goals. In this model, the context is constituted by local, culturally-specific practices that circumscribe who has access to learning to read and write which kinds of texts for which purposes. Individual differences may affect the process, but only within the constraints and possibilities afforded by the cultural, historical context.

While approaches to literacy based in an autonomous model assume that literacy is context-free, an ideological approach seeks to understand how literacy forms and practices have evolved to serve culturally specific purposes. Street (1995) presents ethnographic sketches of literacy in a variety of international settings and at different historical periods to emphasize the deeply contextual nature of literacy practices. For example, he describes how forms of literacy that are valued in schools are culturally produced and rooted in essayist textual practices of Western academic elites. Such an autonomous definition of literacy grounds the literacy package we studied in this district. Street (1995) argues that through the "pedagogization" of literacy, autonomous, objectified conceptions of literacy are naturalized in practice and, as we argue here, reified in literacy packages.

In a social practice approach, students use reading and writing to access the world as meaning-making subjects, not as objects of instruction (Coles, 1998, 2000; Edelsky, 1991; Freire & Macedo, 1987). However, in settings dominated by skills-based pedagogies, students are constrained in what they are enabled to do with and through text. In this study, for example, teachers interpreted and used the commercial materials to support reading pedagogies that denied students a role in the co-construction of social meaning.

We draw on Street's ideological view of literacy to analyze the classroom practices we observed in this study and to situate them in the social and institutional contexts in which they occur (Bloome, 1987; Bloome, Power Carter, Christian, Otto, & Stuart-Faris, 2005; de Castell & Luke, 1986; Edelsky, 1991; Graff, 1987; Irvine & Elsasser, 1988; Scribner & Cole, 1981; Street, 2005). In an ideological model, macro social and political factors, such as who has access to the middle-class social and cultural resources that schooling promotes, are understood to profoundly influence what happens in the micro context of the literacy classroom. Thus, the teachers we interviewed who hold deficit views of their African American students' oral language abilities do so within an institutional and historical context that validates these beliefs. Attitudes toward the use of nonstandard languages in schooling are institutionalized, formally and informally, in local and national language education policies. In this study, those macro social attitudes manifest themselves in teachers' beliefs about students' language abilities and their pedagogical decisions based on these beliefs. Commodified literacy materials grounded in autonomous definitions of literacy preclude the recognition of students' language as valid cultural resources. Students are then offered few opportunities to participate actively in the construction of textual, cultural, or social meaning—to learn to read, in other words.

CONTEXT OF THE STUDY

The data are drawn from a larger study of an urban school district's reading reform process. Northeast City School District (NCSD) is a medium-sized urban district concerned about raising test scores for its more than 30,000 students. In the year we conducted the study, the test scores of several city schools, both elementary and secondary, were so low that the State Department of Education considered placing the schools on its list of low performing schools. Recently, NCSD learned that they have the lowest scores in the state. Only 72 percent of third-graders passed the standardized achievement tests in reading in the year prior to this study. In 2004–2005 that number fell to 57%. In contrast, the nearest suburban school district reported that 86% of its students passed the test. In Northeast City School District in 2005, 87 percent of the students are non-White (Black, 65 percent; Hispanic, 20 percent; and other, 2 percent) while 79 percent of the teachers are White (see Figure 1[1]).

Racial/Ethnic Background	Students	Teachers
Black (Not Hispanic)	64.9%	15.5%
White (Not Hispanic)	13%	79%
Hispanic	20.1%	4.6%
American Indian, Alaskan, Asian, or Pacific Islander.	2%	9%

Total K-12 enrollment: 34,526
Total teachers: 3,035

Fig 1. Racial/Ethnic Breakdown in Northeast City School District by Percentage.

The textbook reform process examined in this study reflects one of this district's responses to accountability mandates from the State Department of Education. In addition, city government was pressuring the district to address the downward spiral of achievement scores that seemed to be driving families out of the city to neighboring suburbs. In response to these pressures, district administration mounted a reading reform effort that began with piloting three new textbook series, one of which would be selected for district-wide implementation the following year.

The administration claimed that one reason for low reading scores was the discontinuity of reading pedagogy in a district with high student mobility. In the previous ten years, four separate series and the packaged phonics drill program, Open Court Reading (1995), had been adopted in various parts of the district. Some teachers echoed administrators' concerns, suggesting that a single, mandated reading series would provide consistency in instruction, particularly for those students who move frequently within the district. In the interview segment below, one teacher, after describing how 50 percent of her students moved in one year, expressed her desire that the district decide on one series:

> That's one of the reasons we need, if you bring anything back (to the District) we need one
> program throughout because each program. . . . it's crucial in this District. Every program

teaches letters in a different sequence. If we were all on the same program . . . (it would be more consistent).

The administration also hoped that a new textbook series would improve reading instruction by teachers considered to be only marginally qualified. One district official believed that all the teachers should be re-credentialed; stating that she wished the district could "start over" with new teachers who were better trained. Administrators hoped that by mandating the use of a scripted textbook series, the quality of instruction would be guaranteed. Teachers in the pilot and administrators all believed that the new reading series would teach reading more effectively.

While the administration had already decided to adopt a new textbook, they had not determined how to evaluate the pilot. District administration asked Larson to assist in the evaluation of the textbook pilot by observing and interviewing selected teachers. This observational component was only one part of a larger evaluation that included surveys of teachers, parents, and administrators.

STUDY DESIGN AND METHODOLOGY

We used a qualitative design to explore the teachers' beliefs about reading instruction, their perceptions of the materials, and their use of the materials in practice. In this study of eight inner-city schools, nine teachers were observed (seven White and two African American), both male and female, in grade levels kindergarten through third grade. Principals had selected highly regarded teachers to pilot the textbook series. The pilot teachers received a letter and consent form asking them to participate in the observational component of the pilot process. The nine teachers who participated in this study were the only ones who responded to the letters. District administrators were careful to establish that Larson was not hired by the district and, therefore, outside the official textbook adoption process. The classrooms represented a range of social demographics based on the percentage of students on free-and-reduced lunch (43–100 percent), student mobility indicators, and reading achievement scores (ranging across the nine classrooms from 93 percent to 56 percent, with a median score of 76 percent).

Using ethnographic methods, the teachers were observed twice during the project to document how they used the textbook series. Fieldnotes were taken during each observation. Interviews were conducted and audiotaped following each observation and were transcribed to analyze teachers' beliefs about the teaching of reading, their perceptions of the materials, and their patterns of textbook use. Several additional teachers who declined to be observed were interviewed by telephone and each conversation was documented in fieldnotes.

Some teachers declined to participate, stating that they were uncomfortable being observed, that they received letters of consent too late, or that they thought the decision had already been made by the district. Several teachers alluded indirectly to being over-committed in their schools or to the ongoing union and contract dispute. Textbook publishers and their representatives appear to have contributed to some of the teachers' confusion about the textbook pilot project. For example, pilot teachers received an abundance of extra resource materials from textbook representatives in what seemed to be an attempt to sway their decisions. This created mixed feelings about the textbook adoption process among some teachers, as they believed that the district would not be able to purchase all the materials they had been given. In some pilot schools, publishers also gave manuals and associated supplies to teachers not piloting any series. One publisher even attempted to contact Larson to solicit advance information on the findings of this study.

The following research questions guided this study: What factors do teachers believe contribute to learning to read? How do the teachers in the pilot perceive the commercial packages? How do they use the materials in their instructional practices? The database consists of twenty-four hours of audio taped interviews and full transcriptions of tapes along with comprehensive field notes of all classroom observations. Two observers (Larson & Pope, 1997) conducted several observations in each classroom. Larson and Irvine (1999) coded the data separately to establish patterns and relationships, and then agreed upon a set of categories for analysis. Using the constant comparative method of analysis (Charmaz, 2006; Glaser & Strauss, 1967; Strauss & Corbin, 1990), a link emerged between teachers' beliefs about students' lack of language abilities and how they were observed to use the series and associated materials.

WHAT FACTORS DO TEACHERS BELIEVE CONTRIBUTE TO LEARNING TO READ?

In interviews, teachers stated that in order to read, students need appropriate background experiences and oral language ability. Teachers in the study believed that their students enter their classrooms at an insurmountable deficit (Hull, Rose, Fraser, & Castellano, 1991) and were unabashed about expressing this view, attributing students' reading difficulties to their home environments and lack of middle-class background. As reasons for poor reading scores, they also cited students' lack of oral language and lack of parental involvement. In the following excerpt, one first-grade teacher described her students as coming to school "in the hole":

Learning to read is so complicated. If they can come to first grade knowing letters and knowing some sounds, having been read to, they'll be ready to learn to read. I do not get many children like that in here. They do not come to kindergarten ready for kindergarten. So I'm always looking at children who aren't ready to learn yet. And that's a sad fact. But it's true. Nevertheless, you have to keep on truckin'. They come in, in the hole . . . that you have to dig them out of. That's not a very easy thing to do. I know that people downtown will tell you that it can be done. I'm here to tell you it can't be done.

She believed that her students were not ready to learn when they came to school and that no matter what "downtown" (i.e., district administration) said, she could not bring the students to grade level. Another teacher, referring to what she believed "our population" needed, stated the following:

I think that's something you just have to be diligent about, especially in terms of our population that doesn't have a lot of exposure to stories outside of classroom necessarily. Many students do not know any letters of the alphabet when they come to school at all. It's almost like a foreign language to them.

This view of students as entering school at a deficit was a common belief, whether the teacher was White or African American. This teacher's comment seems to reference the kinds of skills that middle-class children often come to school already knowing (Heath, 1983). Similarly, the African American first-grade teacher in the following excerpt focuses on the importance of appropriate background experience as the main contributing factor to students learning to read:

Background experience is the main factor. How much they've been read to. Whether they've been to the zoo, to the museums. What experiences they bring. Because, I always say I need to write these things down cause I forget, but it's strange how simple things that you just think, "Oh, 6, 7, years old, they know what this is." And then you mention it and no one has any idea what you're talking about. You know? (chuckle) So background experience plays a big part.

The appropriate background experience she refers to is one that middle-class children may take for granted. According to Heath (1983), middle-class language socialization is the model for school-based literacy practices, so poor and working-class children who come without them must learn them in school (see Gee, this volume). As we will suggest later in this chapter, students without middle-class backgrounds are unlikely to learn those skills when instruction is based on materials and practices grounded in autonomous definitions of literacy.

In addition to identifying students' lack of appropriate background experience as contributing to their reading difficulties, all the teachers felt that their students' reading difficulties stemmed from a lack of oral language ability. To some teachers this meant Standard English, while others seemed to suggest that students lacked the ability for language or speaking:

I think the first thing we have to do is that we have to give them the language, help them develop language, not just vocabulary but speaking in sentences, hearing . . . very good examples of language through literature.

Another third-grade teacher with twenty-five years of teaching experience offered the following:

> Sometimes I wonder if these children are used to hearing correctly spoken English for any sounds.

The teacher used the term "these children" to refer to the fifteen students in his classroom, fourteen of whom were African American. Indirect references to this district's student population of predominantly African American students were common across the data. Both White and African American teachers used terms such as "our population," "inner city kids," and "urban students" to label children in their classrooms. Labeling students in this way reifies perceptions that poor children lack language and other cultural resources to the extent that they must be taught with less demanding curricula. It also allows teachers to have lower expectations for academic achievement. In the excerpt below, a first-grade teacher explains her view of student linguistic deficits and how they should be addressed:

> I think ESL should be in every classroom. I think it's teaching of language practices. I think that all little ones need to learn how to speak. And I think here in the city we have students who come in and [are] even further behind with their ability for language and speaking in full sentences.

Her utterance, "here in the city" refers to her perception that native English-speaking children in the city school district need to be taught English as a Second Language (ESL) so they can catch up to the immigrant children in the district who are nonnative speakers of English.

All teachers in the study perceived students' social class and language as deficits, overlooking the cultural and linguistic resources that students do bring to school. Since the 1960s, with the advent of federally funded compensatory education initiatives, the deficit model has been used to explain the achievement gap between middle-class White and poor minority children. Writing in this vein, Bereiter and Engelman (1966) offered an instructional model for teaching "disadvantaged" children not unlike the practices we observed in this study. They argued that African American children show ". . . very close to the total lack of ability to use language as a device for acquiring and processing information. Language for them is unwieldy and not very useful" (p. 39). Labov (1972, 1995) and others critiqued this claim, which is not based on any linguistic understanding of what constitutes a language, and other research that connected language "deficits" to cognitive deficits. Nevertheless, as interviews with the teachers in our study show, deficit notions persist in spite of students bringing what research has shown repeatedly to be rich, varied, and authentic language and literacy practices to school (Gee, 2004; Moll, Amanti, Neff, & González, 1992; Rogoff, 2003). These deficit model beliefs are played out in classroom practices, as the next section shows.

Teachers' perceptions of what their students needed to overcome these deficits drove their pedagogical decisions and their selection of activities from the reading series.

HOW DO TEACHERS USE THE PACKAGED
MATERIALS IN INSTRUCTIONAL PRACTICE?

The commercial reading series presented an elaborate script for teachers to follow, and teachers were under surveillance by the district for close adherence to the textbook and the manual. At the same time, district personnel advised teachers to base their selection of activities on students' needs. In classroom observations, teachers selected some activities and ignored others, relying heavily on their previous practices. In interviews, they explained how they selected activities from the series to meet the perceived needs of their students.

All teachers stated that there were far too many suggested activities in the teacher's manual to possibly accomplish in the suggested time or in the time they had for language arts instruction. Teachers at all levels of experience expressed the tension they felt between the district expectations that they "really do the pilot" and the need to "pick and choose" among the plethora of activities. "Covering everything" or "getting it all in" within a certain time period emerged as a major concern of both experienced and inexperienced teachers.

> There are so many ideas in these manuals that if I did everything, we would never come close. We're not I do not know if we're going to come close, anyway to completing (chuckle) but I wouldn't, I probably, I'd be only half way to where I am now if I did everything in the manual. There's so much to choose from. And all of it is good.

This teacher, like others in the study, did not question the content, scope, or sequence in any of the piloted series, declaring it "all good." The overwhelming criticism of any series was that there were so many ideas that it was difficult to choose. Because there were so many suggested activities, teachers were forced to "pick and choose":

> It's very difficult to squeeze in the pieces and next year if this were the series chosen I would pick and choose a little bit differently. You would see a little bit less than was suggested I do today.

The experienced teachers were concerned that beginning teachers might find the textbook series manual too full of ideas and lack the experience to judge what could be eliminated or what was essential. One teacher with more than ten years experience stated the following:

> Once you get used to looking at manuals, I mean after time, you've taught for a while, you really may not even need a manual . . . I think that it's probably user friendly and I think

that . . . it has lots of activities. The problem is that it probably has too much. And I think that sometimes it would be hard for a beginning teacher to pick and choose what's most— appropriate? Or most meaningful.

Under pressure to complete the list of activities, some teachers omitted optimal teaching practices that they had previously used with the district's encouragement, such as learning centers, collaborative projects, writer's circle, and others, even similar practices suggested as supplementary in this literature-based textbook series. For example, during field observations, teachers commented that learning centers were something they rarely had time for anymore. It is important to note that institutional constraints, such as special events, assemblies, and outside classes (physical education or art) also took time away from the two-and-one-half hour daily language arts period that the district mandates for language arts. A number of teachers made creative use of resource teachers, assistants, and volunteers to gain as much time as possible for a main "lesson." Resource teachers, aides, and volunteers were observed conducting teacher-constructed drills or overseeing students identified as needing special education services on specific tasks.

In the following excerpt, the teacher refers to using the textbook for practice, extension, and reteaching activities, all of which emerge from an autonomous view of literacy as an accumulation of decontextualized skills. Furthermore, she expresses her appreciation that activities were already thought out, saving her the time and trouble of doing it herself:

> I think there's so much to do that I would have to spend 2 or 3 weeks on every story to get every activity done. And when they did introduce the reading series to us they told us that it's not designed to do every single activity that they outline in it, but it's to think of the needs of your children. And I really think that works out really well that way. It gives you so many different things to choose from. It's an excellent resource and it's helped save me time for having to think up activities on my own and what I like to do is I'll use their ideas for practice activities or extension activities or reteaching in class and the workbook pages I'll use for the review.

This teacher was observed in instruction to choose extension activities and workbook pages that focused on reading subskills, such as sound-letter correspondences. Teachers in this study, under time pressure and forced to choose among an abundance of suggested activities, selected language arts activities that were aimed not at the comprehension of whole texts but at developing language subskills. As the next section shows, teachers also justified their selection of activities by referring to deficit perceptions of the oral language abilities of this student population.

To justify their choice of activities from the many offered, teachers consistently referred to their students' need for "pieces of language" and "phonics" to remedy their lack of language ability. In classroom observations of the teachers piloting the textbook series, reading pedagogy was restricted to the teaching of passive decoding skills in which the students were asked to recite someone else's thinking (Nystrand, 1997). Even though the series was literature-based, teachers chose skills-only activities that focused almost exclusively on the word level as a unit of study, with most activities breaking down words into letters and sounds. The following activities were observed in all classrooms: fill-in-the-blank grammar worksheets, phonics drills, spelling tests, vocabulary tests, adjective worksheets, writing prompt exercises, handwriting exercises, letter-sound recognition drills, story sequencing worksheets, character clusters, consonant-cluster and letter-blend drills, alphabetizing, sight-word memorizing, repetition of words and sounds (both oral and written), and whole-class reading exercises. Some of the materials were taken from the textbook series and some were materials the teachers had always used.

No activities were observed in which students read whole texts or participated in activities other than worksheet exercises (see Osborn, this volume). Instead, students were engaged in activities that could be termed "doing reading," meaning that they were practicing isolated skills devoid of meaningful context. Students were learning phonemic awareness, letter-sound recognition, and consonant clusters as discrete activities. What counted as literacy in this context, then, was performance on skills exercises (Edelsky, 1991; Routman, 1996). Students were learning isolated skills that were presented in the textbook, but there was no instruction in which this learning came together into meaningful activity that led to reading or writing.

Teachers in the study understood teaching literacy as delivering a set of technical skills as efficiently as possible, explicitly linking the skills they taught to their perceptions of students' abilities. One male third-grade teacher explained it this way:

> Um, (2 sec) phonics, I believe, if you, phonics are necessary probably for I'd say 70–80 percent of the kids. [They] could learn how to sound out words and how to read through phonics. The remainder of the kids um they use the whole language just straight reading . . . Uh, sight words, I think is important. And, um, syllables, breaking, uh, words into pieces so that they may sound out the words a little bit easier. So I'd say, I'd say, say the basics are pretty much taught with basics. I mean break, break everything down in its smallest, simplest form.

In this teacher's classroom, those students who have access to literacy as meaning making in interaction with text are the 20 percent of students who can do "just straight reading," in the teacher's terms. The majority of the students, however, are taught that what counts as literacy are the pieces that the teacher, echoing macro institutional practices, has determined are the literacy basics: sight words, syllables, and phonics, with the primary pedagogy being to "break everything down in its smallest, simplest form." The textbook series did not disrupt the autonomous model of literacy that the teacher describes in this excerpt or his beliefs that this model is especially appropriate for this group of students.

Phonics-only approaches were clearly evident in all the classrooms. Given the dominant belief that learning to read follows prescribed stages of development (e.g., from oral to written language), phonics was understood to be an essential first step. What we observed in lessons, however, was that other "steps" did not follow. Instruction remained at the level of basic skills and did not extend to more contextual activities in which students used these strategies to comprehend or interpret texts.

Teachers who felt that their students did not come to school "ready to learn" or with adequate skills in oral language (i.e., Standard English) supplemented the textbook with reading activities they had developed over the years; these practices, however, regardless of the comprehension and literature-based activities suggested in the reading series, were grounded in an autonomous model of literacy. Teachers' preferences for using their own previous practices and their judgments about students' limited capabilities governed their selection of activities from the manual and the extent to which they adhered to textbook series recommendations, as this teacher explains:

> Other things are things that I just have always done . . . I like doing those type of activities because it makes them focus more on . . . the . . . spellings . . . you know, of the word and try to really sound things out. And for them it's like a game so they enjoy doing it. So that's something I've always done that is not in the manual. My strategies were basically the same. And that's why I like the program. You know, I still use the same things now, even with the pilot. I like the pilot because it seems to fall right in line with the things that I've done for years.

The majority of teachers in the study supplemented the series with materials from the four programs mentioned earlier that were in place prior to the textbook pilot. Several pilot teachers stated that they have used Open Court exclusively for years to teach reading. For the most part, none of these teachers planned to alter this practice. One first-grade teacher explained it this way:

> We're doing . . . Open Court as well. I do not know if you're all that familiar with Open Court, but you see the cards up there and I do not know if [series publisher's name] would approve that because it's not really a pure pilot, but, I'm doing it because it works. So I'm not going to abandon it . . . I was just afraid to abandon Open Court . . . Because I've been successful with it. And I do not know if . . . Maybe if I just did any kind of phonics everyday, that would be the same thing. But because I have . . . the cards, and the do-this-today, play-the-tape, now-do-this I'm locked into doing it and it's a discipline for me to do it everyday. Maybe it's more training the teacher than it is the student.

This teacher, noting that the structure of the series had the effect of training teachers, echoed the district's hope that a reading series would retrain teachers and standardize instruction. She admits, however, that she will not abandon her previous instructional package, based on skills, in spite of the district's mandate.

In the following excerpt, an African American first-grade teacher explained her use of phonics:

> The manual has so many different activities for you to choose from, um, my thing is getting them to understand phonics and how we use phonics to figure out a word. . . . I tend to rely on phonics. I mean that's—I think phonics is extremely important. And so, my lessons, the phonics, you know, kind of guides me. So I always make sure that at some point during the day that we really, that there is a focus, focus on phonics. And then again, my thing is always looking at, unfortunately, believe it or not, standardized tests? And you want to have the kids prepared so you need to make sure that. So, doing what we did today, with the words in context, kind of trains them you know, for that. But of course your teacher (refers to a beginner), may not realize until they've taught three or four or five years or so that they say, "Hey, my kids really need this so that when it's time for us to really sit down and take the test." I mean remembering the rules, things like that.

In spite of the plethora of comprehension, literature-based suggestions in the manual, this teacher, like many others we interviewed, chose not to use them in favor of her own teaching strategies. In other words, teachers used strategies from the textbook only when they matched their existing practices. During her language arts lesson, the teacher cited above was observed to enact her belief that phonics must come first. She frequently reminded students about phonics rules with the following statement: "One does the walking while the other does the talking," even when the lesson had shifted from language arts into other content areas. Her language arts lesson consisted of students going over isolated words from an upcoming story ("call," "say," "eat," "fish," "to") in which students were asked to repeat each word then use it in a sentence. The lesson followed a strict IRE (initiation, response, evaluation) lesson format in which students responded to test-like questions to which the answer was already known (Gutierrez, 1993; Mehan, 1979; Nystrand, 1997).

In the next section, we bring together interview and observation data from two classrooms to illustrate what happens when the teachers merge, in instructional practice, deficit beliefs about students' language and an autonomous model of literacy.

TEACHING READING BEHAVIORS, NOT READING

Limiting students' participation in literacy events to performing reading and writing exercises amounts to asking students to complete a set of clerical tasks that lead to a formulaic understanding of text (Nystrand, 1997). In classroom observations, teachers in the pilot focused primarily on word-sound correspondence drills and reading behaviors, such as following along in the text, instead of activities in which students actively interpreted text or made meaning of it orally or in writing. A first-grade teacher expressed her belief that students were only capable of completing tasks such as these, but they were not able to "read":

> What I try to do is make sure we read the story every day and make sure I do a lot with the vocabulary and the spelling. The comprehension part of it—they usually do not have a big problem understanding the stories and assessing the stories, um, it's just the reading of the stories that they, you know. At the beginning, when they first start learning how to read, you know, just the attacking the words is the biggest problem.

As we show in the transcript below, reading in this classroom consisted of a whole class read-aloud taken from the piloted reading series in which students were required to all read together without deviation. The teacher focused on reading behaviors rather than the word attack or comprehension strategies she described in the excerpt above. Moreover, students did not read the story themselves; the teacher read to them as they followed along, an activity that was not suggested in the teacher's manual. They comprehended the text based on her oral recitation, but they were not given the opportunity to interpret the text for themselves. In essence, they could not read the story because the teacher did not let them.

During the observation of this classroom, children attempting to read forward to see what was happening in the story were sometimes literally and physically stopped to concentrate on sounds, explicitly told to finger one word at a time in unison:

Teacher:	We're going to start from the first row.
	I want to hear everyone.
	Keep your finger on the word..
	I want to see you.
All:	[Reading] An egg is an egg until it hatches.
Teacher:	What's that word?
	Look at the blend.
	Third row only.
	Where is your finger?
	Okay.
	Paris, we're still in the book even if you're not reading.
	Loud voice in the second row, leader.
	Not too fast,
	Juan, you have to read with everyone else.
	Finger under the A.
	First row, ready, begin.
All:	[Reading] A block is a block until it's a tower.
Teacher:	Finger under the A.
	Second row, ready, begin.
	We need–
	Juan, you're interrupting.
	You've got the right page. Very good.
	You have to read together.

Turn the page.
You're right, the first word is "Nothing."
First row, what's the first word on the page?
Nothing. Okay.
Guillermo, you still have to follow
[even though it isn't his row's turn].
You need to turn when I say turn and then you won't be confused.

Students were vigilantly monitored to make sure they were reading at the same pace. The teacher asked a series of questions ("What's that word?" "Where is your finger?" "What's the first word on the page?"), yet they were allowed no time for students to answer. In fact, the students did not attempt a response because they knew that the teacher already had the answer. Except for the oral recitation of text, students had no turn in the discussion. The teacher focused exclusively on teaching "proper" reading behaviors, such as using fingers as pointers, rather than teaching reading strategies that helped students engage with text.

After this reading period, students were dismissed to their desks to complete a matching worksheet that was not connected to the story but was part of the reading series accessory materials. The teacher read the instructions, then slowly and painstakingly went over each line to make sure they not only had the correct answers, but the same answers completed at the same time. One student secretly traced her finger over the paper where the answers would be on sections that the teacher had not yet reached. She knew not to move at her own pace with her pencil, so she shielded her finger as she answered the upcoming questions on her own.

CONSTRUCTING ACADEMIC DISADVANTAGE

In the following interview,[2] the teacher described what she termed a verb conjugation lesson that she would conduct later in her classroom. She has taught for five years and has had this particular group of students two years in a row, from second to third grade. On this particular day she had twenty-three students in class, seventeen who were African American and six who were White. In our interview, the teacher reported the following:

This [lesson] is a conjugation of the verb "be" which is an interesting idea in itself considering all the Ebonics (laughter) controversy of things. Because I have kids that won't conjugate. I mean they'll use wrong conjugations, ya know, they'll say "he is" or "we is" so this should be interesting today (heh heh) because it's not—it's not natural for some of them to conjugate. So it will be interesting, ya know, to get them to use the correct conjugations of the verb "be."

From this teacher's perspective, the students' language, Ebonics, was the reason for their incorrect or "wrong conjugations" ("he is" or "we is"). The students were, in fact, conjugating verbs, but in their own language, African American Vernacular English (AAVE). Beliefs about students' lack of language ability are reflective of social and institutional beliefs about nonstandard language, and such beliefs, as we will show, may have negative consequences for literacy learning when put into practice. This teacher's beliefs about her students' language abilities influenced her decision to limit her lesson to a grammar worksheet, as the following observation demonstrates.

The lesson began with the teacher at the front of the room using an overhead projector. She was filling in a worksheet taken from the textbook series. She spoke to the students briefly about singular and plural verbs and began the worksheet exercise by reading the first example, "A horse is stuck." The answer was already filled in on the transparency. She read the next sentence, saying the word "blank" where the answer should have been, then called on students to fill in the answer:

Teacher:	A horse is stuck.
	The horses *blank* stuck.
	[Calls on African American student.]
Af. -Am. Student:	The horses is stuck.
White Student:	Horses are stuck.
Teacher:	We didn't say "horse are stuck."
	[To African American students.]
	Would you say "I is hungry?"
	Do we say "We is hungry?"
	No!
Af. -Am. Student:	I do, I do.
Teacher:	But you're not supposed to!
Af. -Am. Student:	I say "I is going."
Teacher:	But you're not supposed to say
	[reaches for an example in the manual]
	I is (going).
	There are words that sound right,
	and there are words that are right with these
	subjects, and you just have to learn them.
Af. -Am. Student:	I was hungry.
Af. -Am. Student:	No. I say, I hungry [laughs].
	[Laughter from his classmates.]
Teacher:	I'm going to wait a minute . . .
	control! [All stop talking.]
	Star Wars!
	Is there a star up there for Group 1?
	Take it down.
Teacher:	Molasses cookies *blank*—is or are—Peter's favorite?
	What would you say?
	[Four or five African American children say "is" from different parts of the room.]

In this example, this teacher's beliefs about her students' inability to make verbs agree with their subjects in Standard English were enacted in a practice that excluded students' language resources as valid in the making of meaning about this text. She positioned African American students as outside ("we/you") the Standard-English-speaking community. In this literacy event, a social distancing process we have called "reciprocal distancing" (Larson & Irvine, 1999) was initiated when she asked questions that elicited what she considered wrong answers from African American students: "Would you say, 'I is hungry'?". When a student answered with an expression that is correct in AAVE, "No. I say, I hungry," eliciting laughter from his classmates, the teacher implemented the classroom disciplinary system called Star Wars.

While the fill-in-the-blank exercise observed in this classroom is problematic as a tool for reading instruction because it is rooted in the autonomous model of literacy, it may not be the most academically disadvantaging aspect of this lesson. The teacher's deficit beliefs about language, combined with an autonomous definition of literacy, in effect denies the students access to meaning-making using their own language and literacy practices. A non-deficit pedagogy would value students as legitimate resources in reading instruction, perhaps not even using the worksheet (see Gatto, this volume) or have used it in a way that assisted students in understanding the grammar of their own language. Students who learn to distinguish the grammatical differences between Standard English and AAVE are better prepared for the school-based literacy they will encounter throughout their education (Christensen, 2000; Elsasser & Irvine, 1985; Lee, 2001; Perry & Delpit, 1997).

As discussed earlier, we draw on a multidisciplinary perspective to define reading, like literacy, as a social practice in which meaning is constructed in the interaction between teachers, students, and text (Baynham, 1995; Bloome & Bailey, 1992; Cazden, 1992; Gee, 2003; Luke, 1994; New London Group, 1996; Street, 1995, 2005). What we observed in this study is the social practice of reading in this context. If, as Rogoff (1994, 2003) argues, students learn through daily participation in all culturally organized activities and it is the "what" that changes, then in the literacy events we observed, they are learning a relationship to text in which they are positioned as consumers of a static body of skills. They are not learning a relationship to text in which meaning is an active construction and interpretation where students are the subjects of meaning making. Students also learn that they are not members of the institutionally legitimized community, that their language and abilities are not adequate, that knowledge resides in the teacher and the packaged materials, and that what counts as reading and as knowledge belongs to the teacher and the institution. Furthermore, students are learning what teachers and texts define as proper reading behaviors rather than reading strategies that will lead to meaning-making and achievement in school-based literacy.

CONCLUSION

To districts in search of a quick-fix approach to low reading achievement, a commercial reading series may seem to be a panacea. Publishers promise a curriculum designed by experts and based on a "scientific," autonomous approach to literacy practices that is in line with government policies, and district administrators are tempted by the prospect of standardizing instruction, "teacher-proofing" the curriculum, and being able to show annual yearly progress, which NCLB mandates to retain federal funding. However, observations of these materials in practice—in this district, at least—show that a literacy package neither standardized the reading curriculum nor trained teachers to be better at reading instruction. The commercial materials in this study offered a script and a variety of activities, not all of them skills-based, but teachers only followed parts of it. They interpreted suggested activities in light of deficit ideologies about students' lack of background experience and oral language while continuing previous practices, many of which they derived from other commercial materials.

The findings from this study corroborate the critiques of packaged materials that show them to promote modes of instruction grounded in autonomous models of literacy (Luke, 1988; Shannon, 1992). At the same time, studying packaged materials as they are used in practice complicates our understanding of their impact on students, teachers, and literacy education. In this context, teacher ideologies about students' and about literacy learning turned out to be the key determinants in how they selected activities from the packaged series.

Commodified packages may support particularly disadvantaging pedagogies in districts serving primarily poor, working-class, and language minority students. Rist's (2000) research, carried out in 1970 but still relevant today, shows how poor children in one kindergarten classroom were systematically excluded from participation in higher-level reading and writing activities. Strickland (1994), too, argues that skills-based instruction targeted at children of color tends to foster low-level uniformity and subvert academic potential, and in this study, we observed students being apprenticed to skills-based literacy practices and reading behaviors.

To succeed in school, students in the classrooms we observed need access to different kinds of literacy practices. Knobel's (1999) research on the multiple literacies of children from different social backgrounds suggests that middle-class children often practice more sophisticated literacy skills at home than they do at school by having access to computer technology, for example. Her research shows that working-class students also possess viable community-based literacies, but their resources are often ignored or disparaged. Therefore, given the structural inequalities that limit poor children's access to middle-class literacies in non-school settings, school may be the only place some children can learn the literacy necessary for school achievement.

In this sense, the packages and practices accompanying them are particularly disadvantaging for the students we observed. The deficit perceptions that teachers hold are reified by the commercial materials and the practices supported by them because students do not, in the end, learn to read in ways that teachers hope or that promote success in school. When teachers implement even more skills practice, a spiral of disadvantage continues. The notion that "these children" can't read (Gee, 2003) persists, essentially blaming the victims for the results of institutionalized practices.

Although we have focused much of this chapter on critiquing teachers' pedagogical practices using packaged literacy, it is not our intention to blame teachers as individuals. Focusing on individuals obscures the larger institutional and social contexts that not only validate, but also impose, the use of commodified materials and the autonomous literacy practices they support. Teachers forced to use the materials (and other packaged series before these) do so in a social and political context, and as the following teacher acknowledges:

> I've had enough of the district and their policies. And do this and do that. And the testing and everything else. If they decide to develop one reading text for the whole district, I'm kind of stubborn. That'll probably just influence me more not to use it. So I do not care what they [say] . . . different kids, different standards.

This teacher's deficit ideology is expressed through her phrase, "different kids, different standards." She means that she does not plan to have the same standards for students she believes are unable to meet them. According to her statement, it is doubtful that the implementation of a packaged series is going to interrupt this ideology. Moreover, she raises the key issue of testing and accountability, key reasons for the district's mandate. This district stands to benefit politically from implementing what appears to be a standardized literacy delivery system. The district can demonstrate accountability to constituents at the local and state levels by committing funds and considerable personnel resources to a colorful, slick, commodified literacy package that promises to raise reading achievement scores, and in some cases has raised scores. If materials, devised by "experts," cannot help teachers raise student reading scores, then the blame falls back on the students, their families, or the teachers. A district may be able to insulate itself from criticism with the exorbitant purchase of a package, a process noted by Shannon (1992).

Standardized tests are a key tool in this political process, especially if they measure competence in the skills promoted by the materials. Luke (1988) writes that some of the packaged instructional techniques may not necessarily be bad pedagogy, but the assessments that accompany these systems are tautological: They provide their own justification and confirm it in the form of test scores.

In Luke's (1988) review of the development of standardized literacy programs that began in the 1940s and 1950s, he anticipates several key findings from the study we report in this chapter. He describes the implementation of standardized systems as forms of control exercised by state education departments that essentially deskill teachers and then re-skill them in particular ways. He speculates about the double bind that postwar teachers may have experienced: The texts provided standardized, "scientifically" sanctioned scripts for instruction, but they were also enjoined to be spontaneous and innovative in adapting activities to local needs. However, doing both is not possible, especially given the constraints of frequent standardized testing and accountability measures. In the study we described, teachers' responses to this double bind were to rely on previous instructional practices, which some teachers said they had learned from other literacy packages. The district's insistence on teachers adhering to a packaged literacy program may, in effect, undermine their goal of helping teachers teach reading better.

As teacher educators, we try to interrupt one small part of this process that we can control, and that is arming new teachers with a theoretical understanding of the differences between autonomous and ideological approaches to literacy (Larson & Marsh, 2005; Street, 1995). We structure our teacher preparation course syllabi so that preservice teachers learn how to identify the theoretical underpinnings of any materials they encounter, to understand what to do to counter these practices, and to know why it is important to do so. However, we are still seeking ways to support new teachers as they face institutional pressures to adopt commercial packages. We are developing formal venues, such as grant-funded activities, to make both new and experienced teachers aware of the presence of deficit ideologies in seemingly innocuous teaching methods. In meetings where these issues are explored, experienced teachers are key members of a team we assembled to offer pedagogical alternatives. Informally, we support new teachers who feel isolated by putting them in touch with a vibrant network of excellent teachers who are willing to talk and work with them, teachers who have been able to resist adopting deficit ideologies and who can talk about how they work in contexts with mandated materials. We are seeking more strategies—formal, informal, and political—which can help new and experienced teachers resist district pressures and packaged activities which systematically ignore students' linguistic and cultural resources and deny them the academic experiences they need to achieve in school.

NOTES

1. Data taken from NYS Department of Education website, August 6, 2006 (http://www.emsc.nysed.gov/repcrd2005/cir/261600010000.pdf). Racial categories used are those of NYS.

2. The following discussion is taken in part from Larson & Irvine (1999). "*We* call him Dr. King": Reciprocal distancing in urban classrooms. *Language Arts*, 76(5), 393–400.

REFERENCES

Apple, M. (1990). *Ideology and Curriculum*. New York: Routledge.

Barton, H., Hamilton, M. & Ivanic, R. (2000). *Situated Literacies: Reading and Writing in Context*. London: Routledge.

Baynham, M. (1995). *Literacy Practices: Investigating Literacy in Social Contexts*. New York: Longman.

Bereiter, C. & Engelman. (1966). *Teaching Disadvantaged Children in the Preschool*. Englewood Cliffs, NJ: Prentice Hall.

Beyer, L. (1988). Schooling for the Culture of Democracy. In L. Beyer & M. Apple (Eds.), *The Curriculum: Problems, Politics, and Possibilities*. New York: SUNY Press. (pp. 219–238).

Bloome, D. (1987). Reading as a Social Process in a Middle School Classroom. In D. Bloome (Ed.), *Literacy and Schooling*. Norwood, NJ: Ablex. (pp. 123–149).

Bloome, D. & Bailey, F. (1992). Studying Language and Literacy Through Events, Particularity, and Intertextuality. In R. Beach, J. Green, M. Kamil, & T. Shanahan (Eds.), *Multidisciplinary Perspectives on Literacy Research*. Urbana, IL: National Council of Teachers of English.

Bloome, D., Carter, S., Christian, B., Otto, S., & Shuart-Faris, N. (2005). *Discourse Analysis and the Study of Classroom Language and Literacy Events: A Microanalytic Perspective*. Mahwah, NJ & London: Lawrence Erlbaum and Associates.

California Department of Education (2005). State approved adopted instructional materials. http://www.cde.ca.gov/ci/rl/im/rlaadoptedlist.asp. Accessed August 28, 2006.

Cazden, C. (1992). Vygotsky, Hymes, and Bakhtin: From Word to Utterance and Voice. In C. Cazden (Ed.), *Whole Language Plus: Essays on Literacy in the United States and New Zealand*. New York: Teachers College Press. (pp. 190–207).

Charmaz, K. (2006). *Constructing Grounded Theory: A Practical Guide Through Qualitative Analysis*. London: Sage.

Christensen, L. (2000). *Reading, Writing and Rising Up*. Milwaukee, WI: Rethinking Schools.

Coles, G. (1998). *Reading Lessons: The Debate Over Literacy*. New York: Hill and Wang.

Coles, G. (2000). *Misreading Reading: The Bad Science That Hurts Children*. Portsmouth, NH: Heinemann.

de Castell, S. & Luke, A. (1986). Models of Literacy in North American Schools: Social and Historical Conditions and Consequences. In S. de Castell, et al., (Eds.), *Literacy, Society, and Schooling*. Cambridge, UK: Cambridge University Press. (pp. 87–109).

Edelsky, C. (1991). *With Literacy and Justice For All: Rethinking the Social in Language and Education*. New York: Falmer.

Edelsky, C. (1994). *Whole Language: What's New?* (with Bess Altwerger & Barbara Flores). *With Literacy And Justice For All: Rethinking the Social in Language and Education*, Second Edition. Bristol, PA: Taylor and Francis. (pp. 108–126).

Elsasser, N. & Irvine, P. D. (1985). English and Creole: The Dialectics of Choice in a College Writing Program. *Harvard Educational Review*, 55. (pp. 399–415).

Freire, P. & Macedo, D. (1987). *Literacy: Reading the Word and the World*. South Hadley, MA: Bergin & Garvey.

Gee, J.P. (2004). *Situated Language and Learning: A Critique of Traditional Schooling*. New York: Routledge.

Glaser, B. & Strauss, A. (1967). *The Discovery of Grounded Theory*. Chicago: Aldine.

Goodman, K.S., Shannon, P., Freeman, P., & Murphy, S. (1988). *Report Card on Basal Readers*. New York: Richard C. Owen.

Graff, H. (1987). *The Legacies of Literacy*. Bloomington, IN: Indiana University Press.

Gutierrez, K. (1993). How Talk, Context, and Script Shape Contexts for Learning: A Cross-Case Comparison of Journal Sharing. *Linguistics and Education*, 5. (pp. 335–365).

Gutierrez, K., Baquedano-Lopez, P., & Turner, M.G. (1997). Putting Language Back Into Language Arts: When the Radical Middle Meets the Third Space. *Language Arts*, 74(5). (pp. 368–376).

Heath, S.B. (1983). *Ways With Words*. Cambridge, UK: Cambridge University Press.

Hull, G., Rose, M., Fraser, K., & Castellano, M. (1991). Remediation as Social Construct: Perspectives from an Analysis of Classroom Discourse. *College Composition and Communication*, 42(3), (pp. 299–329).

Irvine, P.D., & Elsasser, N. (1988). The Ecology of Literacy: Negotiating Writing Standards in a Caribbean Setting. In G. Rafoth & D. Rubin (Eds.), *The Social Construction of Written Language*. Norwood, NJ: Ablex.

Jaeger, E. (2006). Silencing Teachers in an Era of Scripted Reading. *Rethinking Schools*, (20)3.

Knobel, M. (1999). *Everyday Literacies: Students, Discourses, and Social Practice*. New York: Lang.

Labov, W.L. (1972). Academic Ignorance and Black Intelligence. *The Atlantic Monthly*, 229(6), (pp. 59–67).

Labov, W.L. (1995). Can Reading Failure Be Reversed? A Linguistic Approach to the Question. In Gadsden, V. and Wagner, D. (Eds.), *Literacy Among African American Youth: Issues in Learning, Teaching And Schooling*. Cresskill, NJ: Hampton Press.

Larson, J. (2002). Packaging process: Consequences of commodified pedagogy on students' participation in literacy events. *Journal of Early Childhood Literacy*, 2(1), 65–95.

Larson, J. & Irvine, P. (1999). We Call Him Dr. King: Reciprocal Distancing in Urban Classrooms. *Language Arts*, 76(5). (pp. 393–400).

Larson, J. & Marsh, J. (2005). *Making Literacy Real: Theories and Practices in Learning and Teaching*. London: Sage.

Larson, J. & Pope, C. (1997, April). Language Arts Textbook Project: A Collaboration with the Rochester City School District. *Research Report*. University of Rochester, Rochester, New York.

Lee, C.D. (2001). Is October Brown Chinese? A Cultural Modeling Activity System for Underachieving students. *American Educational Research Journal*, 38(1), 97–142.

Luke, A. (1988). *Literacy, Textbooks, and Ideology: Postwar Literacy Instruction and the Mythology of Dick and Jane*. New York: Falmer Press.

Luke, A. (1994). *The Social Construction of Literacy in the Primary School*. Melbourne, Australia: Macmillan.

Luke, C., de Castell, S., & Luke, A. (1983). Beyond Criticism: The Authority of the School Text. *Curriculum Inquiry*, 13(2). (pp. 111–127).

Mehan, H. (1979). *Learning Lessons*. Cambridge, MA: Harvard University Press.

Moll, L.C., Amanti, C., Neff, D., & González, N. (1992). Funds of Knowledge for Teaching: Using a Qualitative Approach to Connect Homes and Schools. *Theory into Practice*, 341, (pp. 132–141).

Moustafa, M. & Land, R.E. (2002). The Reading Achievement of Economically-Disadvantaged Children in Urban Schools Using *Open Court* vs. Comparably Disadvantaged Children in Urban Schools Using Non-Scripted Reading Programs. In annual yearbook *Urban Learning, Teaching, and Research*. Washington: AERA. pp. 44–53.

New London Group. (1996). A Pedagogy of Multiliteracies: Designing Social Futures. *Harvard Educational Review*, 66(1). (pp. 60–92).

Nystrand, M. (1997). Dialogic Instruction: When Recitation Becomes Conversation. In Nystrand, M. (1997), with Gamoran, A., Kachur, R., & Prendergrast, C. *Opening Dialogue: Understanding the Dynamics of Language and Learning in the English Classroom*. New York: Teachers College Press. (pp. 1–29).

Open Court Reading. (1995). *Collections for Young Scholars*. Peru, IL: SRA/McGraw-Hill.

Perry, T. & Delpit, L. (Eds.) (1997). *The Real Ebonics Debate: Power, Language and the Education of African American Children*. Milwaukee, WI: Rethinking Schools.

Rist, R. (2000). Student Social Class and Teacher Expectation: The Self-Fulfilling Prophecy in Ghetto Education. *Harvard Educational Review*, 70(3). (pp. 266–301).

Rogoff, B. (1994). Developing Understanding of the Idea of Communities of Learners. *Mind, Culture, and Activity*, 1(4). (pp. 209–229).

Rogoff, B. (2003). *The Cultural Nature of Human Development*. Oxford: Oxford University Press.

Routman, R. (1996). *Literacy at the Crossroads: Crucial Talk about Reading, Writing, and Other Teaching Dilemmas*. Portsmouth, NH: Heinemann.

Scribner, S. & Cole, M. (1981). *The Psychology of Literacy*. Cambridge, MA: Harvard University Press.

Shannon, P. (1992). Commercial Reading Materials, a Technological Ideology, and The Deskilling Of Teachers. In P. Shannon, (Ed.), *Becoming Political: Readings and Writings in the Politics of Literacy Education*. Portsmouth, N.H.: Heinemann.

Snow, C., Burns, S., Griffin, P. (1998). *Preventing Reading Difficulties in Young Children*. Washington, D.C.: National Academy Press.

Strauss, A., & Corbin, J. (1990). *Basics of Qualitative Research: Grounded Theory Procedures and Techniques*. London: Sage.

Street, B. (1995). *Social Literacies: Critical Approaches to Literacy in Development, Ethnography, and Education*. London: Longman.

Street, B. (2005). (Ed.). *Literacies across Educational Contexts: Mediating teaching and learning*. Philadelphia: Caslon Press.

Strickland, D. (1994). Educating African American Learners at Risk: Finding a Better Way. *Language Arts*, (71)5. (pp. 328–336).

U.S. Department of Education Office of Inspector General (2006). *The Reading First Program's Grant Application Process Final Inspection Report*. http://www.ed.gov/about/offices/list/oig/aireports/i13f0017.pdf, Accessed October 28, 2006.

CHAPTER FIVE

Success Guaranteed Literacy Programs

I Don't Buy It!

LYNN ASTARITA GATTO

"So you'd like me to go from being an outstanding teacher to a mediocre one?" I asked our Reading First support teacher, in response to the directive that I use literacy centers as the independent component of small group instruction. I used individualized centers about fifteen years ago and now my instructional practices had evolved into using silent sustained reading (SSR) as a central organizing practice for my literacy program. During this daily thirty-minute period of time children read self-selected texts at their independent level while I pull small groups for direct instruction. SSR meets various needs through numerous books on tape, Leap Pads, and a huge classroom library of leveled readers. SSR ends with snack and "book talk," where children discuss what they have read with a partner or in a small group. Children that participate in consistent silent reading programs make strong gains in reading comprehension, fluency, and attitudes (Anderson, Fielding, & Wilson, 1988; Donohue, Voelki, Campbell, & Mazzeo, 1999; Krashen, 1993; Pilgreen, 2000). So why would I want them to stop reading independently for a half an hour each day to play skill and drill games without guidance and explicit feedback? A new reading reform? I just don't buy it!

Every week my mailbox is stuffed with sales catalogs for foolproof literacy materials and programs. A multitude of companies claim that their workbooks really teach, and their test preparation and practice materials will give students the foundation and practice they need to succeed on standardized tests. Textbook publishers' expensive sales brochures claim their programs will help students become successful, motivated, confident readers and writers. Even the many professional magazines to which I subscribe are inundated with advertisements for commercial products using "tried and true" methods in order to prepare children for success in literacy. Educators believe the profit-oriented companies materials will teach their students to read (Shannon, 1992).

I am an elementary teacher in a mid-sized urban district with over thirty years of teaching experience. Over those years, I have received a number of local and state awards, including The Presidential Award for Excellence in Science and Mathematics Teaching from the White House and the 2004 New York State Teacher of the Year. Most recently, I was the subject of a documentary, *A Life Outside*, and I was honored as a 2006 Disney Teacher. It's absurd! I have been rewarded for the beliefs and practices that I am being told to stop!

The recent legislation for No Child Left Behind has impacted every classroom across America. Teachers are being held accountable through their statewide high stakes testing at every grade level. Most districts are adopting curriculum and textbook programs designed to prepare students for these tests. When our district's scores are published in the newspapers comparing them to the rest of the county, we are far below the average in all areas. From the superintendent on down to the children, we are all under pressure to perform, which means raising the state and standardized test scores.

Since World War II, literacy has been viewed scientifically, as a subject with a set of skills to be mastered (Coles, 1998, this volume; deCastell & Luke, 1983; Shannon, 1992). In response to the pressures of public outcry for higher standardized test scores, my district has taken a strong scientific approach toward literacy and has adopted a total literacy program. This newly purchased program, which each teacher is mandated to use, provides, according to the district and publisher, a complete literacy program that will meet the needs of all our students for successful instruction. In this case, successful instruction equals high test scores. The major component of this new reading program is an anthology of award-winning literature and an accompanying teacher's manual. The manual guides the teacher every step of the way through the skills-based lessons. In the last two years, our school has become a Reading First grant site for the primary grades (K-3), which mandates assessment tools, professional development, and instructional approaches and materials.

Since I loop from second to fourth grade, I am expected to conform to the weekly testing, phonics-based approach to reading instruction required by the Reading First grant. Teachers must submit the weekly DIBELS scores for the "at risk" students to the Reading First support teacher who, in turn, reports them to the central office administrator. Then, there are weekly grade level meetings during instructional time. Over fifteen hours of instructional time each year is lost while a teacher's aide covers the class for a half hour block so each grade level team can meet with the Reading First support teacher. These meetings are used to disseminate graphs and charts comparing test scores and the required instructional practices and materials. The central office grant administrators believe this total package of instruction and accountability will raise the district's scores and improve the literacy practices of our students. We have become a district dominated by exam-oriented teaching (Street, 1995) in order to follow No Child Left Behind requirements and to keep our funding. But I don't buy it.

According to the state, literacy is defined as reading, writing, listening, and speaking, and my district has determined that literacy can be achieved through the accumulation and use of skills and strategies in those areas. My district provides its teachers with a plethora of commercial programs and products in order to teach reading, writing, listening, and speaking. The district expects that all teachers will use the selected reading program they have purchased and that they will do so as described in the teacher's guide. Most of the supporting materials are test preparation and skill workbooks, overheads, charts, sentence strips, and supplemental remedial kits. But I don't use them.

I define literacy as "shorthand for the social practices of reading and writing" (Street, 1995, p. 2). My approach is to provide experiences and problems that engage students in expanding their existing literacy practices in order to construct and use new ones. Within a community of learner's framework (Rogoff, 1994; 2003), I make sure the children in my class have multiple opportunities for literacy events (Heath, 1982) and practices within social contexts. I do not consider myself the giver of knowledge. I view my role as constructing an atmosphere where the children see themselves as valuable to the process of learning within the classroom (Gatto & Larson, 2004; Larson, 2005).

Underlying my teaching is a theory of learning that is grounded in the work of Vygotsky (1978). To this end, I develop units of study that nurture what Nystrand (1997) calls "substantive engagement," which he defines as a sustained commitment to, and involvement with, academic content and issues (p. 16). It is not enough, however, just for engaging activities to take place; it is equally important for authentic questioning to take place. Nystrand defines such questions as ones that encourage individual interpretations—they open the floor to student ideas for examination, elaboration, and revision (p. 20). Authentic questioning generates in-depth and sustained student conversation, or dialogic instruction.

I encourage dialogic instruction, where the children can express their opinions and disagree with others, self-select the turn-taking during conversation, initiate topics of conversation, offer ideas for activities, and discuss and question concepts (Gutierrez, 1993). These resulting features of dialogic instruction describe a responsive-collaborative script (Gutierrez, Rymes, & Larson, 1995), in contrast to the commercial reading program's script of initiation, response, evaluation, or IRE (Gutierrez, 1993; Mehan, 1979;

Nystrand, 1997). Authentic classroom dialogue within a responsive-collaborative script elicits analytical and interpretive responses from the children, unlike IRE where students respond with recitative answers (Nystrand, 1997).

So far, my "Don't" attitude and "I do not use it" conduct have not been challenged by my school administration. There are a number of reasons for this. First of all, I have three prestigious awards hanging behind my desk! But, even before I received any of the awards, I was considered a successful teacher by the principals for whom I have worked. I must admit, in the last sixteen years I have transferred out of four schools because of the frequent changes in administration, which left me to work with principals who lacked pedagogical vision and leadership skills. Since my district comprises thirty-nine elementary schools, I have had little difficulty transferring to the schools of my choice.

My colleagues frequently challenge me, however. In my present school we prepare for the new school year with the annual textbook and workbook distribution. Grade-level books are stacked in high piles all over the gym. Everyone vies for the few rolling carts in order to pick up and deliver their heavy load of books. As I walk out with just thirty thin paperback spelling dictionaries, some veteran teacher always asks, "Is that all you're taking? Why aren't you taking your books?"

There have even been times when some helpful colleague delivers the books to me with subtle statements like, "You're going to need these," or "I know you do not like to use books, but the kids will want them." I take them and then return them later to the bookroom. I am asked with incredulous skepticism at least once a month by some teacher, "How can you teach without using the textbooks?"

At times I feel marginalized by some of my colleagues. I have overheard some rather unkind comments on more than a few occasions, especially since becoming New York State Teacher of the Year. I have been verbally attacked at faculty meetings. There are teachers in the building that refuse to speak with me, even when I cheerfully call "good morning." And, I know my instructional methodology and outspoken demeanor has been the topic of the Reading First grant team meetings more than a few times.

But, there are many other teachers who ask me to share my approach with them. As I present workshops, teach graduate classes, deliver keynote speeches, and write articles, I try to communicate to others what it is I do in the classroom. This is a difficult task; there is so much that I do that seems implicit and intuitive. My doctoral studies have helped me to better articulate my practice and philosophy to others. The documentary helps people to "see" what I do.

Each year, my students' state and standardized test score averages are equal to or surpass the school and district norms. My students' parents are very satisfied with their children's progress and enthusiasm toward school and learning. In my district there is a high rate of mobility, yet my classroom's yearly enrollment is stable. In fact,

I have had many parents continue to use their old addresses and drive their children to school every day, even after they have moved out of my school's residence zone, just to keep them in my class. In a school of 630 children, where our average attendance at PTA meetings is five to seven parents, I average twelve to eighteen families out of twenty-one students when I hold a special event. Many parents willingly chaperone the numerous field trips I arrange. At every school-wide awards assembly, my class has had significantly more awardees for perfect attendance than any other class.

In this chapter, I describe only the literacy practices that focus on reading, writing, listening, and speaking. For reasons of brevity, I have excluded any description of math, science, and social studies, which I also consider part of the literacy practices in my classroom. Furthermore, a discussion of classroom environment and building a community of learners has also been omitted (cf., Gatto & Larson, 2004; Larson, 2005; Larson & Marsh, 2005 for further elaboration of my practice). I would need to write a whole book, not just a chapter!

So, how do I teach without using textbooks within the confines of the district's mandate to use the commercially produced textbook series? This chapter describes how I created a classroom environment rich in literacy practices without using the prescribed textbooks and commercially produced materials during the fourth grade year of my last looped cohort group. Considering the individual students, planning carefully, selecting appropriate materials and activities, and adjusting activities are all important aspects of what I do to establish a successful literacy program. Luke (1994) describes these decisions as:

> . . . a series of inclusions and exclusions, of decisions about what to teach and what not to teach, what can be said and done with written language and what cannot, about what kinds of texts and competencies are appropriate and valuable. (p. 20)

None of these decisions need to be made when a basal program is used to teach literacy; they have made all the decisions for teachers. The view I will provide is only a glimpse of my decisions and practice.

In this cohort group of students, I had twenty-two children in my class. The racial makeup of the children in the class was comprised of fourteen African Americans, six Caucasians, and two students with Spanish surnames. The class was considered heterogeneous, having been organized on the basis of third-grade test scores, although eight of the children were designated remedial readers, one as special education, and one as ESOL (English for Speakers of Other Languages).

Just as many recent basal programs are organized, my approach also uses themes. However, my themes are for developing motivation for literacy events in my classroom. Unlike the basal programs, where the units are based on such themes as family, fairy tales, super sleuths, meeting the challenge, or immigration, my units are based on authentic activities centered around a theme. Most recently, my fourth-grade students and I completed the planning, constructing, and exhibiting of a walk-in butterfly vivarium (a structure to create conditions for replicating a habitat). This unit was based on introducing and using many new mathematical and scientific concepts, but reading, writing, listening, and speaking permeated every aspect of it.

Many publishers are wise to the integration of subjects and often include what they call "integration connections" sections for each of their themes. But these are just add-ons. I chose the vivarium project because through it the children would need to know about many of the curriculum standards I am required to teach. Describing life cycles and animal habitats, classifying animals, creating environmental awareness, figuring area and perimeter, using averaging, creating models to scale, and drawing blueprints were the science and math concepts that would be used. But, in order to understand any of the math and science, literacy was useful and necessary. In other words, literacy is a practice, something that gets done, not skills to be learned for use at a later date (Barton & Hamilton, 1998; Gee, 2003; Irvine & Larson, this volume; Lankshear & Knobel, 2003; Oakes & Lipton, 1999; Street, 2005; Tharp & Gallimore, 1988).

Before I introduced the project to the children, I collected books on butterflies. The books varied in difficulty from adult field guides and references to picture books. I also searched through magazine issues, both adult and children's, for articles on butterflies. Those reader filmstrips and large picture charts that no one ever uses any more also went into my ever-growing pile of resources. My last stop in the library was to root through the fiction section for any stories that may connect to the theme. By this time in the year, there were many rolling carts available, so I quickly loaded up the cart and headed back to my classroom. I added to these materials by purchasing taped stories on butterflies, videos, models, and coloring and sticker books.

I buy and use very few of the commercial products that promise to teach literacy to my students, but I do buy many materials for my classroom. I spend considerable sums of my personal budget on books, writing supplies, computer and video equipment, subscriptions to children's periodicals, and models. I scour garage sales every summer and shop the dollar stores frequently! I have also gotten quite astute at locating and writing grants (the Toshiba Foundation supported this vivarium project with a $900 grant), to support the purchase of what I consider necessary materials for which my district does not provide. I also borrow extensively not only from the school library, but also from the public library and from other teachers.

I begin every unit by creating an environment for immersion into the topic. Once the butterfly books and periodicals were arranged, pictures posted, and models exhibited, the children began to guess that our next unit would be about butterflies. I confirmed their predictions by announcing my idea of designing, building, and maintaining a butterfly vivarium, to which they enthusiastically and immediately approved. Right away there was lots of chatter among the children. As they posed numerous questions and offered answers and ideas, I struggled to record everyone's words on chart paper.

"Where are we going to build it?" "What are we going to use?" "Is there going to be any furniture inside?" "How are we going to keep the butterflies from getting out?" "How are we going to stop little kids from snatching the butterflies?" "What's the difference between a moth and a butterfly?" "How are we going to get the butterflies?" were just a few of the questions that filled four pages of chart paper. Throughout the unit, we added to the list. The focus for most of the activities in our unit came from the children's questions. Every child knew they had something important to contribute to this unit right from the start.

Next, I passed out copies of Roald Dahl's *James and the Giant Peach* to each child. Many of them had seen the video and emphatically stated that there was no butterfly in the book. They wanted to know what was going on. They had come to rely on having everything we do in the classroom being connected. This was out of character. I wrote the question on chart paper, "Why are we reading a book that has nothing to do with butterflies if we're going to study about butterflies?" and I left it hanging in the front of the room. Although many students were familiar with the novel we were going to read, they now had a purpose. It was no longer just a fairy tale to which they already knew the ending. They were searching for the link to butterflies. The connection between *James and the Giant Peach* and butterflies was that all the supporting characters are insects, which belong to the phylum of insects, as do butterflies. Once the children made the insect connection, I introduced the animal kingdom classification system. The mandated reading program just does not provide this kind of motivation or meaningful connection to content for reading.

And so, our unit had begun with the children's questions, unlike a basal or commercial theme, which begins with the publisher's questions. In fact, the basal series from which I am supposed to teach has a chapter from this same novel as part of the anthology. But, I cannot bear the thought of sharing only one chapter of a great book with children. How could they possibly understand or emulate an author's voice by reading only one chapter of an entire novel?

Actually, this was not the first Roald Dahl book we had read this year. The children analyzed *George's Marvelous Medicine* and *Danny, the Champion of the World* as I read them aloud during the first semester. When we finished *James and the Giant Peach*, each child selected from a big box of multiple copies of most of Roald Dahl's books. The school librarian had gathered this huge collection for me by putting out a call to other district librarians. We then formed study groups based on their selections in order to further their understanding of Roald Dahl's authorship. Even though the children met in their small groups, we held whole group discussions to examine their theories about Roald Dahl's writing. The program I am supposed to use does not promote in-depth author studies. How are children supposed to connect with authors and their styles if they do not thoroughly study them?

As the children read daily in their author groups, they were also gathering many facts about butterflies as they chose the books from the classroom library on butterflies for Silent Sustained Reading (SSR). One way I do use the student anthology from the basal program is to supply the children with their own copy that they keep in their desks as a resource. Students may choose any story in the anthology at any time for SSR. I begin and end every day with twenty minutes of SSR, where every child and adult in the room reads silently. I often read books for my classes at the university as my choice for SSR. After a few weeks of watching me use Post-It Notes® for marking important passages in the books I was reading, a few children began to ask for the Post-Its®. I questioned their motives, thinking that they just wanted to use them in order to experiment with a new school supply. But instead, they explained they wanted to mark passages and pages for people who might need the information for their individual butterfly reports. Soon, "sticky marking" became standard practice in our classroom.

In the multitude of teacher directions and suggestions of the teacher's guide for the reading program, there is no suggestion for such a practice. Yet, it is something readers do who are reading for information. Not once does this real practice of literacy ever get a mention in the teacher's guide of my basal reading program.

Right after we listed our introductory questions about the butterfly vivarium project we investigated the purchasing of butterfly larvae. One small group of children searched the Internet, another looked through science company catalogs, and a third used the phone book. We placed our order with the company that the children selected by comparing and contrasting the various companies, selections, and prices. Upon the arrival of the butterfly larvae, the children squealed with excitement and conversed eagerly. When all the noise subsided, I asked the children to repeat what I had overheard in the varying conversations. After recording their many comments, predictions, and questions, I focused on "How long it would take until the butterflies would emerge?" "Where are we going to put them so they wouldn't crawl away?" "What do they eat?"

Each child received a container with a larvae and an accompanying blank journal book. Just as real scientists, they were going to collect and record as much data about their larva as they could. Each day I used my own larva to model illustrating and labeling, note taking, and data collecting, such as measuring the length of the larva, and timing how long the wings took to dry out. The children were focused on finding out as much information as they could!

A few days after our larvae arrived, we took a trip to our city zoo. We carefully inspected and took notes on how the bird aviary was designed and set up to create an authentic habitat. It gave the children a vision of what our vivarium might look like and the kinds of things we would need to do in order to simulate a habitat for the butterflies. We also met with the education director, who had an extensive background in working with butterflies. He answered all the children's questions and then posed some of his own for them to think about. He also gave us seeds for some of the essential plants for feeding and stimulating egg laying for the butterflies. He reminded the children to search for the other kinds of plants we would need in our vivarium. We left the zoo with a clear picture of our task ahead.

We spent three weeks working on the planning and designing of the vivarium. First the children drew their own idea of what the vivarium should look like and what materials should be used for construction. After the children viewed one another's drawings, we met as a whole group to establish the important aspects that our vivarium should have. In order to determine the size of our vivarium, small groups calculated the area needed to hold eight people. We conducted a survey to determine the average height of the adults and children in our school so we would know how high the vivarium should be. To determine which materials the vivarium should be constructed from we tested the strength, weight, and flexibility of materials suggested by the children. Pro and con lists were compiled to determine the best possible location within the school for the vivarium. We spent hours coming to consensus on the final plans. Once our plans were final we invited the school custodian and principal to our room to view a presentation of our plan and give their input. With their final approval, we began construction of our 8' x 8' x 6' structure. Every child had a part in the construction of the vivarium.

During this twelve-week unit, the children wrote almost daily. Their journals were filled with records of their larva metamorphosis, research notes for their butterfly reports and information that would be helpful in creating a butterfly habitat, explanations for mathematical thinking, visualizations of the vivarium, notes from our visit to the zoo's aviary, interview notes, reflections of readings, and original stories and poems. Our classroom walls and bulletin boards were covered with students' written books and drawings, essays, letters, group posters, and constructed models.

Throughout all this written work, the question of how to spell a particular word came up frequently. Unlike most teachers across the United States, I do not give weekly word lists for preparation of Friday's spelling test. Does knowing how to spell all the words on a test once a week exemplify being a good speller? If a child consistently spells well throughout his/her daily writing, then I would consider that child a good speller. So, I ignore the weekly word lists provided by the reading series company and never give weekly spelling tests.

The one commercial product I order and use each year is a thin paperback-spelling dictionary. This commercial product is one that I do use. It has a page for each letter of the alphabet with a selection of corresponding frequently used words listed down the sides. In the middle of each page are spaced black lines so the children can add words of their choice. The children quickly learn the rule about asking how to spell a word in my classroom: "First the book, then a friend, a good speller next, with the teacher at the end!" In other words, look it up in the speller book, and if it can't be found, then ask two classmates, and only if you cannot get an answer from them, ask the teacher. The bright yellow spelling booklets can be seen in use throughout every day, all year long. But, no one's book is the same; each child's book contains only the additional words chosen by the child.

I also use a word wall for spelling and vocabulary instruction. Unlike the recent commercial products produced for word walls, I use the words from the children's mistakes or questions. During the vivarium unit I noticed almost every child misusing certain homophones such as "there/their/they're" and "buy/by" quite frequently. I immediately set up a word wall to focus on the kinds of mistakes the children were making. The basal program also provides lessons on homophones, but according to the publisher's timing and selection of words, not based on children's need. Word walls kits are now commercially produced and sold. Such a product is useless to me. How would any company know what words my students need for their writing and reading? I do not even know until it comes up, and it is never the same from year to year.

As our study of butterflies intensified, the monarch's yearly migration patterns became a focus of interest for the class after I shared an article in a popular children's magazine. Next, I introduced a short story titled *Radio Man* (Dorros, 1993), a story of a boy whose parents are migrant workers in the United States. The story clearly made a connection to animal migration patterns and human migration. This story is written in Spanish, with the English translation underneath. My two Hispanic students were thrilled to share their reading of the Spanish text with the rest of the class. The sets of paperbacks are the one component of the basal program I do use, but only when they apply to the theme I am teaching.

I then read aloud Jacob Lawrence's *The Great Migration*. In this famous African American artist's book, he tells the story of his family leaving the south with many other African Americans to move north in search of employment. For many days, children reread the story and heard each other's stories about their families' move from the south to the north. It was the perfect opportunity to introduce the difference between immigration and migration when the boy who had recently moved from Jordan to the United States told of his move.

The children's interest in Lawrence's paintings led me to find other books he had illustrated. His books were favorites for SSR for many days, and children placed "dibs" on who would get them next. We also took a trip to our local art gallery to view the two Jacob Lawrence paintings in their collection. Sadly, Lawrence died a few weeks later. When I brought in the full-page obituary from the newspaper, I had to make a trip to the copy machine. Every child wanted a copy of the article.

I am always reading the newspaper for articles to share in order to contextualize the topic of the unit within our community and world events. I have never seen this suggested to teachers in the program's teacher's guide. During this unit I read an announcement in our local newspaper for the opening of the photography exhibit "Migration: Humanity in Transition," by the internationally known photographer Sebastiao Salgado. I immediately called to schedule a visit. Due to the graphic nature of the photographs depicting oppression, hunger, and war, the museum officials felt the exhibit may not be appropriate for the children, but I assured them the children would benefit. On the way home from the exhibit, as we sat spread out all over the public bus, the children talked among themselves about what they had seen. That night, for homework, the children wrote their reflections of their visit to the exhibit. Their impressions were personal. One child wrote, "I didn't know that people all over the world migrated. I didn't know that people die when they migrate. I didn't know that people are starving. I'm glad I do not have to migrate."

During the focus on migration, a few students were especially interested in the migration patterns of the monarch butterfly. Actually, I thought they did not believe the monarchs from New York really returned to the same trees in the same Mexican town every single year. They wanted more proof and decided to find it on the Internet (Lankshear & Snyder, 2000). They found a site (MonarchWatch.org) that not only validated the migratory patterns of monarchs, but also described the environmental hazards that caused the destruction and interruption of the monarch's migration. The children wanted to raise money to support the foundation's work in creating a monarch reserve. The rest of the class wanted to help too.

I had them brainstorm some ideas for fundraising. They decided on two projects. They would sell handmade bookmarks (with butterflies, of course!) and hold a raffle. I helped a small group of students search the phonebook for nearby retailers that might donate butterfly knickknacks, and they proceeded to write a letter of request for donations. After addressing the envelopes and mailing the letters, each child took a turn placing a follow-up phone call. The value of all the donations totaled over $250!

I suggested that another way the children might effect a change would be by writing to the Mexican government. The children thought this was a great idea; they had never written to any government before! The children made intelligent suggestions and stated valid reasons for the Mexican government to reduce the heavy traffic and deforestation of the region where monarchs migrate. Their concern and understanding is evident, as in this child's letter:

Dear Mexican Government,

I think that you should just half the tourism in Angangueo, Mexico. I know you are making lots and lots of money from the tourism. If you just let half in the place at one time you will still make lots of money. You can't watch them all at one time and the more tourists, the more dangerous it is for the monarchs. That's why you should cut the tourism in half.

As we worked on the letters, one student wondered aloud how the Mexican government would be able to read the letters since they spoke Spanish. We decided to ask the bilingual class of sixth graders next door to us to translate the letters in Spanish. The two classes who until then, had very little exposure to one another, spent hours together reading the letters, talking about them and rewriting them into Spanish. Literacy was becoming a practice of transformation for my students (Comber, 2003; Freire, 1989; Luke & Freebody, 1997; Lankshear & Knobel, 2004). The letter-writing campaign impacted their identities as literacy learners, their identification with the bilingual class, and may perhaps even change the Mexican government's policies!

It was about this same time that we were finishing the construction of the vivarium, and the reality of the project was becoming apparent. One child commented during a class discussion that "we should make the outside of the vivarium like a museum." When asked for further explanation, he described how a museum has displays and signs, and that's what we should do. Many other ideas followed that initial suggestion, "We could put our models out." "We could put out the microscopes and the kids can look at real butterflies." "We can sell bookmarks and raffle tickets." And so, it was decided we would create a butterfly museum modeled after the museums and zoos we had visited.

In creating the vivarium museum, as we started to call it, the children used the computer for many literacy-based activities. They produced labels, signs, pictures, and short explanations for their ever-growing displays. One child took over, acting as a director, making sure everyone used the same font and size so there would be a professional look to the museum. She kept reminding the others that it has to look like a real museum. From the beginning of the unit I had taken pictures of all our activities, and two girls wanted to use the pictures to make a book showing everything we did. The raffle group used the computer to produce raffle tickets.

Soon our classroom was overrun with all the museum artifacts waiting to be put on display in the hallway surrounding the vivarium. We would be ready to open. But, "How?" asked someone one morning. After much arguing and debating, it was decided that each class in the school would be allowed to sign up for a time to visit. More argument and discussion occurred over "How long should the visits be?" "Which students will be the docents on what days?" "What jobs will the docents do?" and "When do we schedule the visits?" When finally every question was settled to the satisfaction of most, various children used the computers to create forms, schedules, and invitations.

This twelve-week unit involved children and adults working together in order to create the vivarium museum and gain an understanding of many content-related concepts. As the students participated together in this jointly constructed activity, learning was taking place on multiple levels. As the teacher, I learned along with the children. According to Rogoff's (1994, 2003; Rogoff, Turkanis, & Bartlett, 2001) definition, my classroom was a community of learners in which students and teacher work together in goal-directed activity. In "Learning in an Inner City Setting," McNamee (1990) cites one of Gundlach's recommendations for creating a true community of writers and readers is by creating opportunities for a community of speakers and listeners too, something that my students and I accomplish.

During the entire unit, children were given many opportunities to ask questions, argue points, suggest ideas, debate issues, take sides, and challenge one another. But, those opportunities for speaking and listening were usually within the safe confines of our classroom community. The grand opening of the vivarium museum and subsequent exhibition gave the children experience in literacy as a social practice within the context of real life.

Throughout the school year, we made numerous visits to various museums around the city. During every museum visit docents escorted us. The children constructed their own knowledge of what a docent does and knows from their personal interactions with the many docents they met this year. Just like real docents of our city's museums, the children would share their expertise with the public as they escorted visitors through the vivarium museum. They had to communicate with adults, children older than themselves, their peers, and children younger than themselves. They even had to explain and inform the public through the visit and interviews of a local news reporter that came on the morning of our grand opening.

When we watched the afternoon report of our upcoming event for that night, the news station incorrectly reported our school name and the identification of a butterfly. The children's indignation and outrage immediately became cause for action. Two children, selected by the others, called the newsroom and made the director aware of the mistakes and provided the corrections. They were assured that the report would be corrected. However, on the five o'clock and eleven o'clock news that night, the report still ran with the incorrect facts. The children knew then that the news is not always reported correctly. I felt like this was one of the most important lessons the children learned in this unit. They would never read the newspaper or listen to the news with blind faith again. How could any commercially produced textbook reading program teach this to children?

Our grand opening was held in the evening and the children proudly gave tours to their families and central office visitors. They sold bookmarks and raffle tickets, explained how to use the microscopes, and described what could be seen under them, identified the parts and functions of the butterfly using the models, presented the scale models of their vivariums and invited the reading of their letters, essays, journals, and bound butterfly reports. We served butterfly cake, which the children had made earlier in the day by following the directions from a magazine recipe sent in by someone's mother.

Our vivarium museum operated for two weeks, and over 600 children and their teachers visited the museum. Every student had at least four opportunities to present the 45-minute tour. This was their chance to share with an authentic audience their own knowledge about butterflies. It also provided the opportunity for dialogue about butterflies from outside their own classroom community. This experience provided valuable feedback to the children in terms of their own understanding of the content and ability to communicate.

It is a widely held belief that reading and writing must be relevant to children's lives in order for them to develop meaningful literacy practices (Cole, 1985; Gee, 2003; Lankshear & Knobel, 2003; Larson & Marsh, 2005; Luke, 1994; McNamee, 1990; Vygotsky, 1978) which could also be referred to as authentic. Authentic literacy (Oakes & Lipton, 1999) includes activities that allow children to communicate about real things of interest to them and to a real audience. The examples cited in this chapter describe authentic literacy, where the children are producers of knowledge, rather than reproducers of knowledge (Gee, 2003; Lankshear & Knobel, 2003; Nystrand, 1997). Had I used one of the themes from the mandated reading program, my students would have only reproduced the knowledge the company had outlined for them to learn. They would have only learned what was required for the state's standardized tests.

I do give the required district assessments. I hand in the children's results as directed by the district. But these scores are by no means the way I measure how children's practices of literacy are changing within our classroom community of learners. I keep careful and detailed notes on each child. I record the things children do and say. I meet with individual children to confer about their reading and writing, and we look for the different practices they are using over time and how they have changed. I often talk to parents about their concerns and observations. I meet with individual children to confer about their writing, and we look for the different practices they are using over time. In fact, I fill out report cards with each child and we decide together what the grades and comments should be. This way, report cards are meaningful documents to the children, and when parents receive them, their children can explain and discuss the grades and comments. Parent conferences always include the children, and I always begin each one by having the children talk about their learning. After all, if children are supposed to be responsible for their learning, then we must really make them part of the evaluation process.

I also hand in my plan book twice a year as required by my principal. Although not asked for, I also hand in my thematic unit plans every time I begin a new unit. My vice principal delivered a workbook for the fourth-grade English language arts test at the beginning of the year, telling me they would be very helpful in the children's preparation for the test. I advertised free gifts to all the families that attended Open House. Parents enthusiastically received those workbooks—after all, they are not teachers, and these workbooks are great tools for them! They felt as though they knew what to expect on these well-publicized tests and were being provided specific guidance in helping to prepare their children. I do not prepare children for tests, just for life.

Gee (2003, this volume) also offers an example of children's experience with literacy practices through situated, extended, and rich interaction. Do commercial literacy programs provide cultural, social, or historical relevance for children? They certainly claim to develop critical readers. But, does any basal reading program include opportunities for critically analyzing bias, historical perspective, factual correctness, and current world and local events in their stories? It seems diversity in publishers' materials really means pictures of children with differing ethnic backgrounds or children with physical challenges, as well as folktales from other cultures. Publishing companies just do not consider classrooms as places where children participate in communities of practice so that they can interact to increase the complexity of their literacy practices (Lave & Wenger, 1991).

Had I chosen to use the prescribed teaching methods from the basal program my district requires, my students would have been denied authentic and meaningful literacy practices. Had I chosen to use the basal reader as my focus for reading, my students would have been denied an understanding and awareness of a meaningful and important aspect of their own or their friends' histories. And, we would have never felt the sadness we experienced as a group when Jacob Lawrence passed away that school year.

Had I used the commercial reading materials my district expects teachers to use, my students would have never written their eloquent letters to the Mexican government pleading for environmental protection of the butterfly habitats. Had I followed the district guidelines for teaching literacy as autonomous skill, my students would have never understood literacy as a social practice or as critical. By practicing, reading, writing, speaking, and listening within the context of an integrated unit, the fourth-grade drop-off problem described by Gee (2003, this volume) was not a factor for my students. My students ended the school year using more complex literacy practices than when they entered.

Do publishing companies and corporations know what's best for our students? Do teachers feel so powerless that they will allow publishing companies and district officials to tell them how to best provide literacy instruction for their students? Do teachers really believe standardized tests measure teaching and learning? When testing becomes the reason for teaching and learning, it becomes a new parasitic practice (Lave & Wenger, 1991). Is this testing parasite eating away at teachers' personal philosophy of teaching? I refuse to relinquish my beliefs of teaching and learning to commercial enterprise. I believe my students to be literate before they enter my classroom. I use their experiences, interests, history, culture, language, and literacy practices to develop the literacy program in my classroom. The children know they are valued as learners within our classroom. Their ideas and opinions count. Often their questions and suggestions stimulate activities, lessons, or discussions. In my classroom, literacy is the bridge between the exciting and meaningful hands-on unit of study and the minds-on construction of knowledge that is central to providing challenging curriculum.

When teachers take a test-centered approach, their students view literacy not as a process, but as something to test (Nystrand, 1997). Most classrooms using commercial programs for literacy instruction rarely emphasize the process of developing and using literacy practices; instead, they emphasize the skills for increasing literacy as something that can be bought. Shannon (1992) describes teachers and students who use a basal reading series for reading instruction, believing that it has the power to teach (p. 189). He warns that teachers' reliance on commercial reading materials is deskilling teachers.

Commercial programs endorse themselves as foolproof. Who are the fools in foolproof? The companies and districts that align their instruction to commercially produced literacy programs believe it to be teachers! Teachers are not fools. Why do they allow themselves to be considered as such? Why are they allowing themselves to be positioned as deskilled? Teachers do not need commercial publishers and products in order to effectively develop literacy practices in our students.

The implications of teachers developing literacy programs to fit their students instead of fitting their students to the programs are many. First, teachers must assert their beliefs and knowledge in order to do what is right for children. I know many intelligent and hard-working teachers who need to stop asking, "Can we do that?" and just do it! Teachers also need to come out from behind the closed doors of their classrooms. Forming collegial circles, instructional planning teams and co-teaching are good steps towards creating meaningful instructional practices and creating the kinds of meaningful collaboration that skills teachers. Joining a national professional organization and attending the conferences not only expands teachers' classroom practices but also their own learning networks. It was at a national conference where I met a teacher from Kentucky and then, ten years later I flew my whole class from New York to visit hers!

Principals need to support their teachers by providing funds for what is really needed for meaningful literacy learning. Teachers should not have to spend their own money for trade books and materials, and valuable class time should not be spent on fundraisers to pay for field trips. Literacy practices do not just happen inside the school! Principals must also encourage and schedule time for teachers to participate in in-depth professional development and reflection. Principals need to back the teachers in their quest for understanding literacy as social practice and for assisting students in understanding the uses and purposes of literacy.

Reading about theory and literacy practices is not enough for teacher educators to provide for preservice teachers. Modeling the kinds of instructional practices that effectively get children to develop literacy practices needs to occur in teacher education programs too. Preservice teachers must also be exposed to classrooms where literacy is socioculturally situated.

When will teachers, administrators, and teacher educators realize literacy cannot be bought?

REFERENCES

Anderson, R., Wilson, P., & Fielding, L. (1983). Growth in Reading and How Children Spend Their Time Outside School. *Reading Research Quarterly*, 23, 285–303.

Barton, D. & Hamilton, M. (1998). *Local Literacies*. London: Routledge.

Cole, M. (1985). The Zone of Proximal Development: Where Culture and Cognition Create Each Other. In J.V. Wertsch (Ed.), *Culture, Communication and Cognition: Vygotskian Perspectives*. Cambridge, UK: Cambridge University Press.

Coles, G. (1998). *Reading Lessons*. New York: Hill and Wang.

Comber, B. (2003). Critical Literacy in the Early Years: What does it look like? In N. Hall, J. Larson, & J. Marsh (Eds.). *Handbook of Early Childhood Literacy*. London: Sage.

Dahl, R. (1998). *Danny, the Champion of the World*. New York: Puffin Books.

Dahl, R. (1996). *James and the Giant Peach*. New York. Alfred A. Knopf Books.

Dahl, R. (1981). *George's Marvelous Medicine*. New York. Bantam Books.

de Castell, S., & Luke, A. (1983). Defining Literacy in North American Schools: Social and Historical Conditions and Consequences. *Journal of Curriculum Studies*, 15, 373–389.

Donohue, P.L, Voelki, K.E, Campbell, J.R., & Mazzeo, J. (1999). *NAEP 1998 Reading Report Card for the Nation and States*. Office of Educational Research and Improvement. Washington, DC: U.S. Department of Education, March, pp. 98–100.

Dorros, A. (1993) *Radio Man*. New York. HarperCollins.

Freire, P. (1989). *Pedagogy of the Oppressed*. New York: Continuum.

Gee, J. (2003). *Situated Language and Learning: A Critique of Traditional Schooling*. London: Routledge.

Gutierrez, K. (1993). How Talk, Context, and Script Shape Contexts for Learning: A Cross Case Comparison of Journal Sharing. *Linguistics in Education*, 5, 335–365.

Gutierrez, K., Rymes, B., & Larson, J. (1995). Script, Counterscript, and Underlife in the Classroom: James Brown Versus Brown V. Board Of Education. *Harvard Education Review*, 65(3), 445–471.

Heath, S.B. (1982). *Ways With Words*. Cambridge, UK: Cambridge.

Krashen, S. (1993). *The Power of Reading: Insights from the Research*. Englewood, CO: Libraries Unlimited.

Lankshear, C. & Knobel, M. (2004). Planning Pedagogies for i-mode: From Flogging to Blogging via Wi-Fi. Published jointly in *English in Australia*, 139 (February) and *Literacy Learning in the Middle Years*, 12(1), 78–102.

Lankshear, C. & Knobel, M. (2003). *New Literacies: Changing Knowledge and Classroom Knowledge*. Buckingham, UK: Open University Press.

Lankshear, C., & Snyder, I., with Green, B. (2000). *Teachers and Technoliteracy: Managing Literacy, Technology and Learning in Schools.* St. Leonards, Australia: Allen & Unwin. (pp. 23–47).

Larson, J. (2005). Breaching the classroom walls: Literacy learning across time and space in an elementary school in the United States. In B. Street (Ed.). *Literacies across Educational Contexts: Mediating Teaching and Learning,* Philadelphia: Caslon Press. pp. 84–101.

Larson, J. & Gatto, L. (2004). Tactical Underlife: Understanding Students' Perspectives. *Journal of Early Childhood Literacy,* 4(1), 11–41.

Larson, J. & Marsh, J. (2005). *Making Literacy Real: Theories and Practices for Learning and Teaching.* London: Sage.

Lave, J. & Wenger, E. (1991). *Situated Learning: Legitimate Peripheral Participation.* New York. Cambridge University Press.

Lawrence, J. (1993). *The Great Migration.* New York. HarperCollins Publishers.

Luke, A. (1994). *The Social Construction of Literacy in the Primary School.* Melbourne: Macmillan Education Australia.

Luke, A. & Freebody, P. (1997). Critical and the question of normativity: An introduction. In S. Muspratt, A. Luke, and P. Freebody (Eds). *Constructing Critical Literacies: Teaching and Learning Textual Practice.* Sydney: Allen and Unwin.

McNamee, G.D. (1990). Learning in an Inner City Setting. In L. C. Moll, (Ed.), *Vygotsky and Education.* Cambridge, UK: Cambridge University Press. (pp. 287–303).

Mehan, H. (1979). *Learning Lessons.* Cambridge, MA: Harvard University Press.

Nystrand, M. with Gamoran, A., Kachur, R., & Prendergast, C. (1997). *Opening Dialogue: Understanding the Dynamics of Language and Learning in the English Classroom.* New York. Teachers College Press.

Oakes, J. & Lipton, M. (1999). *Teaching to Change the World.* Boston. McGraw-Hill College.

Pilgreen, J. (2000). *The SSR Handbook: How to Organize and Manage a Sustained Silent Reading Program.* Portsmouth, NH: Heinemann.

Rogoff, B. (April, 1994). Developing Understanding of the Idea of Communities of Learners. *Mind, Culture, and Activity,* 1(4): 209–229.

Rogoff, B. (2003). *The Cultural Nature of Human Development.* Oxford: Oxford University Press.

Rogoff, B., Goodman-Turkanis, C., & Bartlett, L. (2001). *Learning Together: Children and Adults in a School Community.* Oxford, UK: Oxford.

Shannon, P. (1992). Commercial Reading Materials, a Technological Ideology, and the Deskilling of Teachers. In P. Shannon (Ed.), *Becoming Political: Readings and Writings in the Politics of Literacy Education.* Portsmouth, NH: Heinemann. (pp. 182–207).

Street, B. V. (1995). *Social Literacies: Critical Approaches to Literacy in Development, Ethnography and Education.* London: Longman Group Limited.

Street, B. (2005). (Ed.). *Literacies Across Educational Contexts: Mediating Teaching and Learning.* Philadelphia: Caslon Press.

Tharp, R.G. & Gallimore, R. (1988). *Rousing Minds to Life: Teaching, Learning and Schooling in the Social Context.* Cambridge, UK: Cambridge University Press.

Vygotsky, L.S. (1978). *Mind in Society: The Development of Higher Psychological Processes.* Cambridge, MA: Harvard University Press.

CHAPTER SIX

Fattening Frogs
FOR Snakes

Virtues for Sale

PATRICK SHANNON

Morals matter. Newspapers are filled with articles and editorials about corporate greed, government deception, war, and terrorism. Television feeds us stories about crime, lust, and revenge daily. Pundits explain that the world is in an uproar, spinning out of control. Too many individuals, we are told, cannot determine right from wrong and live by antisocial moral codes. We face, they say, two crises. The first is the present danger—how do we protect ourselves immediately? The second concerns the future—how do we help our children learn to live by sound moral codes?

Into this moral and pedagogical quandary leap the moral entrepreneurs, naming absolute virtues and selling curricula to develop more moral Americans (Nash, 1997). These entrepreneurs transform morals into things for sale (commodities), moral concern into markets, and moral pedagogy into commercialized practice. Rather than oddities, these transformations are natural developments of capitalism, in which new markets for new products must be continuously developed without regard for time, place, or the people involved. At least since the 1980s, protections against the incursion of capitalism into more and more of our everyday lives have been curtailed because neoliberalism has captured the imaginations of many public (and private) officials (Faux, 2006).

As the contributors to this volume suggest, however, not all are convinced that unchecked capitalism offers a livable future for most people. There are signs of dissent outside this book as well. We see these signs in the angst of workers who fear loss of employment to merger, downsizing, or subcontracting (Uchitelle, 2006), in the loud lament of the loss of civic participation (Putnam, 2000), in the odd coalition between Ralph Nader's and Phyllis Schlafly's political groups to fight the commercial exploitation of children, in the campus movements to end sweatshops worldwide, and in the demonstrations among French youth to not become the Kleenex generation to be used and discarded by employers.

In this chapter I intend to explore the transformations of virtue and literacy pedagogy into commodities through an examination of one entrepreneur's efforts. Although there are now many working the virtue markets in homes and schools (e.g., Bill Honig, William Kilpatrick, Thomas Lackoma, Keven Ryan), none is more visible and successful than William J. Bennett, former Secretary of Education and Drug Czar for the Reagan and Bush administrations, and now research fellow at the Heritage Foundation, cofounder of Empower America, and Morning in America radio talk show host. By examining Bennett's production of moral commodities, we can further our understandings of the process of commodification in education, how literacy can be sold to us, and the threat that Bennett and his ilk represents for children and their parents. I begin with the concept of commodity because:

> The wealth of those societies in which the capitalist mode of production prevails, presents itself as "an immense accumulation of commodities," its unit being a single commodity. Our investigation must therefore begin with the analysis of a commodity. (Marx, 1967, p. 35)

COMMODITIES AND FETISHISM

For many people, a commodity appears to be just an object, a thing. That thing has a double nature, however. That is, it has use-value (bringing utility and/or pleasure to people) and exchange-value (commanding other objects or money in transactions of daily life). While use-values are a product of labor and nature (social and physical entities), exchange values are purely social constructs established as ratios of comparable labor among the objects to be exchanged. (This labor theory of value was accepted by Aristotle and Adam Smith despite Milton Friedman's pretense that it was a communist plot.) To make labor comparable across commodities, it must be reduced to a common kind, as undifferentiated and measurable as any other thing involved in commercial production. The human activity of work then must be separated from personal expression or development in order to become one of many comparable factors to be considered in the manufacture of things for sale. This need for "abstract" labor requires a particular set of circumstances in which profit is the highest priority in the production of commodities.

That set of circumstances, capitalism, organizes production in such a way to reduce the costs of production to a minimum (in order to maximize profits). This profit motive impels capitalist manufacturers to seek a "division of labor" (as Adam Smith named it)—a historically specific method of reducing individualized and differentiated work into routine and regular acts, creating new efficiencies. The profit drive, then, creates the powerful forces to homogenize labor and to simplify its form in order to imbue the commodity with the capacity for exchange. Under capitalism, even labor becomes a commodity—a thing that individuals possess, develop, and sell in order to survive and perhaps thrive. Despite their simple appearances as objects, all commodities represent each of these invisible social relationships.

Marx called the invisibility of these relationships "the fetishism of commodities." By this he meant that we lose sight of the social character of commodities and act as if the physical properties of the commodity command a price. Many people (even some economists) believe that the thing itself has the power to establish an object's price, and not the human labor or the social construction of exchange value. Thus, as Marx wrote one hundred and fifty years ago, a "definite social relation between men themselves . . . assumes . . . the fantastic form of a relation between things" (1967, p. 165). Capitalism's (a)moral character is based on this fetishism of commodities—this distortion of reality.

For example, when land and capital used in production are fetishized, they seem to command remuneration through profits because of their physical properties. (Marx described it as, "an enchanted topsy-turvy world, in which Monsieur le Capital and Madame la Terre do their ghost walking as social characters and at the same time as mere things" (1967, p. 169).) Upon inspection, however, it is the rights accorded to the owners of land and capital (by governments through laws) that enables owners to exert a claim on production (on behalf of the contribution to output made by "their" resources or capital goods that is the productive element).

The confusion between this social right and the physical reality of productivity—a central part of the fetishism—obscures the workings of capitalism from public view. It appears that the things—land, machines, etc.—are being remunerated with profits for their contributions, and not their owners, who are accumulating profits. In a sense, however, the transfer is an act of stealing. The physical parts of production are transformed from one state to another, but the surplus value which labor creates (beyond laborers' remuneration) is taken from the laborers. Under capitalism, this government-sanctioned robbery is deemed acceptable (even necessary) by the most precise "scientific" inquiry of economics (Heilbroner, 1985). Through their research, economists endeavor to discover the nature of the system and to naturalize its social and personal values. With government and science behind it, capitalism projects with authority that it is the natural state of civilization that we must preserve at all costs—James Madison's interpretation of that famous phrase—"the pursuit of happiness." Once land, capital, and labor are transformed into commodities, and those commodities are fetishized, all subversive interpretations of the capitalist system disappear.

Each commodity that we encounter, then, can teach us about capitalism as a socially constructed, historical system of production. There is nothing eternal or natural about capitalism (although there are universals within it and a recognizable order to its system). When we consider the commodification of public and private life we must remember its social construction, and not just dwell only on the immediate appearance and illusion of the new commodity created. The values directing that construction include the central role of profits in the structures and practices of our daily life, the rights of owners of the means of production to all the profits from commodity exchange, the notion that laborers must be alienated from their work in order to achieve the highest exchange-values for commodities, and the fact that any thing, practice, or idea can become a commodity. Everyone must accept these values in order for capitalism to continue (Marcuse, 1993). The stronger the acceptance of the values and the roles they imply for each citizen, the easier it is for capitalism and capitalists to prosper.

At a cultural level, commodities represent the values of their manufacturers (Schor, 2000). The thing for sale is an embodiment of not only generalized values of capitalism but also of what manufacturers want in the world and how they wish to live with others. Manufacturers produce commodities for profit, of course, but also enter production to make the world better (according to their vision of better). This may seem hard to accept with so many cynical commodities on the market (chocolate cereals, handguns, cigarettes, Elvis statues, etc.). Cereal manufacturers point to the importance of choice in the development of individuals and to the aid that they bring to parents who struggle to get their children to eat breakfast (vitamin contents are displayed on the side of the box). Handgun producers trot out the Second (the right to bear arms) and Fourth (freedom from unlawful search and seizures) Amendments to the US Constitution. Beyond the basic acceptance of capitalism, each commodity expresses its manufacturer's commitment to a freedom of choice, to a quality of life, and to an ideal of how the world should work (Lear, 1994). Even manufacturers who consciously make and sell products they know to be harmful display their values about how the world should work and their elevated position in that world. For example, as John Edgar Wideman (1995) suggests about those who propose barbaric prison conditions, these manufacturers do not believe that their products are produced for people like themselves.

Manufacturers use the appeal to these ascribed values in order to develop brand loyalty. That's why we see so many American flags in advertisements. To an extent, perhaps, this appeal to values is only a sales strategy, but it is also a declaration of the manufacturer's defining features. These values express how they wish to be known and what they believe about themselves (Bourdieu, 1984). Often their espoused values lie in direct conflict with principles of capitalism—lowest costs and highest profits. For example, the Wal-Mart officials contradicted their own "Made in America" campaign because the cost of imported products was less for the company. Nike and other sports apparel manufacturers have been caught in similar contradictions. Consumer advocates exploit this tension by proposing to exchange product loyalty for manufacturers that will abide by a more people-friendly moral code in their conception, production, and marketing of commodities. Rather than an appeal to moral principle, this exchange is economic, playing on the profit motive to drive social responsibility.

To understand the commercialization of moral values, then, we must examine the commodities offered, the markets created, and values promoted through the extension of capitalism into private moral matters. As with any commercial venture, it's important to understand how production is financed, to whom products are marketed, and what is being sold. This is where Bennett's work becomes useful.

MARKETING VIRTUE

With the help of the federal government, the Public Broadcasting System, scores of research assistants, the Heritage Foundation, and many other conservative groups (e.g., Focus on Family, Eagle Forum, Olin Foundation, and the Hudson Institute), William J. Bennett has produced over thirty commodities of virtue over the past twenty years. His efforts began with government service as Director of the National Endowment for the Arts and Humanities during the Reagan Administration. Aiming at higher education, his report *To Reclaim a Legacy* sets several of the tenets of his project. "Although more than 50 percent of America's high school graduates continue their education at American colleges and universities, few of them can be said to receive there an adequate education in the culture and civilization of which they are members" (1984, p. 1). In this title and short proclamation, Bennett names several of his values, begins to create a market, and implies a solution to a social problem (albeit, not a commercial one). That is, he names a singular definition of culture and civilization (the legacy), he concludes that colleges and universities are inadequate and damaging our youth, and he suggests that attention to this crisis is required. Eight years later, in his memoir of his work for the Reagan and Bush administrations, he made this charge more bluntly: "We are in the midst of a struggle over whose values will prevail in America" (1992, p. 9).

At first consideration, it may seem ungenerous to suggest that Bennett's efforts in this struggle are the commodification of virtue, but his relentless generation of new products (books for adults, anthologies for adults and kids, recorded versions of both; a television show; a website, books from the website, dolls from the television and website, etc.) demonstrate emphatically his intention. Moreover, Bennett's reply that he didn't take a vow of poverty when he was asked if he would continue in the second Bush administration (if there had been one), states clearly that he measures his success by his income. His salary as a government official (which is public record) was well over $100,000 per year, with a generous expense account. During those years of "poverty," Bennett honed his argument and vigorously attempted to create a market for virtue education. Within a four-year span, he declared and promoted the notion that all levels of the American education system, from preschool to graduate, were inadequate, and even dangerous—not just for the young, but for all Americans.

Bennett's efforts to create and define his market for a particularly type of virtue and literacy are sophisticated. *Our Children and Our Country* (1988) presents twenty-four speeches that Bennett made to various groups while he served as Secretary of Education. Across these speeches, you can see how he crafted his message, tailoring at first to those who will be immediately receptive, and slowly developing it for a much wider audience. It is interesting to compare his subjects and tone across these speeches. Although Bennett still enjoys his reputation as a "straight-talker," he clearly chose his words carefully. For the liberal National Press Club, he announced his intention to bring the three Cs—content, character, and choice—to the forefront of discussions about education. He concluded that elementary schools were "doing pretty well," and secondary schools and colleges were missing opportunities to capitalize on this strong start. Yet, when he addressed the conservative Focus on Family group, he opined, "If the family fails to teach honesty, courage, desire for excellence, and a host of other skills, it is exceedingly difficult for any other agency to make up for its failures" (p. 63). For the Eagle Forum, he concluded "those who claim we are now too diverse a nation, that we consist of too many competing convictions and interests to instill common values, are wrong" (p. 75). That middle C, character, was most important, and if some families do not instill it, then society would be obligated to do so.

His speech at the Manhattan Institution in 1986 supplied the name for these problems—moral literacy. Comparing moral literacy to E.D. Hirsch's cultural literacy (the argument that Americans must have a common knowledge of facts in order to communicate with each other), Bennett concluded, "If we want our children to possess the traits of character we most admire, we need to teach them what those traits are. They must learn to identify the terms and content of those traits." True to his conservative convictions, Bennett maintained that teaching moral literacy does not require new courses or more funding. Rather, existing English and history classes could be redesigned to fit this need. "We have a wealth of material to draw on—material that virtually all schools once taught to students for the sake of shaping character" (p. 81). According to Bennett, "a grassroots movement for education reform that has generated a renewed commitment to excellence, character, and fundamentals" (p. 9) will lead this reform.

By the end of the 1980s and into the 1990s, Bennett worked to extend the market for moral education beyond his conservative constituency, tying it to individual betterment and general social and economic security. For example, he released a series of books intended to spread his interpretation of the causes of this social decline. The titles convey their content: *The De-Valuing of America* (1992), *The Index of Leading Cultural Indicators* (1994), *Body Count* (1996), *The Death of Outrage* (1998), and the millennium issue of *The Index of Leading Cultural Indicators* (1999). Although each book offered some unique information, all hammered Bennett's singular theme that liberal American institutions are not prepared or willing to deal with the social problems released during the morally bankrupt 1960s and 1970s. Then, in order to gain social recognition and redistribute cultural and economic wealth, minority groups and their liberal allies subverted the traditional American standards on drugs, promiscuity, divorce, crime, popular culture, and laziness. The result, Bennett concluded, is a society in which more and more people lack impulse control and empathy for others. This de-valuing of self and society, he argued, led to an America in which citizens could no longer feel secure in public or even in their homes.

To promote his solution, Bennett disparaged existing conservative and liberal solutions to what he argued were growing social problems. He concluded that advocates for prisons without compassion, the death penalty, and more guns for self-protection were concerned only with curtailing the consequences of social ills, and not with addressing their causes. Extreme solutions—debtor prisons for the lazy, death to the sexually active (through HIV), or more guns for citizens—could not address the root causes of the problems. Advocates of such solutions, he maintained, are only interested in punishment and underestimated the scope of the problems. Liberals who pointed toward social factors that conditioned antisocial behavior simply made excuses for individuals' indefensible choices. Although he acknowledged that some people have more than others, Bennett argued that poverty and racism are no longer serious problems in America because economic opportunities at the turn of the 21st century made poverty a personal choice (and not a social condition) and laws against racism had curtailed its consequences.

With the market clearly defined, Bennett applied a name to it:

> Moral poverty is the poverty of being without loving capable responsible adults who teach right from wrong; the poverty of being without parents or other authorities who habituate you to feel joy at others joy, pain at others pain, satisfaction when you do right, remorse when you do wrong; the poverty of growing up in a virtual absence of people who teach morality by their own everyday example and who insist that you follow suit. (1996b, p. 27)

This statement completed the market circuit. Adults must teach the young to be moral through developing moral literacy, and newly literate populace will put an end to moral poverty. In this way, every American citizen became implicated in one way or another in the problem and its solution. While some adults work from an adequate set of moral principles to instill moral literacy within their children, clearly other adults present a mixed moral pedagogy of the young.

Until the middle of the 1990s, Bennett seemed convinced that the majority was moral, while a minority (mostly minorities and the poor) was not. "When the American people are asked what they want from schools, they consistently put . . . help them to develop reliable standards of rights and wrongs that will guide them through life" (1988, p. 9). Yet, Bennett seemed startled to find that many Americans were not alarmed when President Clinton was charged with "political" indiscretions. In *The Death of Outrage: Bill Clinton and the Assault on American Ideals* (1998), Bennett chides that majority to be "angry at the proper things and the proper people." The lack of outrage, Bennett claims, was a sign that America was worse than he thought—most Americans are morally illiterate or at least alliterate, and thus there was a need for a curriculum to direct American adults and children toward the proper moral values.

VIRTUES AS COMMODITIES

The need for a curriculum to teach moral literacy in order to eliminate moral poverty supplied incentive for Bennett to move from public servant to private entrepreneur. His first effort was *The Book of Virtues: A Treasury of Great Moral Stories* (1993), which spent over a year on the *New York Times* bestseller list. In that book, he named the essential American virtues as: self-discipline, compassion, responsibility, friendship, work, courage, perseverance, honesty, loyalty, and faith. To avoid confusion over what these labels might mean, he provided an explicit definition for each based on his reading of "the corpus of Western Civilization, that American schoolchildren once upon a time, knew by heart" (p. 15). Although Bennett warned that virtues are not like "beads on a string or marbles in a pouch" that can be possessed, he maintained that these ten would supply the moral anchoring for each American. In order to obtain these anchors, Bennett invited all to read the stories he placed in his anthology: "Parents will discover that reading this book with or to children can deepen their own, and their children's, understanding of life and morality" (p. 14). Of course in order to read them, one must buy the book.

The structure of *The Book of Virtues* is simple, because Bennett believes that the morals reside in the text itself. Reading, for Bennett, is not a process of interpretation. Rather, reading is an act of discovery in which the reader uncovers the treasure that the author intended. After a very brief introduction (taken almost verbatim from the Manhattan Institution speech), each virtue received a chapter—a two-page introduction/definition, followed by scores of short stories, poems, letters, excerpts, and fables on that theme. Through the shear weight of repetitive example, Bennett assumes that readers should be convinced of the value of these virtues. Moreover, once valued, readers would habituate themselves toward each virtue by "marking favorite passages, for reading aloud to family, for memorizing pieces here and there" (p. 15). Readers would then have "specific reference points . . . and a stock of examples illustrating what we see as right and wrong, good and bad—examples illustrating that, in many instances, what is morally right and wrong can indeed be known and promoted" (p. 12). Bennett used a metaphor—the chapters as rich quarries of virtues, which readers are to mine—in order to portray the effort and reward in his character education. Upon completing all the chapters, readers and listeners become morally literate and good Americans.

In this way, *The Book of Virtues* promised to deliver both virtues and moral literacy to those who purchased it. For if the approved virtues were indeed in the texts waiting to be discovered, then they were/are for sale—things to be acquired through a two-step process. First, buy the book, and then, read the book. Owning and reading *The Book of Virtues* makes the virtues property to be used at the now morally literate owner's discretion. Lost in the fetishism of this commodity is the human center of morality and literacy education. The possible value of interaction between text author (Bennett only wrote 26 of the 831 pages in the book—the rest are public use documents) and reader is erased in the extraction of the singular correct interpretation of virtue encoded explicitly in the text. As a result, the text—the thing—seems to be the moral agent, not the author or reader. And Bennett was and is ready to sell that thing (now in multiple editions and media forms) to every family and every schoolteacher. Perhaps it is important to note that only 28 of the more than 200 texts included in *The Book of Virtues* required permission fees to be paid. Salaried assistants gathered these documents and presented them for Bennett's selection. Both acts kept costs down in order to maximize profits.

For $30 (hard cover), Bennett promised a virtuous America that he considers to be the last best hope of Western Civilization. The dust jacket presents affirmations for the book from Margaret Thatcher, Rush Limbaugh, and Roger Staubach, suggesting the political slant of the virtues offered inside the covers. And in fact, Bennett's selection of virtues is skewed in favor of his conservative political agenda. His choices of virtues for each text are clearly open for debate. For example, although he quotes Plato frequently and declares that his virtues reflect the best of Western Civilization, Bennett does not follow Plato's lead. Plato distinguished four cardinal virtues: wisdom, courage, temperance, and justice. Bennett ignored Plato's intellectual virtue, wisdom, and reinterprets his political one, justice. For example, Bennett suggested that Frederick Douglas's 1852 Fourth of July speech on the hypocrisy of celebrating Independence Day in a slave nation is about responsibility; he selects courage as the virtue of Susan B. Anthony's symbolic vote in the

1872 presidential election; and he characterized Mary Wollstonecraft's (1792) *A Vindication of the Rights of Women* as a demonstration of faith. Each of these texts expresses its author's plea for justice in a world controlled by Bennett's heroes.

At times, Bennett acknowledged that his choices in texts were political. "Some of the history that is recounted here may not meet the standards of the exacting historian. But we tell these familiar stories as they were told before, in order to preserve their authenticity" (p. 14). Contesting Bennett's assignment of virtues, however, is more than a historical quibble. Rather, it is a quest for a different America than the one he presented in his introductions to the sections. If these virtues are to be consumed and used to shape individual and social actions, then the inaccuracies, historical and otherwise, are matters of politics. His representations of history repackage American present as well as its past. When consumers of *The Book of Virtue* encounter another text about apartheid (Douglas's point), democracy (Anthony's point), or women's rights (Wollstonecraft's point), Bennett wants them to ignore issues of justice in order to find his main ideas of responsibility, courage, and faith. In Bennett's virtuous America, citizens should strive to be self-disciplined, responsible, honest, loyal, faithful, and to work and persevere, but to be neither wise nor just.

Because Bennett's definition of reading is to consume the messages from text and then to apply those messages to new situations, it is important to trace his line of reasoning for the texts he selected. Consider his use of Abraham Lincoln's letter to Mrs. Bixby of Boston in the compassion section (p. 177). Lincoln believed that Mrs. Bixby's five sons were killed while fighting for the Union armies. In the introduction to the letter, Bennett quotes Carl Sandburg, a Lincoln biographer—"The letter wore its awful implication that human freedom so often was paid for with agony"—in order to direct readers' interpretation. Lincoln wrote:

> ... I feel how weak and fruitless must be any word of mine which should attempt to beguile you from the grief of a loss so overwhelming. But I cannot refrain from tendering you the consolation that may be found in the thanks of the republic they died to save. I ... leave you ... the solemn pride that must be yours to have laid so costly a sacrifice upon the alter of freedom.

Bennett suggested that the letter shows Lincoln's compassion. And it might, but Lincoln's letter is also self-serving. Mrs. Bixby lost sons to a war that Lincoln declared in order to prevent southern states from seceding during his administration—a war that required the service of only those young American males who could not buy their way out of the draft and in which over 600,000 working-class men and boys were killed. In Bennett's efforts to demonstrate the pettiness of those who have challenged the accuracy of many of the documents he included in his book, he reported that Lincoln had been misinformed about the Bixby boys. Two were killed, one was taken prisoner, and two deserted from the Union Army. Clinging to his agenda, however, Bennett wrote, "Mrs. Bixby's loss and sacrifice hardly could have been greater."

Although I think that Lincoln's letter would be better assigned to the responsibility section (in which readers and listeners could discuss leaders' responsibilities in and for war), I do not believe that teaching virtue was Bennett's primary objective when he chose Lincoln's letter to repackage history for us. Rather than responsibility, courage, loyalty, or any other virtue he might name for the Bixby boys, their mother, or Lincoln, Bennett's real purpose seems to be to prepare America's children and their parents for the next war that a president declares and Congress confirms, or for the many conflicts to which our presidents send American sons and daughters. Bennett framed the Lincoln letter in responsibility in order to tell readers to forget those deserters and think about the glory of the "sacrifice upon the alter of freedom." A similar agenda runs through all of Bennett's books subsequent editions and volumes to *Our Country's Founders (1998), Our Sacred Honor (1997), The Spirit of America (1998), The Children's Book of America (1998)*, and *The Children's Book of Heroes (1997)*. Each shies away from issues of injustice so prevalent in our history in order to embrace a sense of duty to country.

Bennett is selling a different sense of duty as well as those of conservative patriotism. He presents the case for being compliant workers through five virtues: self-discipline, responsibility, work, perseverance, and loyalty. His first order of this business is to reign in our passions and impulses in order to learn to control ourselves. Self-discipline in Bennett's hands becomes self-surveillance, according to his other virtues. If we fail with our self-discipline by acting inappropriately, Bennett implores us to take responsibility for our actions. We alone are responsible for who we are, what we do, and why we do it. We must never be idle. "Even sleeping can be a form of investment if it is done for the sake of future activity. But sleep, like amusement, can also be a form of escape—oblivion sought for its own sake rather than for the sake of renewal" (p. 347). Bennett's answer for idleness is to work and to remember, "There are no menial jobs, only menial attitudes. And the control of our attitudes are up to us" (p. 348). Self-disciplined and responsible in our work, we must persevere— "The world is lost through hesitation, faltering, wavering, vacillating, or just not sticking with it" (p. 528). Finally, we must be loyal even though "we do not have to like those to whom we are loyal, and they do not have to like us" (p. 666).

Separately, these virtues might appear to direct readers along noble paths of reason that could indeed serve the individual (and society) in continuous reflection and development. Collectively, however, these five virtues seem pointed toward compliant workers who will self-monitor their mind and body in continuous service to some larger entity. Moreover, these workers recognize that they are individually responsible for their fate and that they must retain a positive attitude even if they do not enjoy their situation. With these values, workers show up for work daily, ready, willing, and able to do what they are told; they do not hesitate or question the authority or conditions of their work; they do not ask for more money, more time, more safety; and they remain in their work regardless of how they are treated. Unions would be out of the question because they violate the personal virtues of loyalty and responsibility. In this way, Bennett's moral literacy is a capitalist enterprise in more ways than one.

For those consumers who do not master these virtues in one volume, Bennett published *The Moral Compass* (1996) anthology, and a set of children's books with excerpts from his anthologies complemented by Michael Hague's painted illustrations (Bennett, 1995, 1996a, 1997b).

CHARACTER DEVELOPMENT AS
COMMERCIALIZED PRACTICE

Bennett's television program provides insight into both his pedagogy and his sense of moral literacy. His animated PBS show, *Adventures from the Book of Virtues*, ended with its third year of production in 2000. These adventures take place in a fictional world of Spring Valley, where preadolescents Zach and Annie ride bicycles to Plato's Peak and encounter talking animals. Plato (a buffalo, which is presumably Bennett), Aristotle (a prairie dog), Socrates (a mountain lion), and Aurora (an eagle) present tales (similar to the story texts in *The Book of Virtues*) that address the moral dilemmas which Zach and Annie face. In each case, the issues are clear-cut and simple and the morals of the stories fit perfectly. When the children return home, they know exactly how to solve their problems. None of the problems are intended to signify moral anomalies; for example, when the virtue of honesty conflicts with the virtue of compassion or when courage is incompatible with expressions of loyalty or faith. The episodes imply that life is simple to understand once you know which moral examples to apply in each situation. Bennett was part of the production since its inception. Although he does not draw the cartoons or write the stories, he has copyrighted all of the characters, which he leases to the production company.

Although Bennett claims to follow Plato's ideas about essential human nature and the realm of well-defined, abstract, and universal moral truths, he begins and ends his moral pedagogy with Aristotle's notion of moral behavior as habit. That is, children become virtuous by imitating adult examples in everyday life. This strange mix places remarkable demands on adults. On the one hand, adults must be clear in imparting the essence of the virtue found in Bennett's books, but on the other hand, they must apply those virtues in the complexities of their lives. The first demand requires adults to follow Bennett's lead. The second demand is much more difficult. Aristotle's empiricism requires self-critical, relativistic, reflexive logic in order to choose what's right in any particular situation. According to Aristotle, that reasoning is the habit of good moral character to be formed. Within Bennett's pedagogy, however, adults face the challenging task of reconciling his absolute nature of the ten virtues with the messy particulars of their application. Rather than accept this challenge, Bennett denied its importance.

> The reader scanning this book may notice that it does not discuss issues like nuclear war, abortion, creationism, or euthanasia. This may come as a disappointment to some. But the fact is that the formation of character in young people is educationally a different task from, and a prior task to, the discussion of the great, difficult ethical controversies of the day. First things first. And planting ideas of virtue, of good traits in the young, comes first. In the moral life, as in life itself, we take one step at a time. Each field has its complexities and controversies. And so too does ethics. And each field has its basics. So too with values. This is a book in the basics. The tough issues can, if teachers and parents wish, be taken up later. And I would add, a person who is morally literate will be immeasurably better equipped than a morally illiterate person to reach a reasoned and ethically defensible position on these tough issues (p. 13).

After the complexities of life are removed from consideration, what remains in Bennett's moral pedagogy is the notion that absolute morals can be learned by rote and that the application of those absolutes is relatively straightforward. And this is where Bennett's commercialized pedagogy becomes apparent. He has established that American culture is in decline, that adults (teachers and parents) are not always cognizant of the absolute morals needed to stop this decline and return America to moral greatness, and that currently no institution has accepted responsibility to teach character. In order to fill this void, Bennett offers two sets of commodities to direct moral pedagogy. First, he publishes a series of anthologies and picture books to impart the absolute morals; and second, he produces the PBS series, website, and storybooks from the PBS episodes in order to provide adults with simplified daily life examples.

By buying these commodities (PBS will sell you *The Children's Book of Virtues* and six videotaped episodes of the *Adventures from the Book of Virtues* for $74.88), teachers and adults can provide the moral curriculum for children, themselves, and the country. Reading and memorizing the ten virtues, learning to ignore complexity in moral dilemmas, and applying the appropriate virtue to the simplified problem makes one morally literate. Lost in this commercial exchange are the moral reasoning of the authors of these texts and the possible discussions of meaning that readers might construct from the texts (and the contexts). The texts, not the authors, bring the morals, and Bennett, not the adult present at the reading, brings the meaning of the texts. Bennett's representation of virtue as text consumption and teaching as transportation of correct meaning to impressionable but docile minds makes moral pedagogy an exchange between things (not people). Bennett's work positions readers (us) in the overlap between conservatism and capitalism—a rough spot for anyone except the wealthy.

Bennett claims that his moral curriculum becomes more sophisticated as children age. It appears, however, that the moral literacy of the PBS show and *The Book of Virtues* are the beginning and the end of his pedagogy. In *The Educated Child: A Parent's Guide From Preschool Through Eighth Grade* (1999, written with Chester Finn and John Cribb), Bennett offers character education under the chapter heading "Along with Academics." Although the recommended texts for different disciplines increase in complexity, Bennett presents no clear plan for increasing the complexity of students' moral literacy. His checklist to determine if a child's school is performing well is to quiz students on specific facts. (Quick: What happened in 1789? There's only one correct answer, and it's not the storming of the Bastille.) The only explicit moral guidance offered to teachers and parents is that students should be told not to take drugs, not to have sex, not to watch television or listen to rock and roll. Bennett's current involvement in cyber schools through Empower America does not improve on this record.

FIXED VIRTUES VS. DEMOCRATIC DEMANDS

Everyday life is not as simple as Bennett would have it. His denial of the complexities of children's lives simply displays that he writes from a position of cynicism and privilege. Two recent events invite the charge of cynicism. In 2004, newspapers disclosed that Bennett gambled frequently and for such high stakes that casinos provided him with complimentary accommodations whenever he visited Las Vegas or Atlantic City. Some media pundits found his gambling to be a contradiction with Bennett's frequent lecturing of Americans on how to live their lives. Bennett acknowledged the veracity of the charges, but dismissed them as an invasion of his privacy and with a statement that he did not gamble with the "rent money." He had "earned a lot of money and can could do with it what he wanted." In the fall of 2005 while taking calls on his radio show, Bennett responded to a caller's curious inquiry about lost tax income from aborted babies with a statement that if America wanted to lower crime rates, they could abort all Black children. Although he tried to qualify his remarks with a statement that such acts would be reprehensible, who would think such a thought? Both these events demonstrate Bennett's lack of moral character by any reasonable definition as well as a lack of moral principle behind his commercial actions.

Bennett also appears to be naïve in his understanding of children's lives. Bennett's children (who appear on the book jacket *The Book of Virtue*) might not be touched by violence, religious duplicity, corporate greed, racism, and sexism in their daily lives. Many American children, however, do experience or witness these forces daily. These children must recognize, consider, and act in a complex world that is not designed for their support or betterment. Bennett believes that childhood can be bracketed while adults sell them on his ten virtues without reference to how they might apply them to the conditions of their lives. Bennett's sense of childhood, then, is a social construction of his privilege, in which impulse and empathy are designed solely to protect his and his elite associates' position. Compare Bennett's notion of childhood with those which represented in the Children's Defense Funds' State of Childhood Report (2005), the PBS series *American Family: A Journey of Dreams*, or Jonathan Kozol's *The Shame of the Nation* (2005), and the charge of naiveté seems generous.

Bennett is correct—morals and literacy do matter. He is wrong, however, on how to live a moral life within a democracy. Neither virtue nor literacy can be sold or bought, in a healthy democracy in which virtue and literacy are to serve citizens and not just elites (Shannon, 2000a). Fixed moral positions cannot explain the complexities of our lives, and fixed morals are more expressions of power than attempts to improve the lives of citizens in a democracy. Bennett's moral literacy is designed to hide those power relationships from children and adults. In fact, Bennett's commercial moral pedagogues explicitly seek to disable readers' abilities to consider power relationships at all. To paraphrase blues musician Sonny Boy Williamson, Bennett hopes to fatten young and old in order to be eaten by Bennett's privileged class.

In order to reclaim virtue from Bennett's grasp, we need a different type of moral literacy—one that considers both the plurality of positions and the fundamentals of democracy (Shannon, 2000b). Bennett is correct that twentieth-century attempts at democracy have failed. He is wrong, however, that increased recognition of diversity has caused these failures. Rather, the failures were predictable based on the inabilities of conservatives, liberals, and even collectivists to take up issues of diversity productively (Trend, 1996). "What we share and what makes us fellow citizens in a liberal democratic regime is not a substantive idea of the good, but a set of political principles specific to such a tradition: the principles of freedom and equality for all" (Mouffee, 1993, p. 65). Although conservatives and liberals claim their positions to be founded on these principles, their visions of "the good" require them to demand consensus around their positions. Bennett is clear that he wants us to habituate his conservative position of freedom and equality. Yet, democratic politics require adversarial relations among social actors as they advocate their interpretations and their preferred social identities.

> It is the tension between consensus—on the values—and dissensus—on the interpretation—that makes possible the agnostic dynamics of pluralist democracy. This is why its survival depends on the possibility of forming collective political identities around clearly differentiated positions and the choice among real alternatives. (Mouffee, 1995, p. 107)

For democracy to work, individuals must recognize that their identities are not fixed, abstract, or universal, as Bennett maintains. Rather, our identities are multiple and fluid. We are members of many social groups that influence our thoughts, actions, and values in substantial ways, and we vary our hierarchical arrangements of those memberships according to circumstances and intentions. Beyond that recognition, citizens must learn to use their moral power to force clear articulations of positions by forming coalitions to enact their shared concerns (Stone, 1994). Moral literacy can and should play an important role in providing this force. Democracy, then, hinges on the development of individuals' identities that are committed to the value of freedom and equality (blended with the values of their other group memberships), to moral literacies focused on clear articulations of alternatives, and to active participation in civic life. Although these identities cannot be fully specified, they require at least three elements: reflexive agency, the will to act, and respect for the positions of adversaries.

Reflexive agency invites citizens to evaluate the world in terms of their intentions and values, and at the same time, to evaluate those intentions and to reflect on those values. In this way citizens take inventory of their identities, their values, their motives, and their actions; they investigate the sources of those parts of themselves, and they make choices about which ones they hope to enhance and which they hope to diminish. Compare this agency with Bennett's notion that meanings are static, allowing standard reading of texts across time and space. Consider how reflexive agency undermines the authority hidden in Bennett's commercial packaging.

The will to act, which for many has been diverted from public life to private matters of consumption (Schor, 2000), must be redirected through individuals' recognition that their apparently private problems are connected to public issues because their problem is shared by many. As individuals become aware of the political possibilities of their multiple and fluid identities and the real opportunities to form larger, more effective coalitions for accomplishing goals shared across social groups, the will to act in civic life becomes more likely and inviting. Bennett considers morality a solely individual concern—all persons are responsible completely for their actions and the consequences. In this context, collective moral action is out of the question. Recognizing that personal problems are often public issues, however, invites consideration of institutional morality and the will to act collectively on those considerations. This is exactly the morality that Bennett hopes to avoid through his commercial enterprise. Reflexive agency ensures that coalitions will not become fixed power blocks, as basic and secondary assumptions for action are consistently scrutinized.

Because our identities are not fixed, and future intersections of values cannot be predetermined, citizens begin to recognize the need to respect the positions of their adversaries—not to the point of agreement, mind you—but enough to recognize commitment to shared principles of freedom and equality. Perhaps this is how Ralph

Nader and Phyllis Schlafly can find common ground on commercial exploitation of children in schools (Kohn & Shannon, 2004). The limits on this respect must be set by individuals' and groups' commitments to those principles. Anyone rejecting freedom and equality outright stands outside of the democratic process and, therefore, becomes the legitimate object of democratic scorn. William Bennett occupies this space and deserves our scorn.

The social problems we face and the demands of democracy require more than Bennett or any of the other moral entrepreneurs can package and sell to us. Different moral literacies—ones based on reflexive agency, a will to act, and respect for adversaries' positions—will not automatically solve the moral issues facing us. They will not make it easy for children or adults to choose moral courses of action. They will, however, prepare us to look beneath the surface of the particulars of our concerns. They will enable us to see that our problems are not ours alone. They will help us to listen seriously to the moral positions put forth by others. They will help us to understand the conflict that arises out of these various positions and to seek coalition with those others who seem to share a common goal with us on those concerns. They will help us understand how power works and to use our collective strengths to identify and maintain structures that will extend freedom and equality into more aspects of our lives. They will help us to live virtuous lives.

REFERENCES

Bennett, W. (1984). *To Reclaim a Legacy.* Washington, DC: National Endowment for the Humanities.

Bennett, W. (1988). *Our Children and Our Country.* New York: Simon and Schuster.

Bennett, W. (1992). *The De-Valuing of America.* New York: Simon and Schuster.

Bennett, W. (1993). *The Book of Virtues: A Treasury of Great Moral Stories.* New York: Simon and Schuster.

Bennett, W. (1994). *The Index of Cultural Indicators.* New York: Broadway Books.

Bennett, W. (1995). *The Children's Book Of Virtue.* New York: Simon and Schuster.

Bennett, W. (1996a). *Adventures from The Book of Virtues.* New York: Simon and Schuster.

Bennett, W. (1996b). *Body Count.* New York: Simon and Schuster.

Bennett, W. (1996)c. *The Moral Compass.* New York: Touchstone.

Bennett, W. (1997a). *The Book of Virtues For Young People.* New York: Simon and Schuster.

Bennett, W. (1997b). *The Children's Book of Heroes.* New York: Simon and Schuster.

Bennett, W. (1997c). *Our Sacred Honor.* New York: Broaden and Holman.

Bennett, W. (1998a) *The Children's Book of America.* New York: Simon and Schuster.

Bennett, W. (1998b). *The Death of Outrage: Bill Clinton and the Assault on American Ideals.* New York: Free Press.

Bennett, W. (1998c). *Our Country's Founders.* New York: Simon and Schuster.

Bennett, W. (1998d). *The Spirit of America.* New York: Touchstone.

Bennett, W. (1999). *The Index of Leading Cultural Indicators.* Colorado Springs, CO: Waterbrook Press.

Bennett, W., with Finn, C., & Cribb, J. (1999). *The Educated Child.* New York: Free Press.

Faux, J. (2006). *The Global Class War: How America's Bipartisan Elite Lost Our Future.* New York: Wiley.

Gee, J. (1992). What is literacy? In P. Shannon (ed.), *Becoming Political.* Portsmouth, NH: Heinemann.

Heilbroner, R. (1985). *The Nature and Logic of Capitalism.* New York: Norton.

Kohn, A. & Shannon, P. (2004). *Education, Inc.* Portsmouth, NH: Heinemann.

Kozol, J. (2005). *The Shame of the Nation.* New York: Crown.

Lears, J. (1995). *Fables of Abundance.* New York: Perseus.

Marcuse, H. (1993). *One Dimensional Man.* Boston: Beacon

Marx, K. (1967). *Capital,* vol. 1. New York: International Press.

Mouffee, C. (1993). *The Return of the Political.* New York: Verso.

Mouffee, C. (1995). Politics, Democratic Action, and Solidarity. *Inquiry,* 38 (pp. 99–108).

Nash, R. (1997). *Answering the Virtuecrats.* New York: Teachers College Press.

Putnam, R. (2000). *Bowling Alone.* New York: Simon & Schuster.

Schor, J. (2000). *Do Americans Shop Too Much?* Boston: Beacon.

Shannon, P. (2000a). What's My Name. *Reading Research Quarterly,* 35 (pp. 90–108).

Shannon, P. (2000b). *You'd Better Shop Around.* Portsmouth, NH: Heinemann.

Stone, J. (1994). The Phenomenological Roots Of The Radical Democracy/Marxism Debate. *Rethinking Marxism,* 7 (pp. 99–115).

Uchitelle, L. (2006). *The Disposable American: Layoffs and their Consequences.* New York: Knopf.

Wideman, J. (1995). Doing Time, Marking Race. *Nation* (30 October) (pp. 502–503).

Wollstonecraft, M. (1792). *A Vindication of the Rights of Women: With Strictures on Political and Moral Subjects.* Boston: Thomas & Andrews.

CHAPTER SEVEN

"Sameness AS Fairness"

The New Tonic of Equality and Opportunity

KRIS D. GUTIÉRREZ

The first edition of *Snake Oil* (2001) provided a much-needed opportunity to address the persistent inequities non-dominant students, especially immigrant children, experience in California schools. At that time, I discussed the insidious means by which English learners are made vulnerable by anti-immigrant and educational reform policies that normalize academic underachievement and forms of academic apartheid that characterize their schooling conditions. We learned that English-only policies work hand-in-hand with the large-scale implementation of *No Child Left Behind* and its reductive reading programs.

In their instantiation, these policies become a means for socializing large numbers of people toward a new language ideology (or perhaps a refurbished ideology), as well as the rationale for sorting children into categories and curricular programs. Most notably, the centerpieces of the *No Child Left Behind Act of 2001* (NCLB), Reading First and a narrowly defined assessment apparatus, privilege English-only and reductive literacy practices that de-emphasize meaning-making and critical thought in any language.

The current social and cultural educational landscape of educational policy and discourse for poor children in the U.S. is characterized by "marketplace reforms"—that is, reforms that bring the business principles of efficiency, accountability, quality, and choice to establish the educational agenda. Indeed, NCLB has provided the opportunity for extraordinary profit through the implementation of a new set of initiatives that, as Apple (2001) points out, reflect the power of a neo-liberal, neo-conservative, and new managerial discourse in education at work today (p. 87).

As I have written elsewhere (Gutiérrez & Jaramillo, 2006), the road to educational equality via the neo-conservative and neo-liberal agenda (with its testing and mass standardization of the curriculum in schools) leads to a radically different agenda and outcomes than race-based equity reforms. The latter, we argued, focus on a central source of the problem—the underlying historical practices that have contributed to educational, economic, and social inequality (Crosland, 2004; Gutiérrez & Jaramillo, 2006).

In this chapter, I address the deeply divisive views around race, class, and gender justice in education and the larger society, and discuss how issues of equity and difference are addressed in the current educational climate. In particular, I examine how new forms of educational opportunity, proposed through color-blind, merit-based interventions, have promoted a "sameness as fairness" argument that dominates the rhetoric of educational reform and the public sensibility (Crosland, 2004; Gutiérrez & Jaramillo, 2006).

The erosion of the small gains in educational equity advanced in past decades has made it easier to advance the "color-blind" practices of common standards and common culture under the logic of the "sameness as fairness" framework, and to implement English-only and one-size-fits-all curricula. In the service of "color-blind equality," non-dominant communities are flattened out in ways that discount both strength as well as variance in individuals and their communities, and obscure the link between economic disparities, asymmetrical power relations, and historically racialized practices (Crosland, 2004).

I will also call your attention to several rich models of learning in two schools that challenge approaches that strip children of their resources, both sociocultural and intellectual (See also Street, Lefstein, & Pahl, this volume, for discussion of rich learning contexts in the UK). Although the cases are different, each school and community reflects the determination to resist in its own way the normalizing practices engineered by local, state, and national educational policies. And in their attempt to address the unfulfilled promises of educational reform, one school holds tenaciously to its commitment to multilingual and multimodal forms of learning. The other, under attack by ultra-conservatives emboldened by powerful neo-conservative and anti-immigrant discourses, fights to preserve rich instructional practices embedded in cultural and historical traditions, as well as values of cultural amplification and educational sovereignty (Moll & Ruiz, 2002). But first, a discussion of the new educational ecology under which these and other schools struggle to survive.

EQUALITY AS "SAMENESS AS FAIRNESS"

The under-education of children in California, especially those for whom English is not their home language, serves as an illustrative case of the effects of race-based educational practices instituted through color-blind approaches to educational equality. By proposing new forms of equal educational opportunity through color-blind, merit-based interventions, a "sameness as fairness" argument has come to dominate the rhetoric of educational reform—a discourse that has become so powerful and persuasive that it has been co-opted in recent years by those seeking to turn back the small gains in civil rights of previous decades (Gutiérrez, Asato, Gotanda, & Santos, 2002).

One specific response to diversity under the "sameness as fairness" principle has been to commodify instruction and package it in ways that erase difference and ignore the repertoires of practice students bring to learning environments (Gutiérrez & Rogoff, 2003). Here the marketplace elements of efficiency and large-scale accountability facilitate the homogenization of vastly different students, even those who share a linguistic and sociocultural history.

The domain of literacy, the subject matter focus of the neo-conservative and neo-liberal educational agenda, serves as the most significant example of the unequal effects produced by policies that only favor dominant groups with economic, social, and political capital (Smith, Miller-Kahn, Heinecke, & Jarvis, 2003). Of consequence to students from non-dominant communities, the mandated instructional programs are organized around reductive notions of reading and writing processes and practices that dummy-down literacy so dramatically that it no longer looks like literacy. Of significant concern are the short and long-term consequences of the socializing effects autonomous forms of literacy (Street, 1993) have on students for whom schools fail.

Consider the following representative example of writing instruction for fifth grade English learners in many Los Angeles schools. I use this case to illustrate how writing functions neither as a meaning-making practice or a tool for thinking and learning for children in schools deemed "underperforming". Instead, writing has become a disembodied practice in the classroom for both students and teachers; that is, detached from literacy practices and contexts that bring meaning and purpose to people in sense-making activity.

In the following vignette, the teacher and students in a sheltered English fifth grade classroom are participating in what has now become a routine literacy practice during their daily language arts period. Although this is a class of designated English learners, many of the students know some English and all can read, many at grade level. In this example, the teacher tells the students that she is going to say a sentence but that they are not to write the words down when she says them. She tells them that she will say it again slowly, a few words at a time. The students are to repeat the refrain in unison.

DISEMBODIED WRITING

T: The rat ran up the net. Say it.
Ss: The rat ran up the net.

T: Okay. Which word tells us what ran up the net? Raise your hand. Which word tells us what ran up the net? Hector?

Hector: The rat

T: The rat. Write that.

The students write.

T: All right, what did the rat do? Raise your hand. What did he do? Connie?

Connie: Ran?

T: Ran. That's the word that tells us what the rat did. Write it.

The students write.

T: What did the last three words of that sentence tell us?

Adolfo: Up the . . . .

T: What did that tell us?

Adolfo: He ran up the . . . He ran up the . . .

T: What did that tell us?

S: That he ran up the net.

T: What did that tell us?

S: *inaudible*

T: What did that tell us? The last three words of the sentence ?

S: The rat ran up the net.

T: What do those last three words tell us?

S: That he went up the net.

T: What do they tell us?

Students call out random answers.

T: What do they tell us? (She points to the cards on the wall that says "Who? What? Where? Why? When? How?"

S: Why?

T: Do those last three words tell us why? What do they tell us? The rat ran up the net. What do the last three words tell us?

S: How?

T: They tell us how? Up the net tells us how?

S: Who? What? When?

T: When? Up the net tells us when?

Students begin calling out guesses. One of them says "where".

T: Laura?

Laura: Where?

T: Where! Up the net. Doesn't that tell you where? Where he went, right? You guys are just yelling out words, who, what, when. It doesn't tell us that. It tells us where. Write the last three words. (Field note) (Gutiérrez, Berlin, Crosland, Pacheco, Razfar, & Espinoza, 2000).

In this and many classrooms, what counts as writing is a series of activities that no longer resemble the tasks, range, and forms of practice involved in authentic and purposeful writing activity.

Several years after we collected the data included above, prescribed reading programs for children from non-dominant communities have become more prevalent and increasingly synthetic, reaching new heights with new and improved forms of autonomous literacy practices (Gutiérrez, Berlin, Crosland, Pacheco, Razfar, & Espinoza, 2000). One notable example and staple of NCLB is the strongly recommended program Dynamic Indicators of Basic Early Literacy Skills (DIBELS), a program that reduces reading development to a series of measurable one-minute tasks. (Coles, 2003; Goodman, 2005). As Goodman points out:

> Each test has arbitrary benchmarks which get more difficult to achieve in successive grades. The test authors claim that the sub-tests are "stepping stones" to reading proficiency and each prepares the child for the next test. That means that children who fail one test are failing in reading development according to the authors. And in fact children are being retained in kindergarten and first grade solely because they fail one sub-test in DIBELS. In fact, only a small number of states require children to attend kindergarten. So children entering school without kindergarten are already a year behind from the DIBELS perspective. (p. 27)

In light of the pervasiveness of these programs in schools in non-dominant communities, educators, parents, policy makers, and the community members must ask the fundamental question: What are the material effects of such practices on students, teachers, and their communities?

The accepted norm of inequality persists for vulnerable school populations, as the dramatic failure of *No Child Left Behind* and large-scale corruption surfacing around the Reading First initiative exist with impunity (Associated Press, 2006). This point is worth elaborating.

As the Bush administration continues to tout the success of *No Child Left Behind* and Reading First using "scientifically-based" research, it pushes the sale and use of programs and materials—with means whose legality is being publicly questioned (see also Osborn, this volume). Representative George Miller of California, a leading Democrat on the House Education and the Workforce Committee, conjectured the following:

> The Bush administration pushed local school districts across the country to use a reading curriculum that had been developed by a company with close political and financial ties to the administration despite concerns about the quality of the curriculum . . . Corrupt cronies at the Department of Education wasted taxpayer dollars on an inferior reading curriculum for kids that was developed by a company headed by a Bush friend and campaign contributor. (The Carpetbagger Report, 2006)

Recently, the *Los Angeles Times* reported that school districts around the country are using NCLB funds to purchase a program, Ignite, owned by Neil Bush and his family (Roche, 2006). Thus, as the developers of required tests and programs profit, poor children suffer the consequences of the "sameness as fairness" framework at work in the nationalized educational agenda.

RESISTING THE RISING TIDE OF UNEQUAL EDUCATION

There is a perfect storm at work as the national educational agenda and anti-immigrant hysteria combine with neo-conservative narratives of fear around national security, heightened xenophobia, and neo-liberal goals of marketplace reform, privatization, and the larger ideologies of common culture, common language, and common values. As Apple (2004) has argued, the "national standards, national curriculum, and national tests provide the conditions for thick morality as such regulatory reforms are based on shared values and common sentiments" (p. 31).

As a result, the possibility of challenging or deviating from the prescribed curricula becomes increasingly difficult in the "tight-tight" culture of "lower-performing" schools. As elaborated elsewhere (Gutiérrez, 2006), the practical logic of this "tight-tight" culture that characterizes schools with large number of poor children is that the lower the test performance of the school, the more heavily regulated and monitored the mandated policies. That is, there is unprecedented surveillance and regulation of student and teacher behavior and practices. The push toward standardization in educational reform and practice has tightened limits on the autonomy of schools and teachers, yet has disguised these efforts by adhering to the rationale of meeting accountability standards (Crosland & Gutiérrez, 2003). In short, students and teachers in poor and lower-performing schools participate in the most restrictive educational environments.

Working against all odds, there are schools and communities that resist the tide of reductionism that characterizes so much of public education today (see Gatto, this volume, for one teacher's story of resistance). I briefly showcase two schools, one on the southwest side of Los Angeles and the other in East Los Angeles, that exhibit the determination to provide children a quality and meaningful education in the midst of the perfect storm.

Moffett Elementary School, located in the incorporated area of Lennox, is a port of entry community for large numbers of immigrants from Mexico. Lennox School District, until the passage of the English-only amendment, boasted one of the longest histories in providing home language instruction to its students. Since that time, Moffett is now designated a low-performing school, and yet it continues to offer some of the best practices around mathematics, reading, writing, and the arts to Latino, African American, and Pacific Islander students. Using the arts as the medium to build a range of critical skills, the school privileges reforms and interventions that are designed to promote deep learning in children.

For the last ten years, I have collaborated with the school principal, Joann Isken, to offer an after-school computer-mediated learning club, *Las Redes* (Networks) to K-5 children enrolled in the school. I draw on the multimodal literacy practices in which the children participate at Las Redes and contrast them with the disembodied practices illustrated earlier in this chapter.

Every Monday, Tuesday, and Wednesday young children, siblings, and friends mingle outside the library of Moffett Elementary School, waiting eagerly for their amigas/os to arrive and to enter the magical world of Las Redes. Las Redes, organized around cultural-historical theories of learning and development, is a hybrid space in which the elements of informal and formal schooling and play and learning are design principles. In this space, the leading activities of play and the imaginary situation, affiliation, and peer relations promote meaning-making and deep learning (Griffin & Cole, 1984) and privilege the use of hybrid language practices. Here the home language is unmarked in a matrix of hybrid language practices—that is, the use of home, school, and vernacular language practices in the service of learning about oneself and the world, as well as the required content.

But the excitement is not one-sided. The traditional barriers of age, educational experience, social class, and language differences are re-mediated as the naturally occurring ensembles of UCLA undergraduates and children take shape across the 10 weeks of the quarter, as these new friends collaborate on board and computer games, and on the newest addition to Las Redes, digital storytelling (Nixon, 2006).

In this after-school program in a California elementary school, children work in joint activity with college undergraduate students on a wide range of activities, including digital storytelling in which they create a brief movie about something meaningful in the children's lives. In this environment, children, with the assistance of others, engage in meaningful and complex learning activity that utilizes play, imagination, technology, and rich language tools. For example, during digital storytelling children write scripts, import relevant photographs, music, and narration into their stories.

In this rich and playful world, the home language functions as an unmarked language and is considered legitimate in its own right, as well as a tool to build new literacy practices. During digital storytelling, hybrid language practices, that is, the students' use of English, the home language, and various other registers, help children share their stories and lives while creating multimodal storytelling with digital technologies. In this context, we see the kind of literacy learning that is possible when children are allowed access to their full linguistic toolkit to make sense of themselves and their lives in the world (Nixon & Gutiérrez, in press).

Ramon's story was among one of our favorites. What the story below does not illustrate is how proud and excited he was to share his story after weeks of hard and focused work. When I told him one afternoon how much I liked his story, he replied, "I know; everyone loves my story! Can I have five more copies? My mom and my aunt and my teacher want a copy?" Ramon was so motivated to write about his baby brother, Marco, who, as a result of being born very premature, needed ongoing therapy. Ramon loved his brother and was so proud of his ongoing development.

Ramon narrated the following text as the images of his brother that he had brought from home and incorporated into his story were shown[1]:

> Hi, this is my baby brother, [Marco].
>
> He's three years old.
>
> I want to start my storytelling by beginning when he was born.
>
> When he was born, he was premature.
>
> His brain didn't fully develop.
>
> He was the size as my mom's hand.
>
> The doctor gave him some medicine so he could move a lot and not get sick.
>
> Now he goes to therapy so he could walk, play, and eat.
>
> He's big now, and he can move a lot.
>
> I love my baby brother.

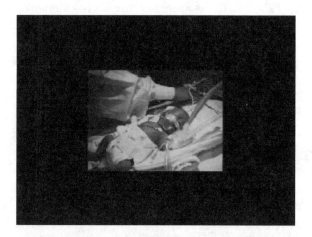

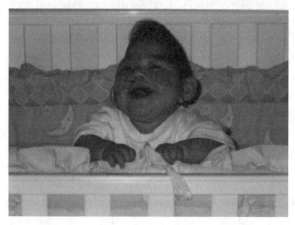

In the creation of these stories, Nixon's (2006) work shows that students increase their knowledge of literacy, technology, writing, and, of import, begin to see themselves as competent meaning-makers. Las Redes and its multimodal literacy activities provide a critical opportunity for children to engage in activities and language practices that are otherwise limited or forbidden by new educational policies and practices.

ACADEMIA SEMILLAS DEL PUEBLO CHARTER SCHOOL

The perfect storm of national curricula, xenophobia, and a thick morality that views difference as deviance has given rise to a new discourse of surveillance and intolerance—a confluence of ideologies that has engendered an even more pernicious response to schools that offer robust learning practices organized around culturally relevant curricula and the valued cultural and historical practices of its student population. One innovative school recently has become the target of a sustained attack lead by a Los Angeles conservative talk show host and conservative political leaders. At issue is the school's focus on including cultural and historical traditions and practices of Mexican and indigenous people as part of its school curricula—a long-standing practice found in schools emphasizing culturally relevant curricula. What is it about Academia that has conservatives rushing to close down the school?

Academia Semillas del Pueblo is a charter school located in "East Los"—the El Serreno area of Los Angeles rich with history, tradition, and the politics of resistance. This particular charter opened in 2002 to provide an alternative to schools that were failing to meet the needs of the community's K-8 grade children and offering curricula devoid of their local and cultural histories. The school's thoughtful and carefully crafted curricula focuses on meeting the state standards and district guidelines by offering an innovative program dense with rich learning activities to a student population that reflects the social and cultural makeup of its surrounding community.

Akin to Cole and Griffin's (1980) notion of cultural amplification, this school is designed to extend children's repertoires of practice (Gutiérrez & Rogoff, 2003) by expanding the curriculum also to include language instruction in English, Spanish, Mandarin, and Nahuatl, the Aztec language. Building on the rich mathematical practices of Mayan communities, Academia Semillas also offers the "base 20" mathematical system. Of interest, the people of Mesoamerica utilized this system at a time when Europeans still utilized the Roman numeral system—a system that was symbolic and had no zero (Lakeoff & Nunez, 2000). In addition, students at Academia Semillas learn about cultures and societies around the world, as well as instruction in visual, performing, and the martial arts.

Like Moffett Elementary—a school with large numbers of English learners and students on free and reduced lunch programs—Academia is having a significant impact on its students, both academically and socioculturally. Two external and independent evaluations document the unique strengths of the school's curriculum and its learning environment. Those evaluations revealed that the school's fifth graders, usually the victims of the fourth grade slump in national achievement data, demonstrate steady progress in standards-based achievement levels, while English learners are developing English language fluency at a rate (28%) that exceeds that of students in the Los Angeles Unified School District (7%). In 2005, 54% of Academia's fifth grade students were designated English fluent, while only 20% were advanced in LAUSD. The school personnel and its evaluators attribute this success to its rich multilingual program and curriculum. Moreover, the school has been recently evaluated by the Los Angeles Unified School District's Special Education audit team that found that Academia's program far exceeded other LAUSD's programs.

Rather than focusing on the gains the school has made or its rich curricula, the school's test scores, scores comparable to similar schools in the district with its student population, serve as evidence for the conservative Right that the school is failing—despite the school's support from the district and county offices and a large number of academic scholars and researchers.

Closing down this school for its alleged separatist practices has become the cause célèbre for the conservative media. As the headlines of one conservative website proclaimed: "Invasion USA: Public Tax Dollars Fund Racist School: K-8 institution backed by groups seeking to retake the Southwest U.S." (WorldNet Daily, June 1, 2006). In the brief column, the web story attempts to discredit Academia Semillas by claiming links to what it terms racial separatists, groups with a mission to take over the Southwest. (In fact, the link is to MeCHA, a progressive student organization with a long history at the University of California and other campuses that is frequently the object of conservative attack.) The website also asserts the inappropriate use of the public's money to fund a school with such questionable links and mission—all claims made without substantiation. In recent months, the school has been the object of investigation by the conservative media (See http://www. kabc.com/mcintyre/default.asp), letter-writing campaigns by conservative politicians, and has even received several bomb threats and uninvited visits from conservative talk show personnel.

Consider the following letter to the Los Angeles United School District Superintendent from a California State Senator calling for an investigation and ostensibly the closing of Academia Semillas for unspecified "questionable practices":

Dear Dr. Romer,

It has come to my attention that some questionable practices are occurring at the Academia Semillas del Pueblo charter school. Based on these reports, I am respectfully requesting that you investigate Academia Semillas del Pueblo charter school, which is a part of your school district.

As you know, LAUSD is the chartering authority for this school and so your district is responsible to hold the charter school accountable. You have full authority to revoke a charter under education code section 47607(c) if there are violations of the law.

[The letter then lists four elements of the Education Code 57607 (c) that outlines the conditions under which a charter can be revoked; the Senator continues:]

(d) Prior to revocation, the authority that granted the charter shall notify the charter public school of any violation of this section and give the school a reasonable opportunity to cure the violation, unless the authority determines, in writing, that the violation constitutes a severe and imminent threat to the health or safety of the pupils.

Charter schools have proven to be very successful and I am in full support of them and their expansion. However, schools that may be abusing their authority and violating the law must be held accountable. I have also written a letter to Dr. [name omitted], Los Angeles County Superintendent urging her to also investigate this school.

I urge you to take the appropriate steps as it is important to preserve the integrity of the law and not allow abuses to occur which ultimately hurts the students and the taxpayers.

Sincerely,

George C. Runner, Jr.
Senator, 17th District (Runner, 2006)

The movement to close down Academia Semillas serves as a powerful and pernicious example of how the "sameness as fairness" principle—the mandate for a common curriculum and common culture—is taken up as a response to any form of difference that offends the growing monolingual and monocultural sensibility of the conservative right and its public. At a time when the public should laud serious attempts to improve the quality of education for students from non-dominant communities, efforts such as those by Academia Semillas are continually thwarted, challenged, and threatened.

On one level it is incomprehensible how some could be threatened by a learning environment in which children, teachers, and parents eagerly engage in learning in an environment mediated by multiple languages, perspectives, knowledges, and a deep respect for its community, its history, and its potential. A visitor to the school would hear children speaking bilingually in English and Spanish, working collaboratively across subject matter areas. And parent involvement is an intrinsic part of the school and community's charter and ethos; all goals articulated and endorsed by district, state, and national educational reforms. And while the school continues to garner support and to develop its academic program, it does so in the larger state and national backdrop of growing anti-immigrant and racist ideologies and practices.

It should serve as an indictment of the failure of our nation to educate its children that what I wrote in the first edition of *Snake Oil* (2001) still applies:

. . . despite the legal and political rhetorical maneuvering, educational reform in California is necessarily about normalizing large numbers of linguistically and culturally diverse children and the social and cultural practices in which they engage; it is also about normalizing their educational practices, and the educators who must implement them. (p. 111)

We should be humbled by schools like Moffett Elementary and Academia Semillas and the students and communities they serve. And we should work vigorously to help such schools thrive and to help those in need of our support: financial, intellectual, political, and moral. Without large-scale changes in current educational policy, large numbers of students from non-dominant communities will continue to be under-served and under-educated in schools with severely deteriorating physical conditions, over-worked and under-valued teachers, a poor curricular diet low in intellectual, social, and cultural riches, all in the name of equality, fairness, and sameness. The "sameness as fairness" framework must be replaced with a race-, class-, and gender-conscious equity framework that will make such inequities visible and a humanist vision of education a reality.

NOTE

1.   This summary does not capture the digitally created story Ramon created.

REFERENCES

Apple, M. (2004). Creating Difference: Neo-Liberalism, Neo-Conservatism and the Politics of Educational Reform. *Educational Policy*, 18 (1), 12–44.

Apple, M. W. (2001). *Educating the "Right" Way: Markets, Standards, God, and Inequality*. New York, NY: RoutledgeFalmer.

Associated Press. (Sept. 22, 2006). Audit Scorches Bush's Reading Program.

The Carpetbagger Report (September 22, 2006). Reading First Finishes Last. (Retrieved from http://www.thecarpetbaggerreport.com/archives/8542.html, October 10, 2006).

Cole, M. & Griffin, P. (1980). Cultural Amplifiers Reconsidered. In D. Olson (Ed.) *Social Foundations of Language and Thought*. New York: W.W. Norton.

Coles, G. (2003). *Reading the Naked Truth: Literacy, Legislation and Lies*. Portsmouth, NH: Heinemann Press.

Crosland, K. (2004). Colorblind Desegregation: Race Neutral Remedies as the New "Equal Opportunity." Paper presented at the Annual Meeting of the American Educational Research Association, San Diego, California.

Crosland, K, & Gutiérrez, K. (2003) Standardizing Teaching, Standardizing Teachers: Educational Reform and the Deprofessionalization of Teachers in an English-only Era. *Educators for Urban Minorities*, 2 (2), 24–40.

Goodman, K. (2005, December). DIBELS: The Perfect Literacy Test. *Language Magazine, 5* (1), 24–27.

Griffin, P. & Cole, M. (1984). Current Activity for the Future: The Zo-ped. In B. Rogoff & J.V. Wertsch (Eds.). *Children's Learning in the Zone of Proximal Development: New Directions for Child Development* (No. 23). San Francisco: Jossey-Bass.

Gutiérrez, K. (2006). White Innocence: A Framework and Methodology for Rethinking Educational Discourse and Inquiry. *International Journal of Learning*, 12, 3–10.

Gutiérrez, K. (2001). Smoke and Mirrors: Language Policy and Educational Reform. In J. Larson (Ed.) *Literacy as Snake Oil: Beyond the Quick Fix*. (pp. 111–122). New York: Peter Lang Publishers.

Gutiérrez, K., Asato, J., Santos, M., & Gotanda, N. (2002). Backlash Pedagogy: Language and Culture and the Politics of Reform. *The Review of Education, Pedagogy, and Cultural Studies*, 24 (4), 335–351.

Gutiérrez, K., Berlin, D., Crosland, K., Pacheco, M., Razfar, A., & Espinoza, M. (2000). Report on the Effects of Coaching on Literacy Instruction in the Venice-Westchester Collaborative. University of California, Los Angeles.

Gutiérrez, K. & Jaramillo, N. (2006). Looking for Educational Equity: The Consequences of Relying on *Brown*. In A. Ball (Ed.) *With More Deliberate Speed: Achieving Equity and Excellence in Education—Realizing the Full Potential of Brown v. Board of Education*. 2006 Yearbook of the National Society for the Study of Education, Volume 105, Issue 2. (pp. 173–189). Malden, MA: Blackwell Publishing.

Gutiérrez, K. & Rogoff, B. (2003). Cultural Ways of Learning: Individual Traits or Repertoires of Practice. *Educational Researcher*, 32 (5), 19–25.

Lakeoff, G. & Nunez, R. E. (2000). *Where Mathematics Comes From: How the Embodied Mind Brings Mathematics into Being*. New York: Basic Books.

McIntrye, D. (2006). McIntyre in the Morning. (Retrieved from **http://www.kabc.com/mcintyre/default.asp**).

Moll, L. & Ruiz, R. (2002). The Schooling of Latino Students. In M. Suarez-Orozco and M. Paez (Eds.) *Latinos: Remaking America*. (pp. 362–374). Berkeley, CA: University of California Press.

Nixon, A. (2006). From Their Own Voices: Understanding Children's and Adolescents' Identities Through the Literacy Practices of Digital Storytelling. Dissertation Proposal. University of California, Los Angeles.

Nixon, A. & Gutiérrez, K. (in press). Digital Literacies for Young English Learners: Productive Pathways toward Equity and Robust Learning. In C. Genishi & A. L. Goodwin (Eds.), *Diversities in Early Childhood Education: Rethinking and Doing*. New York: Teachers College Press.

Roche, W. F. (October 22, 2006). Bush's Family Profits from 'No Child' Act. *Los Angeles Times*. (Retrieved from http://www.commondreams.org/headlines06/1022–02.htm).

Runner, G.C. (2006). Letter to Dr. Romer. (Retrieved from http://www.kabc.com/mcintyre/listingsEntry.asp?ID=438797&PT=McIntyre+in+the+Morning).

Smith, M. L., Miller-Kahn, L., Heinecke, W., & Jarvis, P. (2003). *Political Spectacle and the Fate of American Schools: Symbolic Politics and Educational Policies*. New York: RoutlegeFalmer.

Street, B.V. (1993). Introduction: The New Literacy Studies. In B.V. Street (Ed.) *Cross-Cultural Approaches to Literacy*. (pp. 1–21). Cambridge: Cambridge University Press.

WorldNet Daily. (June 1, 2006). Invasion USA: Public Tax Dollars Fund Racist School: K-8 Institution Backed by Groups Seeking to Retake Southwest U.S. (Retrieved from http://www.kabc.com/mcintyre/goout.asp?u=http://www.worldnetdaily.com/news/article.asp?ARTICLE_ID=50460).

CHAPTER EIGHT

The National Literacy Strategy IN England

Contradictions of Control and Creativity

BRIAN STREET, ADAM LEFSTEIN, AND KATE PAHL

INTRODUCTION

The chapters of the first edition of *Literacy as Snake Oil* painted a gloomy picture of contemporary literacy policy in the United States. Taken together—and recounted rather simplistically—they offer the following account: current literacy policy and programmes reduce literacy and its teaching to a limited and limiting set of technical tools, which are bundled into commercial packages. These packages are sold to schools and parents as a modern form of magical "snake oil" that is guaranteed to cure all educational ills. The research community and government have colluded with commercial publishers in pushing this quick-fix approach, which has damaging effects on children and schools.

These developments were interpreted as a revival of the traditional autonomous approach to literacy, according to which literacy is a set of skills that can be separated from the social contexts of their application, and that accrue cognitive advantages to those who acquire them, again regardless of the contexts of their use (Street, 1984). And the criticisms advanced in *Literacy as Snake Oil* adopted an ideological approach, revealing the power relations in which these business practices are embedded.

Much of this account resonates with recent policy and experience in the UK. We have undergone progressive national centralisation and prescription of literacy teaching, including highly detailed objectives and lesson plans that reflect a technical, skill-based approach to literacy education. Accountability measures have been tightened, including yearly standardised tests, "league tables" of school performance (in which they are ranked like football teams according to the outcomes of standardised external tests), and inspections. Politicians have promised the public that these measures will provide a quick fix, and a "makeover" mentality has captured the popular imagination (Lefstein, in press).

So it is tempting to take up the analysis offered in the book's first edition and apply it to our context, showing in effect how English policy-makers and public have happily imported US snake oil. However, we resist that temptation because we believe that, despite some surface similarities, the English experience presents a more complicated story. In telling that story, we will outline the major components of and developments in recent English literacy policy, provide case studies of the policy's enactment in two schools, and analyse the extent to which "snake oil" provides a good metaphor for what's happening. In particular, we will highlight the positive aspects of recent developments, and the centrality of cultures of enactment—how teachers and pupils actually perform the curriculum together—for understanding how they "take hold" of policy, and its ultimate effects. We begin, however, with a brief review of the introduction of the National Literacy Strategy in the UK and some of the major criticisms that have been levelled against it.

THE NATIONAL LITERACY STRATEGY IN THE UK

Within a year of coming into office, the New Labour government launched a National Literacy Strategy (DfEE, 1998) as a part of its programme towards fulfilling its electoral commitments to the education of all children in school. The explicit aim of the National Literacy Strategy (NLS) was to improve educational outcomes for all pupils and do away with the long tail of underachievement which had dogged the English education system. It aimed to raise overall standards of attainment by raising the standards of literacy in primary schools over five years. The high profile nature of this initiative is illustrated by the promise of the Secretary of State for Education, David Blunkett, to resign if the targets he set for improving literacy levels were not met by 2002 (they were not in fact met and in some cases have still not been achieved, but by then David Blunkett had moved on to other Cabinet offices and no resignations were offered).

The NLS provided a framework of 808 teaching objectives term by term for each year of schooling for children from 5 to 11 years. These objectives were divided into three interweaving strands, focusing on language, at word (sounds, spelling, and vocabulary), sentence (grammatical knowledge and punctuation), and text (comprehension and composition) levels. Word, sentence, and text level objectives were intended to be studied in parallel, and wherever possible in context, in each term and for every age range.

As well as teaching objectives, the framework provided a firm structure of time and class management. It thus gave details both of what should be taught and the means by which it should be taught. Fundamental to the Strategy was "a daily period of dedicated literacy teaching time for all pupils"—what came to be known as the "Literacy Hour." This hour included 15 minutes of shared reading or writing, 15 minutes of focused word or sentence level study, 20 minutes of independent work while the teacher engaged in guided reading or writing with one group of pupils, and a 10-minute concluding "plenary." In what follows we elaborate major criticisms of the Strategy, which echo issues that our US colleagues raised in the first *Snake Oil* volume with regard to *No Child Left Behind*.

Shortly after the publication of the Strategy, one of us (Street, 1999), in a discussion on how the NLS appeared to applied linguists, argued:

> It is important to consider the Government's obsession with falling standards and with raising achievement in literacy in the broader context of public attention to literacy over time. Freebody (see AILA website, 1999), amongst others, has drawn attention to the recurrent public crises over literacy (Street, 1999). Brooks (1997) of NFER has produced the most authoritative survey of literacy levels as measured by standard procedures since the [second World] war, and concluded that nothing much has changed, although by broader measures the goal posts themselves have been moved and what counts as literacy currently involves more elaborate and sophisticated skills than previously counted. Against this background we need to ask not only why the Government is so obsessed with standards and crises, but also why they are focusing on such narrow conceptions of literacy precisely at the point when developments point in the opposite direction. Gee and others' analysis of the New Work Order (Gee *et al.*, 1996; Holland *et al.*, 1998) and Kress's (1997) attention to a New Communicative Order suggest alternative directions in which to look when considering what aspects of language and literacy are appropriate for schooling. At the institutional level, we might also consider the plethora of government agencies devoted to setting, monitoring and evaluating literacy standards—NLF; National Curriculum; Qualifications and Curriculum Agency; Office of Standards in Education; Basic Skills Agency—a veritable Foucauldian surveillance. (p. 8)

We suggest that the three levels of analysis incorporated in this passage—the political context, the regulation of teaching, and the conceptualisation of literacy—are essential to understanding the NLS. The transformation of "literacy" into a volatile political and ideological issue sets the stage for the government to "act tough" in introducing a top-down, prescriptive model of instructional reform. The NLS specification of teaching objectives and methods provides convenient measures against which teachers can be held accountable, through the inspection regime, standardised testing, and performance management. Moss (2003) persuasively argues that this is the main thrust of the literacy-hour structure: the division of time and forms of activity "[make] what teachers do in the class both visible and instantly accountable to even the most casual of observers." Critics argue that such attempts to centrally control teaching restrict teachers' enthusiasm and creativity.

With regard to the curricular content—that is, the way "literacy" is conceptualised and constructed by the NLS—concerns have been raised about the way the Strategy narrows literacy to a set of technical skills, atomises components of language, limits textual practices to the linguistic mode, and transforms reading and writing into instrumental activities, Street (1999) pointed out the tendency in NLS documents to privilege aspects of literacy concerned with instruction and control, such as public information and instructional texts, whilst questioning of authority, alternative meanings, and attention to other texts and genres were less in evidence. He suggested that "the National Literacy Strategy is firmly rooted in an autonomous model of literacy (Street, 1984). It assumes decontextualised skills, competencies, basics, a sequence from isolated to more complex and situated units, and it privileges written over oral language" (Street, 1999, p. 9). This led to the NLS failing to draw children's attention to a number of key features of literacy that would have been already familiar to applied linguists and those working in the field of New Literacy Studies.

The Framework pays little attention to contexts for literacy, such as community literacy practices, contrasts between home and school as social practice, and the relations between home and school with respect to literacy learning and activity—issues that, as we shall see below, are now beginning to be addressed. Hannon (1999) has pointed out how much "family literacy" assumes a one-way relationship, with schooled literacy penetrating the home at the expense of a more dialogic relation of the kind evidenced by the work of Gonzalez, Moll and Amanti (2005), Heath (1983), etc., and now, perhaps, apparent in the work of Creative Partnerships (see Pahl, 2006; Heath & Wolf, 2004). An ideological model, on which this more recent work draws, conceptualises literacy as social practice and recognises the often hidden ideological and cultural features of literacy in practice. For instance, recent work on academic literacies drawing upon this perspective has suggested the value of using sociolinguistic and anthropological perspectives to understand the literacy practices and genres associated with writing in educational contexts (Lea & Street, 1999; Ivanic, 1998). This approach is more likely to attribute apparent "problems" with such writing students' concerns around discourse features of writing, such as cohesion, rather than the traditional grammar and spelling issues on which the NLS focuses and for which a "quick fix" appears easier to provide. Attention to register and to the effects and functions of linguistic resources and choices as outlined by Halliday and Martin (1993) and Systemic Linguistics, and to when and how to use resources as suggested by Hymes (1994), Cazden and others in the Ethnography of Communication tradition, could all enhance this rather narrow syllabus and move attention away from quick fixes to more complex pedagogies and curriculum strategies.

Similar criticisms were also developed by Alison Sealey who, at the time, wrote one of the most incisive accounts of the NLS from a linguistic perspective (Sealey, 1999a, 1999b). She addresses in particular the division of the NLS into *Word level work*, subheaded *phonics, spelling, and vocabulary; Sentence-level work*, subheaded *grammar and punctuation*; and *Text level work*, subheaded *comprehension and composition*. From a linguistic point of view, she suggests, this makes it difficult to explore the interrelationships between words, sentences, and texts. "Hence potentially useful conceptual tools such as *discourse, register* and *semantic field*, for example, which cross the boundaries between word, sentence and purpose, are absent or limited, and there is a real danger that language will be represented in an atomised way" (Sealey, 1999b, p. 11). A second problem, she notes, is a tension between descriptive and prescriptive approaches to language, which may be due to the influences of the different authors who have contributed to the package, or it may be a product of the different aims (pedagogic and political) that the strategy has to address. Thus matters of style and choice are sometimes represented as matters of *correctness*, and the vexed notion of *appropriateness* (by whose judgement?) central to the Ethnography of Communication approach signalled above, is taken as given rather than recognised as problematic. A number of the chapters in the original *Snake Oil* book make similar points about the NCLB approach to language as prescriptive and narrow (cf. Larson; Gee; Gutierrez). Applied linguists in both the UK and the US, then, had "grounds for concern that such a high-profile, well-funded, national strategy could initially publish teaching materials which fail to take account of current thinking about basic linguistic issues" (Street, 1999, p. 8).

This concern has recently been extended to those working in fields cognate with applied linguistics but concerned more with non-linguistic features of the modes through which teachers and learners communicate. These include the growing interest in the value of artwork and "visual literacy" that form the focus for one of the case studies in this chapter (see below). For instance, Marsh (2004), president of the United Kingdom Literacy Association, draws upon research on gender and multimodality in UK schools to challenge the limitations of the official strategy:

> . . . the National Literacy Strategy Framework privileges particular types of texts and producers of texts. All references to producers of texts use the words "writer", "author" or "poet", and there is no mention of producers, directors or creators. It could be argued that the term "author" is used in a generic sense to include authorship of televisual and media texts, but the word is most frequently used in conjunction with terms that relate to the written word. (pp. 249–262)

Marsh highlights how the Strategy focuses on and prioritises traditional written texts such as fiction, poetry, myths, legends, and traditional stories, at the expense of digital, visual, and multi-media genres. She calls upon much of the literature cited in this book to propose an alternative approach to the literacy curriculum. She begins with a reference to Kress:

> . . . the primary literacy curriculum needs to reconsider the definition and scope of literacy in a new media age and adapt accordingly (Kress, 2003), recognising that the kinds of texts which are important and relevant to contemporary children's lives are very different from those promoted . . . in the early years of the twentieth century. Thus, the development of a culturally-relevant pedagogy (Ladson-Billings, 1995) is not so much concerned with simply reflecting and valuing children's cultural choices in an effort to ensure that schooling is relevant and meaningful, important as this is, but with ensuring that the kinds of texts that are created and analysed within the literacy curriculum are embedded within popular, socio-cultural literacy practices, practices which are transforming the epistemological foundations of literacy. (Cf. Lankshear & Knobel, 2003, March 2004, pp. 249–262)

How might we identify such popular, "socio-cultural literacy practices" and in what ways could they transform the epistemological foundations of literacy? The second case study explored below provides an example of such a move, as Creative Partnerships and collaborating teachers take on board some of the "snake oil" criticisms and give due credit to the range of modes and social meanings associated with contemporary "literacy."

Some critics have combined the concerns elaborated above—the atomisation of language, the reduction of literacy into a technical skill, the narrow focus of texts and modes—and argued that the NLS replaces the purposive communication that should be at the heart of literate activity with instrumental reading and writing as opportunities to "acquire literacy skills" (e.g., Ashley et al., 2005). Author Phillip Pullman, an eloquent advocate of this view, contends that the NLS robs the experience of literature of its power and appeal:

> Those who design this sort of thing [NLS programs] seem to have completely forgotten the true purpose of literature, the everyday, humble, generous intention that lies behind every book, every story, every poem: to delight or to console, to help us enjoy life or endure it. That's the true reason we should be giving books to children. The false reason is to make them analyse, review, comment and so on. (Pullman, 2003)

The preceding critiques of the NLS are based primarily upon analysis of policy documents and curricular frameworks. While such an analysis provides insight into policy-makers' declared objectives, conceptualisations of literacy, and assumptions about teaching, and furthermore into the teaching and literacy practices enabled and constrained by the policy, it does not and cannot provide an account of how teachers and pupils actually enact these policies in their day-to-day classroom interactions. Moreover, since teachers' consumption of policy is to a large degree mediated by commercial textbooks, our analysis of enactment also needs to look at the way such textbooks and teachers' guides have translated policy into actual lesson plans, with their accompanying texts, activities, and tasks. To extend the snake oil metaphor, just because governments and publishers may have offered teachers snake oil does not necessarily mean that the latter have followed the instructions on the bottle. For example, they may have diluted it with other elixirs, tried it once but discarded it when the results were disappointing, and/or applied it selectively alongside other medicines.

The following two case studies look at the way policies have filtered down through the various levels of the system, focusing in particular on how teachers have taken hold of and enacted literacy initiatives. The first case study is taken from a yearlong ethnographic study by Adam Lefstein of the enactment of the National Literacy Strategy in one struggling primary school during the 2003–2004 academic year.[1] The second, based on research by Kate Pahl, describes an Arts-Council funded initiative, designed to support collaboration between artists and schools and to foster creativity within schools.

THE ENACTMENT OF THE NATIONAL LITERACY STRATEGY IN ONE STRUGGLING SCHOOL: HIGH PRESSURE, HIGH COMPLIANCE, MIXED RESULTS

Low Tide Primary School

In the following case study we examine Miss Goodwin's teaching of apostrophe placement in two consecutive Year 5 literacy lessons at "Low Tide Primary School."[2] The lessons exhibit many of the criticisms articulated above regarding the NLS. Sentence-level work—in this case, punctuation—is isolated from word and text levels, and especially from any meaningful context or rhetorical purpose. The placement of apostrophes is treated as a technical skill, employed independently of social or communicative practices. However, as we will argue below, this outcome is not wholly attributable to the NLS—indeed, we will see that paradoxically the enacted curriculum was in many ways more problematic than the prescribed one.

The study from which these two lessons are extracted included participant observation in the school (focusing on literacy in four Key Stage 2 classrooms), formal and informal interviews, audio-recording of lessons, and individual and group feedback conversations on the basis of transcripts of classroom interaction. The research site, "Low Tide Primary School," is a relatively large (almost 400 pupils) community primary school serving a village which has for all intents become a suburb of a Southern English city. The majority of the pupils come from working-class backgrounds, and the ethnic background of over three quarters of them is White British.[3] 80 percent of the pupils in the case study classroom were born in the same local hospital.

The confidential Ofsted "PANDA" (performance and assessment) report sent to head teacher Kathy Boyle at the beginning of the 2003–2004 school year portrayed a gloomy picture of school achievement standards (according to Standardised Assessment Task tests). Compared to similar schools (with between 8 and 20 percent eligibility for free school meals), pupils' attainment was in the bottom quartile (but not the bottom five percent) for all subjects at both Key Stages, with the exception of Key Stage 2 English, which was in the bottom 40 percent. Moreover, whereas the five-year national trend reflected a slight rise in scores, the school trend exhibited a downward trajectory. In January 2004 the school received the (failing) inspection grade of "serious weaknesses."[4]

Kathy Boyle was hired in the middle of the preceding school year in order to bring the school up to the expected levels of performance. She had a reputation for renewing failing schools: she assumed her previous post at a nearby school after it had been found to have "serious weaknesses" by Ofsted. Four years later Mrs. Boyle was credited by the local paper with engineering a "dramatic turnaround." Relations between Mrs. Boyle and the teaching staff at Low Tide were tense at the beginning of the school year. One central area of controversy was performance management negotiations over attainment targets: teachers believed that Mrs. Boyle's targets were unreasonable, setting both them and their pupils up for failure.

The Year 5 (10 year-olds) teacher in the lessons analysed below, Miss Goodwin, had 6 years of teaching experience at the start of the study. She stood out as a strong and vocal member of the staff, with a sharp tongue and few inhibitions. She was especially outspoken in her disdain for the "authorities": the NLS, Ofsted, and the new Head teacher. She originally "fell into teaching by accident," as a way of getting into a degree course in drama (she was advised that her A-levels weren't high enough to be accepted to drama without the education degree). However, she lost patience with academic study of drama, which she felt was too theoretical, and was drawn to the hands-on character of teaching. Over the course of the year she began to talk about leaving teaching or transferring to a different school, especially in the context of discussions about the school's underachievement.

Though Miss Goodwin was vocally anti-establishment, she was, like most of the teachers at the school, largely compliant with the NLS objectives and literacy-hour structure. The following two lessons, in which she teaches her class the rules for assigning apostrophes, are typical in this regard. In what follows we describe the lessons, examine the patterns of curricular enactment reflected in them, and discuss implications for our above critique of the NLS.

Dicken's Novels: Revising the Use of Apostrophes

The first lesson involved reading an excerpt of the story "Getting Granny's Glasses" and then learning about apostrophes. The second lesson was wholly devoted to apostrophes. The major stages in the lessons were as follows:

First lesson:

1) Reading and responding to the story "Getting Granny's Glasses." Pupils read the story out loud, then discuss three questions, initially in groups and afterwards in the forum of the entire class: "Find clues that it's a story from another country"; "Who is telling the story?" and "What questions do you have about the story?" (12 minutes, 30 seconds)

2) Introduction to apostrophes. Pupils highlight all the words with apostrophes appearing in the story. Miss Goodwin collects the highlighted words and records them on the board in two lists. Asks pupils why they think she's separated the words into two lists. Establishes that the words have been sorted into cases of contraction and possession. Explains the meaning of each, and quizzes the class as to which letters are replaced by the apostrophe (for the contractions) and what belongs to whom (for the possessives). (16 minutes, 45 seconds)

3) Exercise in creating possessive apostrophes. Pupils write on white boards "the [something] belonging to [their name]" and then convert that phrase into the possessive "[their name]'s [something]." Miss Goodwin collects orally pupil examples. (3 minutes, 20 seconds)

4) Dictations. Miss Goodwin dictates sentences (with apostrophes). Pupils write down the sentence, adding apostrophes where appropriate. After each dictation the class reviews and justifies the correct answer (e.g., extracts 1 & 3 below). (10 minutes, 40 seconds)

5) Recording evidence. Pupils are instructed to write in their books (copying from the board and filling in examples as requested): "Today we found out about apostrophes. Apostrophes can show where letters are missing. e.g., ____. Or where something belongs to someone. e.g., ____." (9 minutes, 50 seconds)

Second lesson:

6) Review. Pupils write on their white boards a sentence with a contraction, and then a sentence with a possessive apostrophe. Miss Goodwin collects answers orally. (5 minutes, 10 seconds)

7) Dictations. As in the preceding day. (6 minutes, 30 seconds)

8) Explanation of rule for plural apostrophes (elaborated in extract 4 below), and a series of demonstrations of plural possessives. (8 minutes, 45 seconds)

9) More dictations, including now plural possessives (e.g., extract 5 below). (10 minutes, 25 seconds)

10) Independent work: pupils work on exercises from a pupil workbook (differentiated by literacy group), recording answers in their English books. (22 minutes, of which 6 minutes, 40 seconds is devoted to getting organised and explaining the tasks)

11) Plenary: whole class solve orally "challenger" questions from the workbook (e.g., extract 2). (3 minutes, 30 seconds)

Below we discuss the part of the lessons devoted to apostrophes, focusing in particular on the whole class discussions of common problems (sections 2, 4, 7–9, and 11). Again the focus on apostrophes offers a telling case of the enactment of the NLS, where literacy teachers are being called upon to provide detailed technical knowledge of features of English orthography as part of an overall concern with literacy skills. The following extract is typical of the interactional pattern recurring in these sessions in Miss Goodwin's class. In this particular instance, Miss Goodwin dictates the sentence, "We didn't clean the stain from Jack's overcoat," to the children, who are instructed to record it on their white boards, adding apostrophes as necessary.

Extract 1. (Section 4—UFG 040426, 35:22–37:17)[5]

1 MISS GOODWIN: OK, put your hand up if you've found any in that sentence.
2 [3] I should see every hand up ( ). Louise, what did you find?
3 LOUISE: Didn't.
4 MISS GOODWIN: Good. [2] Contraction or possession?
5 DAVID: Possession. [2]
6 -: [Contraction.
7 MISS GOODWIN: [Didn't.
8 MANY: Contraction.
9 MISS GOODWIN: Short for?
10 A FEW: Did not.
11 MISS GOODWIN: We didn't.
12 -: Clean the stain from Jack's.
13 MISS GOODWIN: What was the other one? Hands up, please. Stop calling
14 out. [2] I'd like to see some different hands. Some people haven't spoken to
15 me yet. [1] Helen.
16 HELEN: Jack's.
17 MISS GOODWIN: Good. [recites slowly as writes on board:] We didn't clean
18 the stain from Jack's overcoat. What belongs to Jack?
19 MANY: The overcoat.
20 MISS GOODWIN: If I hadn't put the apostrophe there what happens to Jack?
21 DAVID: Jakes.
22 MISS GOODWIN: Think about it.
23 -: Because it ( ) contraction.

24 MISS GOODWIN: Think, don't call out answers, think. What does a "s"
25 normally show?
26 DAVID: Is.
27 MISS GOODWIN: [slowly and firmly:] Don't. Call. Out. How many times
28 have I said that this lesson? [1] Think and put your hand up. [3] Theresa.
29 THERESA: More than one thing.
30 MISS GOODWIN: More than one. So, if I don't put the apostrophe in there,
31 what have I got more than one of?
32 LARA: Overcoats.
33 -: No, Jacks.
34 MISS GOODWIN: Jacks. I've got lots of jacks, yes? So, I've got to put that in,
35 to show that there's only one Jack and the overcoat belongs to him,
36 otherwise I've got lots of Jacks. OK, next one. Who got both of those? [1] Good.

This routine is repeated such that pupils know exactly what to expect, and sometimes call out answers before Miss Goodwin has finished posing the question. The
basic structure is an interactional sequence composed of 7 steps:

1) Teacher poses problem.
2) Pupils solve problem individually.
3) Teacher asks for answer.
4) Pupil(s) provide answer.
5) Teacher prompts for justification (i.e., the rule employed).
6) Pupil(s) provide answer.
7) Teacher validates answer.

In the case of extract 1 (and most of the problems in this lesson), the sentence
includes two missing apostrophes, so steps 3–7 are repeated for each problem.

Learning the Rules for Apostrophe Placement

From this extract and similar interactions a logical method for solving apostrophe
problems can be explicated. Below is a graphic representation of this technique
(Figure 1).

The first stage is to classify the problem as either a contraction or possession (or
a case of plurality not needing an apostrophe). This happens in lines 4–8. Immediately
after Miss Goodwin poses the question David blurts out "possession." The other
pupils momentarily hesitate, but, since his answer is not accepted—Miss Goodwin
repeats the prompt "didn't" to signal that she has not yet received the correct answer
(and many undoubtedly know the correct response)—they answer "contraction." The
rule for a contraction is that the apostrophe replaces letters which are missing when
two words are "squidged together." Thus, the proof of a contraction is stating which
two words have been contracted (and, occasionally, which letters are replaced by the

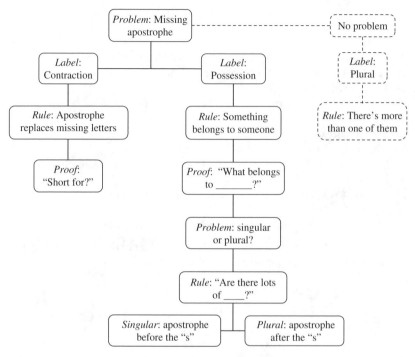

Fig 1. A logical Map of the Method for Assigning Apostrophes.

apostrophe). Miss Goodwin prompts the class to provide that proof with the brief "short for?" (line 9).

In all the problems with more than one apostrophe presented during this lesson, one was a contraction and the other a possession. Thus, "Jack's" is assumed to be possession by process of elimination. Identifying what belongs to Jack (line 18) provides proof of the validity of this assumption. The next section (lines 20–36), regarding what would happen to Jack without an apostrophe, relates to the right-hand side of Figure 1. The main clue that a word might be a candidate for an apostrophe is that it ends with the letter "s". There are conceivably—according to this method—three explanations for the s-suffix: a contraction (e.g., it's), a possessive (e.g., Jack's overcoat) or simply a plural noun (e.g., houses). Miss Goodwin creates the counterfactual "Jacks" (without an apostrophe) to demonstrate the importance of the apostrophe: "I've got to put [the apostrophe] in, to show that there's only one Jack" (lines 34–35). This explanation is a rare instance of attention being given to the relationship between the punctuation and meaning.

A further reason for checking whether a word is plural or not—one Jack or lots of Jacks—relates to the placement of the apostrophe in plural possessives, an issue introduced on the following day. According to this rule, after ascertaining that a noun is a possessive (i.e., something belongs to it), you must ask whether it is singular or plural (and thereby know whether to place the apostrophe before or after the *"s"*). In extract 2 below this rule is invoked. This interaction is taken from the end of the lesson on the following day (section 11). The class is looking together at the (more difficult) problems under the heading "Challenger" in a workbook. For each problem the pupils must fill in the missing apostrophes (for most of the problems: one possessive and one contraction).

Extract 2. (Section 11—UFG 040427, 54:42–56:00)

1 MISS GOODWIN: Next sentence. Shhh. [2] "Its made of hundreds of animals
2 bones." Lots of *"s*-es" in there. Drew.
3 DREW: Bones. [2]
4 MISS GOODWIN: Is it just telling you there's more than one bone, or is it telling
5 you that something belongs to those bones? [7] Does anything belong to those
6 bones?
7 DREW: No.
8 MISS GOODWIN: No, it's not one. That's just an "s" to show that it's more than
9 one. Beatrice.
10 BEATRICE: It's.
11 MISS GOODWIN: It's is the first one, which is short for—
12 -: It is.
13 MISS GOODWIN: 'It is made of hundreds of animals bones.' Keith.
14 KEITH: Hundreds. [1] No.
15 MISS GOODWIN: What belongs to the hundreds?
16 KEITH: No. Animals.
17 MISS GOODWIN: Animals. Good. 'It's made of hundreds,' just saying that
18 there's more than one hundred. Animals' bones. How many animals?
19 LARA: Lots.
20 MISS GOODWIN: Lots. How many bones?
21 LARA: Lots.
22 MISS GOODWIN: So, where's your apostrophe going to go?
23 LARA: Before. [1]
24 A FEW: After.
25 MISS GOODWIN: After, to show that there's lots of animals' bones. Otherwise
26 you'll end up with an animal owning lots of bones, won't you? OK.

It is the existence of numerous plural words ending in *"s"* that make these "Challenger" problems so tricky. And pupils fall for the traps set by both "bones" and "hundreds" (lines 3 and 14). In both cases Miss Goodwin asks what or if something belongs to the candidate possessive (lines 5 and 15), thereby testing the accuracy of the incorrect pupil answers. Of course she has already given away the fact that there is something wrong with the responses by not immediately accepting them.

Correct answers receive immediate validation, commonly through repetition of the answer (lines 11, 13, 17, 20, 22, and 25). Note that the children give short, one-word responses, and Miss Goodwin elaborates the rule and/or proof that validates their answers (e.g., in lines 16–18, Keith gives the correct answer, "animals," and Miss Goodwin explains the justification for why his previous answer of "hundreds" was incorrect).

The Problem of the Missing Apostrophe

What is the significance of this explication? One reader looked at Figure 1 as I was working on this chapter and appeared unimpressed. "So they're learning the rules for using apostrophes," she said. While there is a family resemblance between accepted rules of punctuation and the logical system underlying Miss Goodwin's teaching in this lesson, they are different in important ways. The class isn't learning how to decipher apostrophes encountered in their reading, or to punctuate their own writing; rather, they are learning how to cope with a specific type of school exercise: the problem of the missing apostrophe.

This problem has a number of distinguishing characteristics. First, and most significant, the problem is framed by the *a priori* knowledge that apostrophe(s) are missing (and, often, their precise number). Thus, in extract 1, after Miss Goodwin says "put your hand up if you've found any [apostrophes]" she adds, "I should see every hand up" (lines 1–2). The implication is clear: every sentence is missing an apostrophe. And, indeed, over the course of the lesson, there were no exceptions to this rule. This prior knowledge frames the task for the pupil: look for a word to which an apostrophe can validly be assigned.

Prior knowledge of apostrophe deficiency is also the context in which the problem appears. The problem is not occasioned by participation in communicative activities, that is, by the need to express oneself or to understand another.[6] Nor is the problem of the missing apostrophe a simulation of proofreading. The logical map for proofreading would differ significantly from that outlined in Figure 1. Only in the problem of the missing apostrophe, for example, does it make sense to group contractions and possessives into the same system. In the course of reading or writing there is little chance of confusing them.

A second aspect of the problem of the missing apostrophe is that it appears in isolation from all other possible problems. Indeed, it even excludes them. For example, (about a minute before excerpt 1) the children are recording from dictation (and placing apostrophes in) the sentence, "We didn't clean the stain from Jack's overcoat." David asks, "How do you spell stain?" Miss Goodwin instructs him not to worry about it: "It's the apostrophe that's important today."

A third aspect of the problem is that it is intolerant of exceptions. Possible deviations from the map are either excluded or made to conform to the rules being taught. For example, during the second lesson (section 8) Miss Goodwin solicited plural nouns from the class in order to demonstrate the use of possessive apostrophes with plurals. She calls on Chad, who offers, "mouse." Miss Goodwin replies, "Right. [1] Then, now, a difficult one, because if you've got lots of mice, you say mice, not mouses, don't we? Pick another one." The problem of course is not that mice cannot possess something—e.g., the mice's hole—rather, that the word "mice" doesn't end in "s", and the rule being taught is that in plural nouns the apostrophe is added after the "s". This example emphasizes that the technique taught is better suited for solving problems of missing apostrophes, where the main dilemma is whether to place the apostrophe before or after the terminal "s", than for expressing relationships of possession in composition.

When an exception accidentally passes through Miss Goodwin's filter, it is made to conform to the rules, as illustrated in extract 3. Miss Goodwin dictated the sentence, "I'm always borrowing Dickens' novels from the library." This sentence is anomalous, since according to the technique as described in Figure 1; the apostrophe should be placed before the "s", that is, "Dickens's novels".[7]

Extract 3. (Section 4—UFG 040426, 41:12–42:06)

1 MISS GOODWIN: Two again, what were they?
2 -: [Always.
3 -: [I'm
4 MISS GOODWIN: 'I'm' is the first one, short for?
5 A FEW: I am.
6 MISS GOODWIN: I am. And the second one, hand up.
7 A FEW: Dickens.
8 MISS GOODWIN: Dickens. The books belonging to?
9 A FEW: [Dickens.
10 A FEW: [Dickens.
11 MISS GOODWIN: The books belonging to?
12 A FEW: [Dickens.
13 A FEW: [Dickens.
14 MISS GOODWIN: Dickens books [writes *Dickens's books* on board], it's the
15 book belonging to—
16 A FEW: Dickens.
17 -: Dickens.
18 MISS GOODWIN: Why is that apostrophe 's' there?
19 -: Because it's a name.
20 -: [Dickens ( )
21 -: [(There's be loads of Dickens.)

22 MISS GOODWIN: What is his name, Marcus?
23 MARCUS: Dickens.
24 MISS GOODWIN: Dickens. The book belonging to Dickens [2] is totally
25 different, you're saying his name is Dickens, and we're not. The book
26 belongs to Dicken, [1] so it's Dicken's book.

Part of what makes this example so striking is that the literacy groups in this class are named after famous authors, among them Dickens. Miss Goodwin later explained to me that she regretted giving the pupils the sentence, which appears in a commercially published activity workbook, immediately after dictating it. In an interview she said, "I thought, I don't want to do this because it's going to confuse them because it's not the rule—it's not following the exact rule we're doing." The solution—changing Dickens' name to Dicken—exchanged potential confusion about "the exact rule we're doing" with confusion about Dickens' name. But note the consistency: "It's the apostrophe that's important today."

Later, in an interview, Miss Goodwin and Adam Lefstein discussed the rules for making names ending in an "*s*" into possessives: *Dickens'* or *Dickens's*?

MISS GOODWIN:	We looked it up because [the other Year 5 teacher] said that to me, what do you do? And then I don't know which one of the books it was. It said to do it as we told them with the apostrophe and the "*s*".
MR. LEFSTEIN:	I looked it up too. I wasn't sure.
MISS GOODWIN:	You see, you're right, people do it differently.
MR. LEFSTEIN:	It's optional.
MISS GOODWIN:	I would say to teach it with the "*s*" because then it fits with what—the rules that you're teaching. We stuck with that.

What's interesting is that Miss Goodwin and her colleague didn't decide to teach both options, but rather chose to stick with one "correct" rule.

We have highlighted three distinguishing characteristics of the problem of the missing apostrophe: it is framed by *a priori* knowledge that an apostrophe is missing, it is isolated from other problems, and it is intolerant of exceptions. What can be learned from the lessons about how to solve the problem? There are a number of implicit messages. The most obvious one is that there is a logical system of rules that will yield the correct answer if followed exactly. Second, proficiency in the use of this technique improves with repetition. Third, mastery of the technique is at least in part a function of speed: Miss Goodwin frequently calls out the questions at a brisk pace with the expectation that pupils respond in unison. These implicit messages, combined with the lack of exceptions, relative inattention to meaning, and no time to pause and reflect, lead to an image of apostrophe placement as a technical method, which is employed mechanically, without thinking (i.e., Kress's "do[ing] it by rôte").

Pupil Strategies

This account of the lesson and the system of punctuation rules being taught is incomplete without at least cursory analysis of pupil responses. In particular, the high frequency of pupil errors observed in these lessons is puzzling. Pupils offer incorrect answers in lines 5, 21, 23, 26, and 32 of extract 1; in lines 3, 14, and 23 of extract 2; and in lines 2 and 19 of extract 3 (and also pupils' "Dickens" answers in lines 10, 12, 17, and 23, which, although actually correct, are treated by Miss Goodwin as errors). There are roughly as many erroneous answers as correct ones. Why are there so many incorrect responses? And how does Miss Goodwin deal with them?

One possible explanation is that the pupils are simply finding the rules for how to solve the problem of the missing apostrophe difficult to understand and/or apply. While it may be the case that many of the pupils do not fully grasp the technique, this explanation does not adequately account for the errors observed. Why would a pupil who "doesn't get it" be constantly among the first to call out answers, even after repeatedly getting the wrong answer? It seems more reasonable to assume that understanding and misunderstanding are simply not salient issues in most of the cases of error.[8] David, Lara, Drew, and Keith seem to be calling out the first answer that comes to mind. Consider how quickly they respond. They frequently offer their wild guesses even before the rest of the class has had a chance to think about the question. Miss Goodwin's admonitions to think (in lines 22, 24, and 28 of extract 1) suggest that she shares my interpretation. The problem is not that they have carefully considered the question and obtained an incorrect answer; rather, they have simply not thought.

Understanding these pupils' actions requires consideration of how Miss Goodwin reacts to them. In the course of my explication above I noted that Miss Goodwin tends to immediately validate correct answers, but pauses for 1–2 seconds before responding to erroneous answers. Usually, during this brief pause, the pupil either corrects her or his initial guess (e.g., Keith's correction of "hundreds" with "animals" in line 16 of extract 2), and/or other pupils provide the right answer (e.g., in line 24 of extract 2 a few pupils correct Lara's "before"). Then, once the correct answer has been furnished, Miss Goodwin validates it and explains why it is correct (or, alternatively, why the other answer was incorrect). This interactional pattern is the basis for the pupils to guess, check Miss Goodwin's response and correct their answer (hereafter the guess-check-correct strategy).[9]

Since most of the questions posed lend themselves to binary oppositions— contraction/possession, plural/singular, x belongs to y/y belongs to x, before/after the "s"—the guess-check-correct strategy is quite straightforward. Rather than thinking about the answer, simply offer one of the terms of the question. If it isn't accepted, offer the other one. Rather than following the logic of punctuation, these pupils are following the logic of the interaction. It is noteworthy that, though Miss Goodwin expresses exasperation at the pupils' use of this strategy and chides them to stop and think,[10] she implicitly enables the use of the strategy by the way she responds to error.

Snake Oil?

The preceding lesson exhibits many of the criticisms articulated above regarding the NLS. Sentence level work—in this case, punctuation—is isolated from word and text levels, and especially from any meaningful context or rhetorical purpose. The placement of apostrophes is treated as a technical skill, employed independently of social or communicative practices.

However, to what extent are NLS policies responsible for this outcome? Should Miss Goodwin's compliance with highly prescriptive NLS regulations be blamed for the isolation of literacy from meaning? Should we encourage the Miss Goodwins to resist such Snake Oil? Our answer to these questions is complicated. On the one hand, the literacy-hour framework and accountability system appear to have contributed to the atomisation of literacy and the focus on getting the right answer respectively. On the other hand, close study of the ways in which Miss Goodwin enacted the curricular materials shows that tighter adherence to the NLS prescriptions would have yielded a more thoughtful lesson with a more nuanced view of punctuation.

Miss Goodwin does not follow any specific curricular prescriptions in these two lessons, but does draw from three different commercial textbooks. The NLS objective she addresses is S5: "To revise use of apostrophes for possession (from Y4 term 1)." The teachers' manual for the Collins' *Focus on Literacy* programme, which provides the general structure for Miss Goodwin's planning (and from which the story excerpt "Getting Granny's Glasses" is taken), prescribes revising the use of the apostrophe only on the last day of the five-day unit, during focused word/sentence level and independent work (i.e., about 35 minutes). The manual and accompanying pupil's book only discuss possessive apostrophes; contractions are not mentioned. Miss Goodwin broadens the NLS objective, extending the revision to both possessives and contractions, and allocates almost two entire lessons to a topic for which only half a lesson was prescribed by the manual.

The structure and main activities employed in these lessons do not appear in any of the materials employed. They seem to have been developed independently by Miss Goodwin, or adapted from lessons on other topics (see the discussion of similarities with *Grammar for Writing* activities below). Into this general structure—composed of an introduction, explanation of rules, and practice through dictation and independent workbook exercises—Miss Goodwin inserts fragments from two pupil workbooks: Letts' *Key Stage 2 Differentiated Activity Book Literacy Year 5* and

Coordination Group Publications' *National Curriculum English Literacy Workbook: Year Five*. She draws from these books examples and exercises, which she often recontextualises, for example transforming pupil exercises into dictations. Similarly, the rules she teaches are not found in any of the curricular materials upon which she has drawn. Indeed, Miss Goodwin might have avoided some of the problems created by "Dickens' novels," for example, had she taught the rules as detailed in the *Focus on Literacy* teacher's manual:

> What are the rules for using the apostrophe? The easiest way to remember this is that the apostrophe always goes immediately after the owner, e.g., *Granny's glasses*: *Granny*, the apostrophe and then the *s*. This rule applies equally with plural owners, e.g., *the men's coats*: *the men*, the apostrophe and then the *s*. If the word is plural and ends in *s* there is no need for a second *s*, e.g., *the boys' shoes*. With a name ending in *s*, e.g., *Mr Jones's car*, we usually add an *s*. (p. 67)

The NLS has produced materials on teaching apostrophes, most notably unit 27 in the Year 4 section of *Grammar for Writing*.[11] Although these materials are not among the resources used by Miss Goodwin, contrasting their recommendations with what transpired in the lesson is illuminating. First, the similarities: both emphasize a number of activities in which children identify whether an apostrophe is used to signal possession or omission; both engage children in collecting and classifying apostrophes appearing in a narrative text; both require children to add missing apostrophes; and both involve dictations to dry-wipe boards. Moreover, the NLS includes the following advice for how to establish whether an apostrophe is a possessive or contraction (what I called "proof" in my explication of Miss Goodwin's system).

> If the children have difficulty in deciding whether an apostrophe is one of omission or possession, ask them whether the word after the apostrophe, e.g., *coat* or *forgotten*, belongs to Dad. Where the apostrophe is used as omission, it can be replaced by the full version, e.g., *Dad has forgotten*.

Alongside these similarities, there are some nuanced differences, which together reveal a drift away from the "rhetorical" approach to grammar (Kolln, 1996) favoured by the NLS and towards a more traditional, decontextualised grammar teaching. First, in the NLS "Collect and Classify" activity, which requires that the children locate apostrophes in a narrative text and divide them into two columns (possessives or omission), the manual instructs, "Before accepting an answer, insist on an explanation from the child as to why he or she chose that answer." In contrast, Miss Goodwin engaged in a similar activity (in section 2) but with a more procedural emphasis. After the pupils had identified the words with apostrophes, Miss Goodwin decided on her own how to divide them into groups. She then posed the question, "Who can think why I've separated those like I have. Look really carefully everybody now, no pen should be moving. Why have I separated the words into those two lists?" Rarely did she insist on explanations for pupil answers, instead providing them herself.

Second, whereas the NLS instructs teachers to prepare "a short text in which some of the apostrophes are missing or in the wrong place," the problem of the missing apostrophe in the Miss Goodwin's class appeared in the often absurd phrases or sentences, devoid of any meaningful context, appearing in the workbook exercises. On a related note, the NLS unit also briefly discusses why a writer might choose to use an apostrophe for possession, in order to make "writing more economical."

Third, whereas dictation in the NLS involves saying "a sentence including a word with an apostrophe and ask the children to write two of the words on their dry-wipe boards," Miss Goodwin sometimes dictated fragments, and required pupils to record the entire phrase or sentence dictated. Finally, whereas Miss Goodwin avoided exceptions to the rules, the NLS instructs teachers to "make certain the list [of examples of possessives] contains some regular plurals, e.g., *boys'* and some irregular plurals, e.g., *children's*."

These differences add up to a shift away from a rhetorical approach to punctuation—in which rules are explainable, relate to meaning, and facilitate expression—to a more traditional approach, in which the emphasis is upon getting the right answer. This outcome complicates the view of the NLS we developed in the first section of this chapter, by highlighting the complexities of the enactment of policy and curricular documents in the minute details of classroom interaction. In the second of our case studies we follow up these contradictions and complexities in the enactment of the NLS, showing how recent attempts to open up the literacy curriculum and afford teachers greater autonomy may involve similar issues around teacher and pupil mediation of—in this case—"creative partnerships" in their classrooms.

CREATIVE PARTNERSHIPS IN THE UK: "THE CURRICULUM PULLS BOTH WAYS"

From the inception of the Labour government in 1997, there have been a series of initiatives in the UK designed to promote creativity, running counter to, and in some cases, at the same time as, initiatives to standardise literacy teaching in schools. In 1999, the National Advisory Committee on Creative and Cultural Education published *All Our Futures: Creativity, Culture, and Education*, which argued that a national strategy for creative and cultural education was essential to unlock the potential of every young person. Following this report, in 2000, the Qualifications and Curriculum Authority (QCA) commissioned a review of creativity in other countries, and developed a creativity framework, part of a three-year project designed to advise schools on how to develop pupils' creativity (QCA, 2003). Creativity began to be seen as both a way of boosting the UK's economic regeneration and a good way of delivering learning.

These initiatives have recently received a boost, as policy-makers have begun to promote "creativity" in response to criticisms about the rather formal and time-laden character of the NLS. In May 2003, the Department for Education and Science (DfES) outlined a new vision for primary education in a document called, *Excellence and Enjoyment: A Strategy for Primary Schools* (DfES, 2003). This new "Primary Strategy" was a contrast to the top-down approach of the Literacy and Numeracy strategies, offering a more flexible approach to teaching, encouraging teachers to be creative and innovative in their approach to the curriculum. Likewise, the Office for Standards in Education (Ofsted), which administers school inspections and as such is typically identified with enforcing the standardisation agenda, published the results of a small survey to identify good practice in creative pedagogy in schools (HMI/Ofstead, 2001).[12]

In this climate, Creative Partnerships was set up as a joint initiative between the Department of Culture, Museums, and Sport and the Department for Education and Science in May 2002, to develop long-term partnerships between schools and cultural and creative organisations. The project ran as a pilot programme from 2002–4, in 16 areas of the UK. Phases 2 and 3 followed, from 2005–6. Between May 2002 and July 2005 Creative Partnerships ran 3,767 projects. The programme is planned to continue until 2008, with 36 areas around the UK involved. A research programme is now underway, following a national call for proposals, including a national evaluation of the pilot phase of the project by the National Foundation for Educational Research (NFER). Subsequently, an inspection of some Creative Partnerships schools by Ofsted resulted in an overall confirmation that the Creative Partnerships initiative had developed some very positive practices, particularly in the area of developing children's speaking and listening and collaboration skills (Ofsted, 2006).

PREVIOUS RESEARCH ON CREATIVITY
IN SCHOOLS IN THE UK

Research on the impact of creative artists in schools has focused on the possibilities that work with artists offers children's learning and literacy skills. Most of this has resulted in research focused on what Creative Partnership-funded initiatives have done to change teaching and learning in schools, in an effort to demonstrate their positive effects. Heath and Wolf (2004) produced *Visual Learning in the Community School*, which consisted of a fine-grained analysis of ways in which artists, by supporting children to look more closely, enabled children to leap forward in their ability to maintain their visual concentration, as well as use extended discourse in their talk (Heath & Wolf, 2004). Likewise, Safford and Barrs (2005) describe instances of positive collaborations between artists and teachers in London. For example, their research study described how children in schools which were struggling with behaviour, in areas of socio-economic disadvantage, turned around their behaviour difficulties through drama work and role play using film making techniques. Craft, Cremin, and Burnard (2006), in their study of pedagogical thinking and creativity, uncovered some key elements of creative teaching. These include allowing teachers and children time for reflection in the crowded curriculum and fostering the quality of "standing back" and watching children as they take risks and explore unexpected avenues. Creative approaches to learning included posing questions, play immersion and making connections, being imaginative, innovative, risk-taking, and involving children's agency and self-determination. Jeffery and colleagues (2006) have looked at creativity in a European context, and argued that creative approaches to learning let in learner identity, allowed learners to collaborate more closely, and created more equitable approaches in the classroom.

The picture from the UK, then, seems to be that there are shifts in the discourse and possibilities are opening up for learner autonomy. Research, cited above, has documented ways in which teachers are "letting go" of pedagogic control, and spaces can be opened for more creative possibilities (Craft, Cremin, & Burnard, 2006). The focus on creativity worked well when all the stakeholders agreed on what they meant by creativity; however, in some cases partners had different conceptualisations of the term, leading to problematic consequences for schools. Hall and Thomson (2005) traced the focus on creativity in UK educational policy, through analysing one creative initiative in a primary school, but argued that it continued to be seen as located outside mainstream structures rather than within the national curriculum. The challenge, then, is to see how a focus on creativity within the classroom can significantly open up spaces where mainstream schooled literacy practices are in some way altered, developed, or bring in new practices and identities.

A research project was commissioned by Creative Partnerships in Barnsley, Doncaster, and Rotherham to study the impact of collaboration with a group of creative artists on teaching and learning in a school in Barnsley, Yorkshire. The research aimed to look at ways in which the impact of the artists in the school enabled different kinds of literacy and language practices to take place. Kate was particularly interested in ways in which teachers "took hold" of the practices initiated by creative artists. What did teachers do with the art practices when developing curricula for their students? How were art practices discursively constructed in the classroom? How did teachers, having worked with artists, then develop their own understandings of art practices, and integrate them into the curriculum, after the artists themselves had withdrawn?

Here, we present a slice of data from the research project. The data included 18 teacher interviews, 8 classroom observations, interviews with children from the class, and interviews with the creative artists involved. Kate focused on the concept of the multimodal event, and the multimodal practice, from Lancaster (2003) as a lens from which to look at instances of practice. She also looked at ways in which teachers' talk instantiated ideologies connected to concepts of creativity. By focusing on practice, as a heuristic for creative activity, it was possible to pinpoint ways in which both teachers and pupils instantiated what had been creative practices in their work. In her work with Creative Partnerships, she acknowledged that the definition of creativity is contested, and in a recent review (Banaji, in press) creativity has been identified as a "woolly" concept interpreted differently by different stakeholders.

The link between literacy and a creative arts approach was explicated in the earlier study by Heath and Wolf (2004), cited above, in which the argument was made that focusing on the visual enables children to push their creative and critical thinking and thereby develop their capacity for metaphorical language. In the study of the impact of a group of artists within a school, Kate was interested in the relationship between literacy practices and events, and the way creative practices stretched these events and practices with the theoretical perspective that practices were observable and could be traced within texts (Street, 2000; Pahl & Rowsell, 2005). Therefore, in this discussion, we look closely at practice. We then argue that the practices Kate observed were transformed in particular ways, and these transformations tell us about ways in which teachers "take hold" of particular practices. Kate traces examples by which an idea initiated by an artist was taken hold of by a teacher and then became part of classroom practice. She uses the expression "take hold" from the work of Kulick and Stroud (1993), who in their study of the uses of literacy by a group from Papua New Guinea, were able to identify ways in which literacy brought from outside was adapted by locals and used to obtain their own desired outcomes. Rather than being a general "good thing," literacy was used instrumentally, and in doing so, transformed. This is the understanding Kate acquired of the use of art practices in the classroom.

Rather than see creativity as a general force for good, which is understood as a way of transforming schools from dull Grandgrind type places to more cheerful sites, she focused on particular events and instances of practice. The focus was particularly on instances in relation to discussions around a material practice, such as the making of an object. Where a material practice is described, Kate used interviews and discussions to try to trace back how the material practice was conceived, and probe the meanings such practices had for participants. This theoretical and methodological apparatus also then made understanding of the concept of creativity more focused, and specific.

As the artists initiated art practices, these were used by the teachers, and could be seen in their work. In order to describe this process, Kate saw this as a kind of tree, branching off into many fronds. In her analysis of these events, practices, and discourses, she used a form of fractal analysis. That is, she saw how one kind of practice branched off and replicated across domains. She traced a particular event from the interview with the artist who initiated the artistic practice, to the teachers who "took hold" of the practice, to the students who then described their experience of the practice to me. She noted in particular how the teachers interpreted the practice and then made it their own.

The particular practice analysed here involved the procedure by which children were sent home with a disposable camera to capture their favourite toy or person. These photographs then came back and were blown up on the photocopier and turned into black and white images. The children then coloured them in. In some cases, the children used these as starting points for abstract art. In other cases, they were used for story making, both oral and written. The final result was a magazine, *My Home, My School, My Barnsley*, which included many of the images, plus writing by the children about their social worlds. One of the key aspects of the project was that it was not defined as being about literacy; although literacy practices were embedded within the activities, the final focus of the project was on a magazine, which was produced jointly by the teachers, the children, the parents, and the artists involved in the project.

THE ARTISTS

Kate interviewed two artists, Kay and Alice, about their work in the school. The artists described the process of taking photographs. Kay was primarily a photographer, who also worked with image and colour. Kay said:

> I got the children to draw what their photos are going to be of.
>
> Some of the pictures were photos blown up and then painting over it.
>
> One of the huge parts of the project for the school is about the community and the involvement of the parents in and the school out, crossing the line as it were. (Interview, February, 2005)

The artists described ways in which they worked with parents, children, and teachers to create different representations of the community. First they used cameras, then they blew up the photographs and the children coloured them in using black and white photocopies. The focus of the artists when they talked about their work was on the parents, and how they encouraged them to be involved, as much as on the teachers and the children. The magazine would describe to the outside world the theme of its title, *My Home, My School, My Barnsley*, and would be for the parents as well as for the children at the school.

The Teachers

The teachers all described these practices in interviews, with enthusiasm and in detail. The artists' interventions had resulted in many different kinds of practice. A year 1 teacher, Sarah, who had replicated the photography project, described the process of doing this:

> Sarah: We set off with the training day with the parents. And then we used it with the children and they had their own little disposable cameras and they took some round school first to practice and then they actually had their own, well they went home and we asked them to plan some photographs they wanted to take and we said photograph things that you like places that you like, toys that you like whatever. (Interview, November, 2005)

Sarah was clear that she wanted the children to work collaboratively, so her next project involved using large sheets of paper for the children to draw their abstract art. This seemed to happen organically. She described the ways in which she developed the ideas, and her chief discursive expression was the phrase "things just happened":

> Sarah: I would never ever thought of doing photographs. I mean some of the things we planned and some of the things just happened. I mean I hadn't planned to do that I was just— like I said we had done so much focused small detailed drawings and things and lots of the work was on their own or with a partner we had not actually done the big work and big paintings and the collaboratives [pictures] . . .

Her way of taking hold of the process was to encourage the children to create large-scale collaborative images using abstract ideas emerging from the photographs. This multimodal event she described as the "collaboratives." The teacher then focused on collaborative work as her outcome from the creative project. The focus was also on the practices, visual, oral, and written, and how they emerged from the photographs. However, the focus for the teacher was ultimately the way in which the project developed collaborative work, joint talk, and shared activities.

Another teacher, Jenny, who worked in year 2, described how she had developed her own art project, an environment box project, as a result of the activity within the school and the focus on art. She wanted to develop teamwork with the children, and also to develop a learner focused approach to teaching. She described the benefits of the project to me in an interview:

> . . . it gives them all the skills of co-operating and working as a team and speaking to each other and communicating and listening, so I think that its definitely benefited them, this notion of speaking with a partner and consulting with a partner. (Interview, March, 2006)

Her current project utilized the focus on art practice but, much like the year 1 teachers, her focus was on collaboration and, in this case, she used the project to develop collaborative talk. The teachers, then, took hold of art practices for their own ends, to try to develop curricular goals that they had identified within their class, including literacy and oral language as well as visual representations. This kind of goal, that of collaboration and oral discursive skills, was identified as being one of the key outcomes of the Creative Partnerships intervention in a recent inspection report (Ofsted, 2006).

The Children

Kate also interviewed 15 of the year 1 children, now in Year 2, who had experienced this teacher-led art practice. They had experienced the taking home of the cameras and the making of new kind of multimodal text, drawing on the photographs, talking with the artist, the teacher, and each other and writing for the magazine. These images involved the taking of a picture at home, and then the duplicating of these images in school. Children's identities came strongly to the fore when these pictures were recalled. The enhanced affordances offered of taking the picture opened up different kinds of cultural spaces (Pahl, 2006). Lucy described trying to take a picture of her dog:

Lucy: Yeah. I took one of me dog.
Kate: (laughing) You didn't!
Lucy: It wouldn't sit still though. It just kept moving. Me dad's sat him down and put lead on him and hooked him to door and he got stuck so I took photo quick so and then when I took it back to school we had picture and we got to copy it on a piece of paper bag piece of paper and then we got to colour it in. (Interview, March, 2006)

Lucy's focus is on the actual process of taking the photograph and how hard it was for her to photograph a dog that would not keep still. When the children took their photos back, the teachers initiated the process of turning them into artwork. The children described the process of taking the pictures in relation to their memories of what was happening at the time, as Sally described here:

Kate: Did you turn them [the photographs] into a picture?
Sally: Yes, we took a picture and then with Kay from Heads Together we coloured it in with some pastels. With some tracing paper.
Emma: She came in and we got to pick one of our pictures and I had another one and I did that one and I think it was of my dolls on my bed and she photocopied this big picture of it. (Interview, February, 2006)

This description locates the practice of photocopying the images as a next stage on from the art practice of taking the photographs. One of the children then described the abstract artwork that came out of this process, which was the teacher-led part of the project. Emma looked again at the big pictures the teacher had encouraged them to do, the collaborative picture, which was an abstract of the shapes they made from the photographs and commented:

Emma: You know how a slug leaves a trail, I were doing a fish.

Here, the child has taken hold of the art practice of turning things into other things, from the photograph to the painting and then to the abstract shape, and has identified the way in which the fish leaves a trail. The children in the main focused in their interview on what they engaged with, rather than the specific multimodal events and practices. However, in some cases, the description of the multimodal event was very specific. Angel (Year 3) described how she and her friend had responded to this technique the year before:

Angel: She had a picture in front of her, of t'fountain and she got a pen and she went round it. She did 2 of them and then she did one white, a blue, and she did water . . .
Kate: Are they photocopies or real pictures?
Angel: Photocopies. We had the photocopy at school, and we had a picture and then we went up and photocopied it. (Interview, June, 2006)

The process of taking the picture, then turning it into black and white, then photocopying it, is described by the child in relation to the actual multimodal practice of taking the photograph and blowing it up on the photocopier. The child has focused on the events and practices. It was also evident in the data that many children focused on the subject of their images, which tended to instantiate their home identities.

By contrast, while the teachers do focus on multimodal events and practices in the first instance, their talk turned quickly to wider goals of collaboration and learning which they had identified as stemming from the art practices. They moved from practices to values and skills instantiated within the practices, wider goals which were for them critical to the development of the creative learning they wanted to achieve in the school. Creativity, in this instance, was harnessed to the greater good of curricular outcomes, including literacy. By analysing the spread of the practice, its changes and developments can be tracked. The teachers took hold of the project with wider aims for the children, and the art practices were a way to achieve wider goals of collaboration, independent learning, and decision-making. In this way, "literacy" became embedded in broader learning issues than just encoding text or "reading," for which the earlier NLS was criticised.

One key aspect of the project was the way in which teachers and children identified that the process blurred curricular boundaries. The Year 2 teacher, Carol, who did the final magazine, commented that,

They couldn't work out whether they were doing history or art or literacy or numeracy they had no idea they used to sit there and go what lesson are we doing? Oh, we are doing the magazine and I think that became much more important and it actually broke down the barriers between subjects so that they were learning in a completely cross-curricular way that was the biggest thing. (Interview, November, 2005)

The final product, the magazine, which Angel's year was involved with, did include a strong literacy element; however, the focus was on the activity, the project, rather than individual subjects. Angel also explained to me how the project was divided up:

Angel: That part is about Joseph Locke, that's about art, this is about Barnsley, and maps and all that.

Kate: OK, so that's the different aspects.

Angel: There's four parts, that's about art, that's about Joseph Locke park, that's about Barnsley and that's about, um, maps . . . (Interview, June, 2006)

Creative Partnerships in the UK has undoubtedly opened up new spaces for teacher autonomy and freedom. The discourses around creativity continue, however, to be muddied in particular ways in the UK. On the one hand, the collaboration with what is called "The Creative Industries" is seen as contributing to long-term productivity and economic prosperity. On the other, the curriculum pulls both ways. Teachers are encouraged to pursue innovative ways of delivering the curriculum—as long as their test scores are high. Schools that "perform" creativity well, as reflected in school displays and nice "products," are rewarded for good behaviour (Thomson, Hall, & Russell, in press). What is more difficult is to tease out the benefits of long-term collaboration between artists and teachers in terms of the triangle in which teacher, artist, and child all play a part. How does each of those players interpret and construe creative approaches? Creativity is not in itself a necessarily good or bad space, but offers a kind of space that can be described in different ways. One metaphor is the concept of creative approaches dissolving into everyday teaching practice, as teachers make habitual alternative ways of delivering the curriculum involving art, drama, or other creative media. The other is the one described here of "taking hold." In the case of Creative Partnerships, the outside intervention appears to support a way of enhancing pupil agency while giving teachers more scope to develop a curriculum in which literacy was part of a wider picture: a magazine, an exchange project, or a collaborative discussion. The challenge is to examine those spaces in the curriculum where things are moving, given the label of being "creative," and to deliver an account of what that teaching and learning actually look like, of the kind evident in the research described here.

CONCLUSION

In both of the case studies described here there is ambivalence, some blurring of boundaries and also uncertainty as to how "literacy" is defined amongst the complex communicative practices now being enacted in schools. More precisely, the cases have demonstrated how the actual practices of the classroom do not just replicate the intentions of policy-makers, curriculum designers, and testers. In the case of the Creative Partnerships project, teachers were seen to "take hold" of the external designs in their own local ways. Likewise, in the punctuation lessons, the class's interactional routines can be seen to be just as important as the curricular prescriptions (if not more so) in terms of the approach to literacy and punctuation that ultimately emerges from the lessons. This finding is supported by the other lessons in both Lefstein and Pahl's larger studies: NLS curricular prescriptions have been assimilated into existing interactional dynamics and local meanings.

While the accountability mechanisms that might appear to justify the metaphor of "snake oil" on analogy with the US situation have led to criticism that schools are sometimes producing evidence of attainment at the expense of actual learning, they have also been instrumental in getting teachers to reconsider pupils' potential achievement and the effectiveness of their own practice—the adapted "elixirs" have perhaps been of some value. In the case of Low Tide Primary School, the external interventions—the NLS, SATs, PANDA and Ofsted—have in fact constituted the primary impetus for necessary change at a school that systematically failed its working-class pupils. If accountability measures had not been put in place, the teachers and pupils at Low Tide—and presumably many other schools around the country— would have been content with their low performance.

Likewise, with respect to a different kind of external intervention concerned with "creativity," the outcomes depend on the enactment, how the teachers take hold of the ideas, rather than in the treatment itself. It is not so much the diffuse notions of "creativity" that causes positive outcomes as the opportunity the intervention provides for enhancement of teacher professionalism and of learner identity.

The problem, then, might be better formulated as one in which current accountability measures are seen as blunt instruments—intervention has taken the form of a bludgeon where a more subtly negotiated set of tools would be more appropriate. The challenge is how to reconfigure performance management, testing, and inspection practices so that they are also catalysts and vehicles for teacher reflection and deliberation. Central control of teaching is problematic, but employing "creativity" as its opposite term may be no less problematic. Literacy as "snake oil" can be taken hold of in positive ways, and a more nuanced, social practice approach may be enacted by teachers at the same time as it may be subverted by traditional classroom interactional patterns. The case studies analysed here suggest that the key to productive enactment of both prescriptive and laissez-faire approaches is teacher professionalism.

NOTES

1. The methodology and outcomes of this study are reported in Lefstein (2005).
2. The name used for the school, teacher and all pupils are pseudonyms.
3. The largest minority group is "Black or Black British—Caribbean" (3.0%).
4. It is noteworthy that most studies of the NLS (and of teacher-curricular interaction) have focused on "best practice" research, in which cases are selected precisely because they are perceived to be successful. Since current policy was designed to provide support—and pressure—to struggling schools, the case of Low Tide Primary School offers an important perspective (cf. Nicolaidou & Ainscow, 2005).
5. See Appendix 1 for guidance on transcription conventions for this and all other extracts.
6. Indeed, the texts missing apostrophes read as if they were written specifically for the purpose of exhibiting apostrophe deficiencies. Consider, for example, the "Challenger" paragraph (part of which is discussed in extract 2), which is the only text more than one sentence long: "Lets look at the dinosaurs skeleton. Its made of hundreds of animals bones. I cant believe theyve all come from one animals graveyard. Its makers mustve dug up loads of animals in the countrys mountains."

    These sentences are packed with instances of apostrophe-rich but awkward constructions. Wouldn't "dinosaur skeleton," "animal bones," and "country mountains" have been more effective than "dinosaur's skeleton," "animals' bones," and "country's mountains"?
7. The sentence is also problematic inasmuch as it is not a very good example of possession. Arguably, one could write "Dickens novels" (with no apostrophe) where Dickens is an adjective that describes the novels: What type of novels do you like to read on vacation? I love to lose myself in a Dickens novel.
8. These pupil guesses are somewhat reminiscent of Bloome, Puro, and Theodorou's (1989) descriptions of "procedural display." However, in Bloome and colleagues' example, pupils bid for turns in the hope that they will not be called upon. They engage in what Bloome et al. term, "mock participation": "making it seem as if he knew the answer when he did not. If he had not been called on by raising his hand he could have made it seem to the teacher and peers that he had indeed known the answer" (p. 281). In the case discussed here, Miss Goodwin's pupils neither attempt to appear knowledgeable nor seek to avoid being called upon—they interject their wild guesses even before the turn is allocated.
9. Dickens describes this strategy in *Hard Times* (1854):

    "Very well," said this gentleman, briskly smiling, and folding his arms. "That's a horse. Now, let me ask you girls and boys, Would you paper a room with representations of horses?"

    After a pause, one half of the children cried in chorus, "Yes, sir!" Upon which the other half, seeing in the gentleman's face that Yes was wrong, cried out in chorus, "No, sir!"—as the custom is, in these examinations.

    "Of course, No. Why wouldn't you?" (pp. 50–51)

10. Pupils "call out" constantly during these lessons, and their interjections are usually accepted by Miss Goodwin. She rarely admonishes them for calling out when their answer is correct.
11. Also relevant are a series of "Activity Resource Sheets" available on the NLS web site at http://www.standards.dfes.gov.uk/literacy/teaching_resources/nls_framework/year4/term2/?level=sentence.
12. These initiatives culminated in a revised "Primary Framework for Literacy and Mathematics," which was released as this chapter went to press in October 2006 (see http://www.standards.dfes.gov.uk/primaryframeworks/).

REFERENCES

Ashley, B., Blake, Q., Fine, A., Gavin, J., Morpurgo, M., Powling, C., Prince, A., Pullman, P., Rosen, M., & Wilson, J. (2005) *Waiting for a Jamie Oliver: Beyond a Bog-Standard Literacy* (Reading, National Centre for Language and Literacy).

Banaji, S., Burn, A., & Buckingham, D. (in press) *Rhetorics of Creativity: Literature Review*. Report commissioned by Creative Partnerships, UK.

Bloome, D., Puro, P. & Theodorou, E. (1989) Procedural Display and Classroom Lessons, *Curriculum Inquiry*, 19(3), 265–291.

Craft, A., Cremin, T. & Burnard, P. (2006) Pedagogy and Possibility Thinking in the Early Years. UKLA Paper.

Department for Education and Employment (DfEE) (1998b) *Teachers' Notes On Shared And Guided Reading And Writing At Ks2*. London: Her Majesty's Stationery Office.

Department for Education and Employment. (1998a) *National Literacy Strategy*. London: Her Majesty's Stationery Office.

DfES (2003) *Excellence and Enjoyment: a Strategy for Primary Schools*. London: DfES.

Dickens, C. (1987) *Hard Times: For These Times*. Harmondsworth: Penguin.

Gonzalez, N., Moll, L., & Amanti, C. (2005) (eds.) *Funds of Knowledge: Theorizing Practices in Households, Communities, and Classrooms*. Lawrence Erlbaum: Mahwah, NJ.

Halliday, M.A.K. & Martin, J.R. (1993) *Writing Science: Literacy and Discursive Power* (London, Falmer Press).

Hannon, P. (1999) Rhetoric and Research in Family Literacy. *British Educational Research Journal*, Vol 26(1), 121–138.

Heath, S. B. (1983). *Ways with Words: Language, Life, and Work in Communities and Classrooms*. New York: Cambridge University Press.

Heath, S.B. & Wolf, S. (2004) *Visual Learning in the Community School*. London: Creative Partnerships.

Ofsted (2003) *Expecting the Unexpected: Developing Creativity in Primary and Secondary Schools*. HMI 1612 E-Publication: Ofsted.

Hymes, D. (1994) Towards Ethnographies of Communication. In J. Maybin (ed.) *Language and Literacy in Social Practice*. Maidenhead: Open University Press.

Ivanic, R. (1998). *Writing and Identity: The Discoursal Construction of Identity in Academic Writing*. Amsterdam: John Benjamins.

Jeffery, B. (ed.) (2006) *Creative Learning Practices: European Experiences*. London: The Tuffnell Press.

Kress, G. (2003). *Literacy in the New Media Age*. London: Routledge.

Kress, G., Jewitt, C., Bourne, J., Franks, A., Hardcastle, J., Jones, J., & Reid, E. (2005) *English in Urban Classrooms: A Multimodal Perspective on Teaching and Learning*. London and New York: Routledge/Falmer.

Kolln, M. (1996). Rhetorical Grammar: A Modification Lesson. *English Journal*, 85(7), 25–31.

Kulick, D., & Stroud, C. (1993) Conceptions and Uses of Literacy in a Papua New Guinean Village. In B.V. Street (ed.) *Cross-cultural Approaches to Literacy*. Cambridge: Cambridge University Press.

Ladson-Billings, G. (1995) Towards a Theory of Culturally Relevant Pedagogy. *American Educational Research Journal*, 32, 465–491.

Lancaster, L. (2003) Beginning at the Beginning: How a Young Child Constructs Time Multimodally. In C. Jewitt & G. Kress (eds.) *Multimodal Literacy*. New York: Peter Lang Publishers.

Lankshear, C., & Knobel, M. (2003). *New Literacies: Changing Knowledge and Classroom Learning*. Philadelphia: Open University Press.

Larson, J., & Marsh, J. (2005) *Making Literacy Real: Theories and Practices for Learning and Teaching*. London: Sage.

Lea, M. R., & Street, B. V. (1998). Student writing in higher education: An academic literacies approach. *Studies in Higher Education*, 23(2), 157–172.

Lefstein, A. (2005) *Teacher Enactments of the English National Literacy Strategy—An Extended Case Study*. Doctoral dissertation, Educational Studies, King's College London, London.

Lefstein, A. (in press) Literacy makeover: educational research and the public interest on prime time. *Teachers College Record*, 110(7). (http://www.tcrecord.org/Content.asp?ContentId=13450).

Marsh, J. (2004). The Primary Canon: A Critical Review. *British Journal of Educational Studies*, 52(3), 249–262.

Moss, G. (2003) Texts and Technologies of Accountability: Making New Pedagogies for New Times. Unpublished paper presented at the University of Wisconsin.

National Advisory Committee on Creative and Cultural Education (NACCCE). (1999) *All Our Futures: Creativity, Culture and Education*. London: Department for Education and Employment.

Nicolaidou, M. & Ainscow, M. (2005) Understanding Failing Schools: Perspectives from the Inside. *School Effectiveness and School Improvement*, 16(3), 229–248.

Ofsted (2006) *Creative partnerships: Initiative and Impact*: Ofsted.

Pahl, K. (2006) Birds, Frogs, Blue Skies and Sheep: An Investigation into the Cultural Notion of Affordance in Children's Meaning Making. *English in Education*, 40(3), 19–34.

Pahl, K. & Rowsell, J. (2005) *Literacy and Education: The New Literacy Studies in the Classroom*. London: Paul Chapman.

Pullman, P. (2003) Isis Lecture, *Oxford Literary Festival* (Oxford). Downloaded from http://www.philip-pullman.com/pages/content/index.asp?PageID=66 on 3.10.2005.

Qualifications and Curriculum Authority (2003) *Creativity, Find it, Promote it!* http://www.ncaction.org.uk/creativity/about.htm (Accessed 11.12.06).

Qualifications and Curriculum Authority (QCA) (2005) *Creativity: Find It, Promote—Promoting Pupils' Creative Thinking and Behaviour Across The Curriculum at Key Stages 1 and 2—Practical Materials for Schools*. London: Qualifications and Curriculum Authority.

Safford, K. & Barrs, M. (2005) *Creativity and Literacy: Many Routes to Meaning*. London: CLPE.

Sealey, A. (1999a) *Theories about Language in the National Literacy Strategy*. Coventry, Centre for Elementary and Primary Education, University of Warwick.

Sealey, A. (1999b) Implied Theories of Language in the National Literacy Strategy. In T. O'Brien (ed.) *Language and Literacies* (BAAL/Multilingual Matters, Clevedon, Buffalo) pp. 10–12.

Street, B. V. (1984). *Literacy in Theory and Practice*. Cambridge Cambridgeshire; New York: Cambridge University Press.

Street, B. (1999) The NLS: Some Theoretical and Textual Considerations. In T. O'Brien (ed.) *Language and Literacies* (BAAL/Multilingual Matters, Clevedon, Buffalo) pp. 8–10.

Street, B. V. (2000) Literacy Events and Literacy Practices: Theory and Practice in the New Literacy Studies. In M. Martin-Jones & K. Jones (eds.) *Multilingual Literacies: Reading and Writing Different Worlds*. (Amsterdam/Philadelphia, John Benjamins Publishing Company) pp. 17–29.

Thomson, P, Hall, C. & Russell, L (2006) An Arts Project Failed, Censored or . . .? A critical incident approach to artist-school partnerships. *Changing English*. 13(1), 29–44.

Thomson, P., Hall, C., & Russell, L. (in press) If These Walls Could Speak: Reading Displays of Primary Children's Work.

CHAPTER NINE

Complex Literacy Landscapes

Veiled Meanings and Contested Identities

NANCY ARES AND EDWARD BUENDÍA

In the work reported here, we examine the social and physical divisions in Salt Lake Valley in the western US, where citizens designate historically developed and locally maintained partitions of the local area as the Westside versus the Eastside, reflecting the physical geography of the area. As in most urban centers across the globe, these socially constructed boundaries denote divisions along racial, ethnic, class, and even religious lines. While terms such as these and others—the South Side of Chicago or the North End of Boston—refer to different geographical spaces, they also function as local knowledge that defines the identity of individuals and groups associated with these places.

Historically, these different designations have come to mark for some inhabitants of these spaces a sense of collectivity, place, and belonging. They are deployed in a manner to denote, "That's them, not us." However, these codes can also denote a pejorative assemblage of meanings that inscribe particular people and spaces with a sense of "Other-ness," so that competing meanings may exist side by side within a city. Often, as was the case in Salt Lake Valley, these spatial-ontological constructs are so embedded in the imaginations and language of their citizenry that they serve as short hand to name the unarticulated racial and class markings of its inhabitants. We explore the consequences of educators' deploying the Eastside and Westside constructs in their discourse about students and themselves, as well as the relations among discourse, technologies, and practice, for their decisions about literacy programs to adopt as part of a whole-district reform effort.

We give a brief history of the development of the Eastside and Westside con-structs, and tie them to their usage in Salt Valley School District elementary schools. While the Westside and Eastside constructs have been produced and sustained over time by city planners, politicians, the media, and city inhabitants themselves, we argue that these terms are more than just spatial signifiers that mark a place or an origin. We show that they are codes underpinned by local knowledge, or what we will frame as discourse, that index racial and class meanings as well as construct places within institutional and city spaces. We argue that principals and teachers also actively par-ticipate in producing and sustaining these spatial constructs that inscribe students and spaces with particular encoded meanings of race and social class. Further, we explore how these acts of encoding were important in guiding choices of particular literacy programs for particular places and people in the Valley, as well as shaping educators' choices regarding which other educators and schools they saw as "like" themselves and, thus, appropriate to collaborate with around literacy practices.

To illuminate the productive quality of educators' employing local spatial con-structs, we explain and theorize the knowledge and practice, particularly about liter-acy programs, produced by a collection of eight elementary schools that were situated physically between the areas constructed as the Eastside (largely affluent, White) and the Westside (largely poor, racially and ethnically heterogeneous) and that comprised a third space that existed in the division of schools and students in Salt Valley City District. This new social space is developing because increasing ethnic/racial, linguis-tic, and socioeconomic diversity, expanding from west to east across the Salt Lake Valley, is creating a spatial border that is shifting over time. Parts of the Eastside are now a destination for immigrants both from outside the Valley (for example, inter-national students attending local universities, and their families) and from the Westside. These eight schools and their neighborhoods are spaces that have histori-cally been homogeneous White and middle class. Now, they are quickly becoming demographically heterogeneous (the District experienced an average 8% yearly increase in students of color between 1997 and 2003, and by 2004, White students made up 49% of the total student population).

The schools in this corridor, or borderland, identified themselves as not Eastside or Westside. Instead, they identified themselves as constituting what some termed Central City. This local knowledge base was a hybrid of local and national discourses, and distinct from that found in both Eastside and Westside schools, particularly the nostalgic frameworks of educating that are prominent within Eastside schools that are holding on to historical, pastoral notions of student and school; and at-risk dis-courses that are prevalent within Westside schools. Instead of invoking the local meanings in identifying themselves, educators in Central City schools called up national discussions about urban, at-risk schools, avoiding associations with locally familiar terms that embodied historical race- and class-based judgments about people. The dynamism found in their construction of social space included their complex and varied choices of literacy programs and entry into collaborative relationships with other schools based on those choices.

SPATIALIZED AND SPATIALIZING PRACTICES

We foreground the spatial (i.e., relational), historical, and institutional dimensions of school knowledge to explain the hybrid nature of the Central City schools' discourse and literacy program choices and practices. From this point of view, both process (actions) and form (configuration of objects and relations) are constituted and reconstituted through the enactment of spatial practices. Those practices can be spatialized in that they can be based on unexamined notions of what is "natural" or "appropriate," and are thus reproductive. Such reproduction leads to a re-instantiation or reification of historically developed social relations. On the other hand, spatializing practices can involve both production and reproduction, depending on the purposes people have for engaging in them. It is this productive quality that entails possibilities for transformation. Here, intentional actions to invoke existing social relations serve like spatialized practice in reproduction of knowledge and practice, while work to transform social relations involves production of new or hybrid assemblages of objects, bodies, knowledge, and discourse.

Drawing from Nancy Fraser (1991), we emphasize that the relations that compose the space of schools, as well as the historical practices that have emerged as effects of these relations, necessitate, in part, that educators produce spatial categories that identify students (e.g., low or middle income; limited English proficient; high or low achiever). For example, funding formulas schools are given by state and federal entities and the required reporting to those agents require such identifications. This was made particularly salient in Salt Valley District as they engaged in a whole-district reform effort aimed at responding to increasing demographic diversity among their students. Further, the intermingling of legal and administrative mandates, local historically derived discourses, and structures in the district's reform effort lead educators to create this new Central City space in particular ways. A key understanding that emerges from examining these educators' production of knowledge, discourse, and practice is that spatialized and spatializing practices are not only linked to historical, social, and economic forces, but that they involve individuals' and groups' embodied acts. The discontinuity seen in the knowledge, discourse, and practice in the Central City schools compelled us to explore that space as a space of possibility in the midst of a reform aimed at changing district, school, and teacher structures and practice so that the increasingly multicultural mix of students and families in the Valley would be well served.

METHODOLOGY

Theoretical Framework

Our examination of spatialized and spatializing practices in the literacy program choices among Central City schools aims to illuminate the dynamic relations operating in this borderland area. Connecting those choices to socio-historical, socio-political spaces in Salt Lake Valley ties spatial patterns in compensatory versus enrichment approaches to literacy to the historical development of discourse, knowledge, and practices as embodied acts. To do so, we draw from the work of Henri Lefebvre (1991), Edward Soja (1996), and Michel Foucault (1972, 1977) and argue that space does not exist *a priori*.[1] Space is a social construction that is produced through material relations, practices, interactions, and talk and bodily acts. Discourse, knowledge, and bodies are coordinated through processes that reproduce and produce historical relations. This coordination can be seen in the spatialized and spatializing practices of educators, as, for example, their discursive framing of students and themselves, choices of curricula, and orchestration of school and classroom activities and interactions constitute material and ideal experiences of schooling.

The material world of technologies also has an important role in the production of space, as it interplays with knowledge. Rose (1996) argues, "Human technologies are hybrid assemblages of knowledges, instruments, persons, systems of judgment, buildings and spaces, underpinned at the programmatic level by certain presuppositions and objectives about human beings" (p. 26). From this view, technologies are inherently spatial as they are coordinated to produce material and ideal relations. Through the forging of these relations, technologies function as spatialized and spatializing objects. However, technologies are integrated into practices by knowledge. Embodied practices impose order upon objects and structural relations to work within the logic of historically developed knowledge. Thus, for this chapter, rather than literacy programs being seen simply as collections of print and other media, packaged or teacher-created, or reading and writing exercises, they are viewed as part of the integration of knowledge, objects (e.g., texts, assessments), practice, and people based on ontological and epistemological assumptions about students and teachers.

Data and Analyses[2]

As part of a large-scale study of Salt Valley District's comprehensive reform effort, we interviewed groups of teachers four times each from all elementary schools (60 teachers, 26 schools) and conducted four individual interviews with the school principals over a two-year period. School reform documents and improvement plans were also collected. Our analysis followed Gee (1999) and Huckin (1988), drawing on critical discourse analysis and qualitative grounded theory. Codes, categories, and themes were arrived at through discussion, independent coding of a common subset of the data, identification of emergent themes and searches for negative examples, and checks for inter-rater agreement. Once sufficient agreement was achieved, we divided up what remained of the data and analyzed it independently.

LITERACY SPACES IN THE CENTRAL CITY SCHOOLS

Our historical mapping of the public life of the Westside and Eastside discourses as they were employed in the media during the period of 1900–2000 showed how the Westside has come to be underpinned by overtly racialized and criminalizing meanings, whereas the Eastside has existed, for the most, in a precarious silence, with a few intonations, at times, of a pastoral space (Buendía, Ares, Juarez, & Peercy, 2005). Alongside the dominant knowledge of the Eastside and Westside, this production of spatial knowledge was bound tightly to the structural organization of the city. Specifically, patterns in the organization of the city's built environment (e.g., placement of rail yards and freeways, historically developed zoning laws) and occupational (i.e., social class) dimensions also follow a racial- and class-oriented pattern. Today, the built environment is such that houses that range in cost from the millions to the hundreds of thousand dollars are situated up and around the rim of the eastern- and northern-lying foothills. This area is commonly referred to by locals as the "the Eastside" or "the benches." As you travel westward, down the foothills toward the Great Salt Lake, other Eastside neighborhoods begin, still located on the benches that are composed of houses priced in the two to three hundred thousand dollar range. This residential area has a mix of upscale sidewalk cafés and restaurants that are intermingled with single-family housing.

Proceeding westward, a multi-acre train yard dissects the city. More heavy-industry-oriented buildings and older businesses can be found within the train track lines as well as various ethnic supermarkets, such as *La Michoacana-Productos de Mexico*. An elevated freeway that runs north-south parallels the central railroad lines that cut the city in half. It marks, for many city residents, the beginning of another neighborhood, commonly referred to by locals as the "Westside." Houses situated between the freeway and the airport are larger yet markedly less expensive than those on the Eastside of the freeway. Within this neighborhood, a mix of ethnic restaurants, primarily Mexican, and convenience stores are intermixed with various fast food chains, strip malls with dollar discount stores, and major chain supermarkets. The area is interspersed with both large and small churches, with some dating back to the turn of the 20th century while others show the markings of new construction.

Many of the business and church storefront signs are written in English, Spanish, or Tongan.

CONTINUITY IN DISCOURSE, PRACTICE AND TECHNOLOGY IN THE WESTSIDE AND EASTSIDE SPACES

Discursive practices of educators in the Eastside and Westside schools were also tightly tied up with the historically derived built environment. That discourse calls on the knowledge of the Westside and Eastside that is produced by educators who self-identify, and are identified by others within the school district, as Westside and Eastside teachers and schools. That knowledge was put into motion by educators naming those from, and those inhabiting, the Westside as "deficit," "uninterested in education," and "at-risk." This knowledge of the Westside was a racialized discourse of deficiency that, at times, explicitly named race and social class, and, at other moments, avoided identifying the racial identifiers, using instead the Westside signifier as a proxy to denote the racial and classed dimensions of this knowledge.

Our analysis also showed how the Eastside construct was a marker that generally rendered race invisible. It was coupled to propositions of the "enlightened," the "invested," and the "intellectually prepared" student and population in the few instances when it was elaborated upon. Its explicit use, however, was generally subdued in comparison to that of the Westside. It, too, was employed as a proxy to name and discuss race and class, as well as to coordinate people and resources to produce a differentiated space called the Eastside. For schools in both spaces, the constructs and their deployment by educators propelled the coordination of practices and technologies, including literacy program choices.

Converging technologies and practices. The reform, as a set of practices and the coordination of material objects and bodies, was the most recent catalyst in sustaining this spatial knowledge of East versus West. Schools were required to base curricular and instructional decisions on achievement, attendance, and other data disaggregated based on race/ethnicity and class designations. Federal and state funding mechanisms bolstered these practices (e.g., Title 1, the state's Highly Impacted Schools monies). As such, the reform's mandated literacy curriculum reorganization and grouping with other schools based on literacy program choices were efficiently connected to pre-existing school technologies that helped to reproduce and instantiate the space and knowledge of the Eastside/Westside. They were both a spatialized and spatializing technology in producing these distinctions. That is, the reform was initiated within the existing logic of the Westside/Eastside binary (the spatialized quality) and operated to organize other practices and technologies so that they corresponded to this knowledge (the spatializing element). As a result, the division between Eastside and Westside schools and students was reproduced so that the difference was not solely conceptual, but so that it also had real, material technologies that corresponded to this knowledge. The alignment of "words and things" (Foucault, 1972) confirmed for educators that the distinctions between these schools and students were indeed authentic.

Literacy Programs and Clusters. The hub of most of the reform's activity was the adoption of new literacy programs. Schools opted for four literacy series that varied in price and emphasis. The integration of these technologies within particular schools and not others also buttressed the historical spatial distinctions so that the new literacy technologies and practices associated with them were spatialized. Federal and state monies functioned as spatializing elements that spurred, in part, the spatial consolidation of the expensive, compensatory literacy programs (e.g., Success for All, California Early Literacy/Extended Literacy Learning) within schools that were identified and self-identified as Westside. Only two schools in this space opted for the less prescriptive Scholastic-Houghton Mifflin series, a formal series and more of a balanced literature model or framework (i.e., open-ended and varied phonics instruction, authentic literature readings and resources). Meanwhile, schools that identified as Eastside chose the more flexibly oriented Literacy For All model, a program that had no designated publishing house or set series. It was the most flexible, or least prescriptive of the literacy programs found in the Valley. Also, it was a curriculum negotiated and constructed by the teachers themselves, under the auspices that, first, they did not have the money for the expensive the pre-packaged programs and, second, these did not fit the needs or profile of their students. Finally, the clustering of schools, or entry into collaborative professional development groups, based on choice in literacy program was another spatializing practice, one that strengthened the reproductive nature of the discourse and other technologies in play. The effect of these activities was Eastside clusters and Westside clusters, a result of a set of reproductive spatialized and spatializing practices.

CENTRAL CITY SCHOOLS—SPACES OF DISCONTINUITIES AND FLUX

While discourse, knowledge, and practice in Eastside and Westside schools were invoked in ways that largely reproduced social spaces, Central City educators were found to engage in spatializing practices that produced hybrid discourses and knowledge, and a set of literacy practices and clusters across schools that reflected the messiness of the constitution of social space. As indicated earlier, a collection of eight schools caught our attention in the process of data analysis initially because they did not claim an Eastside or a Westside label. The result was a discursive ambiguity that characterized their talk, as educators did not explicitly claim a label and rarely used the existing binary to identify themselves and their schools. As we explored this interesting discourse, we looked to see what relationships might tie the schools together. What piqued our interest in critically examining the cultural geography of the Valley and its schools was the fact that the 8 schools all lie physically along that corridor over which the eastward-moving line of increasing diversity is crossing most recently.

Situated between the flatter, more crowded downtown and the steeper, more spacious foothills, these schools have demographic profiles similar to Westside schools; however, the changes in their student populations and surrounding communities have happened more recently than schools who are physically on the west of the downtown area and who explicitly claim Westside as an identifying signifier. These schools provide a telling case of how spatializing practices can be both productive and reproductive. Central City teachers and principals didn't re-instantiate historically constructed divisions, but instead participated in the production of a new construct and hybrid discourse that was beginning to emerge in this space outside schools as well (a community center in the area had adopted the name Central City some years before the construct surfaced in school documents). This new code served to identify as unique the space in the Valley that was experiencing the most rapid and recent demographic shift.

Central City is an area of conflict, convergence, and negotiation—a contested space. Educators were engaged in spatializing the area through the practices, technologies, and knowledge they adopted in response to students and families bringing unfamiliar languages, sociocultural norms, and practices to these formerly Eastside schools. Through the coordination of knowledge, practice, and technologies, schools were actively constructing this dynamic space, particularly their students, as new and different. As a result, the roles of teachers and principals were undergoing rapid change, and educators grappled with language to redefine their personal and professional roles and identities. The fact that the existing binary was not invoked, particularly the Westside category that has historically been attached to people of color, highlights the fact that the binary functions to do more than name students and families; educators also invoked the constructs to identify themselves. Thus, it may be that educators were seeking a new code that allowed them to retain their image of themselves as "not Westside." As we show, the patchwork pattern of literacy programs and clusters, as an effect of the relations among discourse, practice, and technology, make clear the messiness and dynamism of constituting changing social spaces.

Naming themselves, placing themselves. As part of the district-wide reform effort, all schools were mandated to produce school improvement plans. For the Central City schools, the categories of East- and Westside were not invoked anywhere in these documents. Instead, our analysis revealed a mixture of not invoking any category (two schools), or using terms other than East- or Westside. In three schools, the signifier "inner city" was linked to ethnicity/race, poverty, language, and instability, similar to the Westside code. Most interesting in terms of local dynamism in spatial/linguistic constructs, in two school improvement plans the term Central City was prominent in the self-definitions: "located on the edge of Central City," and "an elementary school located in the Central City area." One of the schools placed its street address in the same sentence in which the term Central City was used, helping the reader locate the school and "Central City" geographically. The students were described as "neighborhood" versus "magnet gifted and talented," with text helping to clarify to whom Central City refers: "While most children walk to school, the magnet program has students car-pooled from all over the city." The other school tied the term Central City to a description of the movement of students in and out of the school: "Between 150–170 students transfer to [School] each year, with most coming from [three other Central City schools]. Between 120–150 students transfer to other schools, with the largest percentages attending [two Eastside schools]." Again, this use of Central City as a category was accompanied with discursive markers to alert the reader as to where the school was and that Central City students were arriving and Eastside students were leaving. As such, the category was being defined by both place and the descriptions of people who inhabited it, coupling mobility with the Central City term. Thus, in schools, this locally developing code that may serve, some day, as a third signifier to characterize both a part of the city and its inhabitants.

SPATIALIZED AND SPATIALIZING PRACTICES

This evolving discourse signaled to us that possibilities existed for disrupting the historically developed divisions and pattern of compensatory/Westside versus enrichment/Eastside literacy programs. The assemblage of knowledges, technologies, and practices revealed in these educators' acts made particularly visible that there is considerable agency in the construction of space. It also is a telling example of the ways in which spatialized and spatializing practices are not only linked to historical, social, and economic forces, but that they involve individuals' and groups' embodied acts, that space is personalized and invested with personal meanings.

Discourses and technologies. For example, in interviews, teachers at one school cited other, nearby schools as being like them: "One thing I'd like to see is neighborhood, neighboring schools maybe like Elkhorn, Roosevelt, and Alpine meet like once every couple of months on a grade level, you know. . . . We service similar communities and it might be very interesting to see what's working in their classrooms and their schools, and take some of that information and use it here." These teachers pointed to other schools that fit within a shared, unnamed category, as well as within the same geographical area, that seemed to match their image of themselves and their students. In other Central City schools, both teachers and principals talked vaguely about "in certain school settings," or "this school in particular" such that no spatial signifiers were used that coupled demographics with geography; the focus was on demographics only:

> E.P.: I asked people from the state office to come down and talk about test scores for people with the demographics that we had. . . . she talked about what they were seeing in schools with demographics like ours. What are some strategies for demographics like this? . . . And they said well, you know, for schools like this you score in a range of this to this.

Rather than using the larger East/West discourse, talk such as this pointed vaguely at kinds of students to describe these schools. Importantly, a particular range of observed test scores was tied to schools as demographic profiles, coupling technologies of categorizing people by ethnicity or race with those of categorizing schools by achievement ranking. As a result, by invoking technologies and knowledge they deemed appropriate for "schools like this," these schools were becoming spatialized. The discourse is one of turning to data of a particular type to identify a social space that then leads educators to "strategies," so that guidance in choosing practices comes from an existing, technical knowledge base rather than relying on themselves or on students and their communities for insight as to how to proceed.

Reaching outside the Valley. Not only were local discourses being hybridized; so were national discourses, especially about students of color. Elements of the deficit discourse so pervasive in schools identified as Westside were deployed in Central City schools, but the staff at all of these schools conceptualized their roles and defined their students in terms that corresponded to the spatial-ontological construct of "inner-city" and "at-risk" students (see also Irvine & Larson, this volume). This use of a different set of terms that also served as shorthand for referring to race and class highlighted the tense negotiations teachers and principals seemed to be grappling with, where they invoked nationally salient terms that labeled their students with constructs whose meaning is clear but not stated, but avoided using local constructs that would also situate their schools and themselves spatially within the Valley. The reaching outside of the Valley to national discourses of "inner city" and "at risk" terms allowed them to talk of their students while shielding themselves from being identified as Westside teachers. Personalizing this space, investing it with personal meaning, seemed to mean that educators intentionally avoided using the local construct, given the well-understood but implicit social consequences for their self-identities. As was the case with their Eastside and Westside counterparts, educators in this space of the District invoked constructs that masked the racial and class differences being alluded to, evidence that across the Salt Valley direct reference to racial and class difference was avoided. However, the use of "inner city" and "at risk" also signaled that Central City educators were identifying their students in deficit terms, constructing them as lacking, while working to distinguish themselves somehow from Westside educators whose identities were tied to Westside students (see also Irvine & Larson, this volume). In addition, there was a pragmatic aspect to calling on the national discourses, as they provided a knowledge base from which to draw to choose "appropriate" literacy technologies and practices. As shown next, these enunciative acts had material consequences for educators' choices of literacy programs.

Literacy curricula. The ambiguity in educators' discourse and the ways that schools described themselves in school improvement plans was mirrored in the choices of technologies of schooling and reform made by educators in the Central City area. Schools adopted a variety literacy programs that ranged from the rigidly scripted SFA and CEL/xLL curricula to more flexible programs such as the Scholastic literacy program and the Literacy For All (LFA) program that was constructed by schools on the Eastside. Looking across the adoptions, we found a strong relationship between the discourses circulating within these schools about students and families and their adoption of particular literacy programs. The schools in the Central City that aligned themselves with the SFA and CEL/xLL shared a similar knowledge base as Westside schools who framed students as "needy" and as "socially deficit," whereas schools who participated in the LFA program with schools on the Eastside of the city enunciated a complex discourse that emphasized, at times, the "at risk" status of students but also the need to connect the curricula to the strengths and insights that students and families brought to school. Note the differences in tone in the following excerpts from, first, two schools that adopted a rigidly scripted, compensatory program also found in Westside schools, and second, two schools that adopted the more balanced, enrichment programs found on the Eastside:

Principal: I've decided that one of the things is, at this school in particular; there are so many social services issues . . . I think some of them [teachers] are barely keeping their head above water just dealing with kids, there are so many critical issues here. (Elementary principal)

Teacher: Somehow parenting seems to have disappeared. . . . And that means everything. . . . We opened the door, took responsibility away from the parents and the learning and teaching is suffering. (Elementary teacher)

Also:

Teacher 1: The thing is you really can't learn about a culture, or really know a culture until you've been in it and you've been there. I mean you can read about it but that's not the same as actually being there and being a part of it.

Teacher 5: I don't know if that's our job either. Just teaching more acceptance.

Teacher 1: I see myself—our job is to teach them how to function in our society and also our society to function in a world society where everybody needs to work together and if we can get them to accept other's differences but to learn how to live within this society I think you're going to be—

Teacher 2:   I think we're kind of missing the boat because we have some experts in the parents, in the children, and we're missing the boat because we're not using our experts to help us to understand what diversity is all about, what acceptance is all about. (Elementary teachers)

The conflicting messages in the second group of teachers' talk, all of whom taught together, highlighted the nature of the identity work educators were engaged in as they grappled with knowing their students, reconfiguring their roles, and reconsidering the purpose of schooling. It may be that the mixture of both positive and deficit discourses regarding the communities they were serving, along with their sense of themselves as "not Westside," influenced their decisions to adopt a less structured literacy program that kept open the possibility that they could still be "experts" who make professional judgments rather than implementers of teacher-proof curricula. These contradictions and tensions in the relations between discourse, practice, and technologies in the evolving Central City area illuminate the messiness and dynamism of the production of space.

School clusters. The choices of literacy programs and the accompanying clustering of schools functioned to reproduce the division of Eastside versus the Westside as salient knowledge, so the Central City schools did not have a third option in the clustering that reflected their contexts, even though they saw themselves as not clearly Eastside or Westside schools. They did not recognize each other as a collective, either, that had shared interests and student populations around which they could collaborate to craft or choose a literacy program. These schools were forced, instead, into the binary that existed, clustering with either Eastside or Westside schools. Five of the schools adopted the SFA or the CEL/xLL program and participated in clusters with schools that identified themselves as Westside schools. Reasons for choosing these clusters centered on finding "other schools doing what we wanted to do . . . we share training costs" (principal interview), thereby both identifying themselves with Westside schools' technologies and practices, and sharing resources or reducing costs. Connected to educators' use of national discourses of students of color as "at risk" and "inner city," these schools were able to accomplish pragmatic things in terms of deciding how to allocate resources based on the direction those constructs provided about choices of "appropriate" programs. Importantly, they also placed themselves within the spatial relations forged through discourse, practice, and technology that located them with others they perceived as having similar students and purposes.

The three remaining schools within the Central City corridor aligned themselves with the clusters composed of schools on the Eastside. While their discourses about their students were tied to national discourses of "at risk" and "inner city," their choice of cluster placed them with Eastside schools, creating some tension among discourse, practices, and technology. One principal indicated how the decision to join those schools was made: "So many of the schools in [the literacy cluster] have a unique approach that works for them." She went on to contrast the less prescriptive, teacher-created, enrichment approach in this program with the more scripted compensatory programs that required a strict structure and consistency across grade levels that was "not for them." In addition, these principals conferred with each other and with a district person who "interviewed us and thought we'd be a great fit, " a clear indicator of being identified and identifying themselves as "like" Eastside schools. This hybrid discourse was made up of those found in schools on the Westside (at risk, deficit-based) as well as on the Eastside (rejecting rigid literacy programs). Thus, the choice to cluster embedded these schools in complex and contradictory spatial relations.

SUMMARY

The material relations among discourse, technologies, and practice in this area of the Valley show more fluidity, tension, and negotiation than those in the other two areas. In particular, the durability of the Westside construct seems to have been challenged when educators were faced with applying the term to themselves. Central City teachers' and principals' use of nationally significant rather than locally constructed terms that serve as shorthand for deficit-based markers for race and class makes clear the spatial relations of this space. The Central City construct did not have continuity like the Eastside (academically able students, involved parents; enrichment literacy program) or Westside (immigrant, needy, deficient students and families; compensatory literacy programs), or an historical set of relations among discourses, practices, and technologies that defined places and people, because the space was in flux. The binary that helped distinguish East from West wasn't appropriate here, as it invoked relations that were settled long ago and were continually reified in both school and broader city discourses. In the unsettled space of Central City, educators' moves in personalizing space served as a critical factor in decisions about literacy program choices.

As a result of the spatial relations that involved competing epistemological assumptions about teachers and students, Central City schools featured a cobbled-together landscape of literacy programs and a splintering of the teachers across literacy clusters. Spatialized and spatializing technologies and practices were such that educators' coordination of bodies, technologies, and discourse brought together an unsettled mix of reproductive and productive knowledge and material relations. As a potential space of transformation, our analyses indicate that, for teachers, Central

City may have possibilities; for students and families of color, this is likely not the case. The splintering of educators in collaborations outside Central City militates against building a community of educators connected by a sense of place and belonging. It militates, too, against families and students being invited/included in what Bhabha (1994) terms an "insurgent act of cultural translation . . . [that] does not merely recall the past as social cause or aesthetic precedent; it renews the past, refiguring it as a contingent 'in-between' space, that innovates and interrupts the performance of the present" (p. 7).

In terms of compensatory and enrichment literacy programs, understanding the patterns of adoption across geographic areas as resulting from the relations among socio-historical and sociopolitical discourse, practice, and technologies illuminates the complexity inherent in educators' decision making. The personalizing moves educators made, where they readily took up national-level deficit discourses and adopted prescriptive literacy programs but eschewed drawing on local constructs that would locate them in the historically developed social space, gives some valuable insights into ways we might disrupt the landscape of literacy programs across time and space. Teachers' senses of self and of belonging to a community may serve as an important site for productive actions with potential for transformation of conventional practice, as long as that sense is tied to a clear understanding of the historical, social, and political implications of the coordination of technologies, practices, and discourses that shape decisions about literacy programs and curricula that are most powerful for supporting students' learning.

Learning and knowledge production rather than reproduction then could involve a process of moving outside of the school walls and exploring the various social relationships in which alternative meanings about populations and space are in circulation. A rearranging of the existing school technologies (i.e., literacy pedagogies, instructional conversations) that are focused on different ends and different subjects (e.g., Westside and/or students and families of color as sources of insight and important learning resources) would be in order. Educators may be able to envision practices of possibility as lying around them within other contexts of relations (i.e., counter-narratives in the media, relations that question the impacts of federal technologies), rather than within their belief systems or new technologies aiming to create more efficient modes of meeting particular population of students' needs. It was clear in the Central City data that teachers aligned themselves with somewhat different relations of power in representing themselves as not-Westside. They drew on readily available national discourses, technologies, and associations with other schools to organize their work. Still, their ability to create a new designation and space for themselves and their students may be very difficult considering the ways that schools institutionalize discourses and technologies to manage people and things, as well as the investments by individuals across the city that are well-served by continuing to draw on the historical Eastside/Westside division. If Central City educators were to question how and in what spatial contexts communities and students of color define themselves in ways that differ from those of institutions, including schools, it could help them to ask: How might we talk about and realign ourselves differently in order to draw on communities of color's positive self-representations and rethink the categories that we continuously deploy?

NOTES

1. See Edward Soja (1996), an insightful interpretation of the points of convergence and divergence between Lefebvre and Foucault, in the chapter "Heterotopologies: Foucault and the geohistory of otherness."
2. For a detailed presentation of our methodology, please see Buendía, Ares, Juarez, & Peercy (2005).

REFERENCES

Bhabha, H. (1994). *The location of culture*. New York: Routledge.

Buendía, E., Ares, N., Peercy, M., & Juarez, B. (2004). The geographies of difference: The production of the Eastside, Westside, and Central City school. *American Educational Research Journal, 41*(4), 833–866.

Foucault, M. (1977). *Discipline and punish: The birth of the prison*. London: Allen Lane.

Foucault, M. (1972) *Archeology of knowledge*. New York: Pantheon Books.

Fraser, N. (1989). *Unruly practices: Power, discourse, and gender in contemporary social theory*. Minneapolis: University of Minnesota Press.

Gee, J.P. (1999). *An introduction to discourse analysis: Theory and method*. New York: Routledge.

Huckin, T. (1995). Critical discourse analysis. *The Journal of TESOL-France, 2*(7), 95–110.

Lefebvre, H. (1991). *The production of space*. UK: Blackwell.

Rose, N. (1996). *Inventing our selves: Psychology, power, and personhood*. New York: Cambridge University Press.

Soja, E. (1996). *Thirdspace: Journeys to Los Angeles and other real-and-imagined places*. Cambridge, MA: Blackwell Press.

CHAPTER TEN

Digging Up THE Family Tree

America's Forced Choice

DAN OSBORN

In this chapter, I will discuss America's Choice, Inc., a for-profit subsidiary of the National Council for Education and the Economy (NCEE) that provides school designs and instructional systems to schools, school districts, and states using a genealogical framework (Foucault, 1975). This is not an efficacy study of America's Choice. Instead, I will explore the events and relationships intertwined in the origins of America's Choice, and notions of literacy embodied within its programs from the perspective of a classroom teacher. In addition, I will discuss consequences of the use of America's Choice for both students and teachers, particularly those in urban schools.

Paired with the high-stakes accountability system of rewards and punishments found in the No Child Left Behind Act (NCLB) and restrictive requirements for Reading First grants, I believe America's Choice represents a forced choice in literacy instruction for many urban schools. In addition, I believe that by focusing on "low per-forming" and "disadvantaged" schools and students, America's Choice serves to per-petuate a parallel tracking system in which students from urban schools receive instruction that focuses on low-level skills in isolation of actual practice, while students in many suburban schools such as mine have opportunities for more authentic cur-ricular and instructional practices.

Sheruich & McKenzie (2005) describe Foucault's notion of genealogy as an ana-lytic tool that can be used to inquire into such programs as America's Choice and to trace its history. The use of genealogy allows for the exploration of political, social, and economic relationships at play in the development of America's Choice, and encourages the consideration of that which is taken for granted, in this case, notions of literacy, curriculum, and instruction. In addition, genealogy allows the analysis of the power relations and technologies inherent in America's Choice.

As a genealogy, this chapter presents something analogous to a family tree for America's Choice. From a distance, the first thing one notices on the America's Choice family tree is its ornamental branches. These branches, which make the tree look good from a distance, are represented by terms like *reading workshop* and *writing workshop*. As you get closer, however, you realize that the branches have been grafted to the trunk. Just as the trunk of a tree contains the bulk of its mass, the bulk of America's Choice is reflected in terms and phrases emphasized in its own marketing materials. Terms like *standards-driven instruction, skills development, systematic instruction, phonics, grammar,* and *diction* highlight the dominant foci of America's Choice instruction (NCEE, 2004). These terms, however, seem to be incongruous with the workshop approach (Atwell, 1998; Calkins, 1994; Graves, 1983) to reading and writing implied by the ornamental branches of the America's Choice tree.

Finally, analysis through genealogy enables us to dig beneath the dirt to find the deep and tangled roots that both explain the origins of America's Choice and continue to give it support. The roots of America's Choice emerge from technical-rational theories of curriculum and instruction and intertwine scientific models of curriculum development focused on efficiency and production (Pinar et al., 2004), with autonomous views of literacy (Street, 1995) that see literacy as a set of discrete, neutral skills to be acquired.

THEORETICAL FRAMEWORK

I approach this study from a sociocultural perspective that knowledge is constructed in social and historical contexts and is distributed across individuals, cultural tools, and institutions (Cole & Engeström, 1993; Rogoff, 2003). From this perspective, learning is characterized as changing participation in culturally valued activities (Rogoff, 2003) and is inherent in all social practice (Lave & Wenger, 1991). A sociocultural approach to learning can be contrasted with a transmission model of curriculum that sees knowledge as being passed from one person to another with learning evidenced by acquisition of knowledge or skills isolated from social activities (Larson & Marsh, 2005).

Given the emphasis on literacy in America's Choice, it is also important that I present my theoretical framework for understanding and defining literacy. Barton & Hamilton (1998) recognize that "any theory of literacy implies a theory of learning" (p. 12). They note that, "like all human activity, literacy is essentially social and it is located in the interaction between people" (p. 3). Literacy practices, therefore, are situated. That is, literacy occurs in social, cultural, historical, and political contexts to achieve specific purposes; it does not exist independently from real social practices that give meaning (Street, 1995). In addition, literacy is inextricably related to power relations (Irvine & Larson, 2001, this volume), which are constructed, maintained, and reconstructed through literacy practices.

Following the scholarship in New Literacy Studies, I believe that rather than a singular literacy, there are multiple literacies (Lankshear & Knobel, 2003; Barton & Hamilton, 1998). The concept of multiple literacies recognizes and is responsive to cultural and linguistic diversity, as well as multimodal forms of texts and images that are part of information and communication technologies (Lankshear & Knobel, 2003). In fact, "there are as many different 'literacies' as there are socioculturally distinctive practices into which written language is incorporated" (Gee, 2004, p. 91). I also recognize that literacy is a set of constantly changing social practices (Barton & Hamilton, 1998; Street, 1995; Lankshear & Knobel, 2003) involved in creating, accessing, interpreting, and responding to varied and multiple texts (both spoken and written), images, and other media to communicate and negotiate meanings within and between a variety of Discourses. Gee's notion of Discourses with a big D (2001a, 2001b) emphasizes that there is much more to literacy than just knowing how to read and write: "A Discourse integrates ways of talking, listening, writing, reading, acting, interacting, believing, valuing and feeling . . . in the service of enacting meaningful socially situated identities and activities" (p. 719).

From a sociocultural perspective, literacy is located in social practices in which people engage to accomplish specific purposes, and cannot be broken down into discrete skills isolated from social, cultural, political, and historical contexts. Just as one does not learn to drive a car by first mastering ignition, then learning how to accelerate, followed by acquiring steering skills, and finally learning to brake, all without ever going anywhere; one does not learn to read and write by accumulating isolated skills like phonemic awareness and letter-sound correspondence without engaging in meaningful reading and writing practices. Literacy learning is evidenced not by an acquisition of skills, but by changing participation in culturally valued literacy practices (Rogoff, 2003).

In my multiage classroom of students who would typically be in second and third grade, I adopt Rogoff's (1994) notion of communities of learners and incorporate many of the characteristics of communities of learners for literacy learning discussed by Larson & Marsh (2005). In my classroom, literacy learning occurs during readers' and writers' workshops, and throughout the day as students and adults in the classroom engage in authentic activities that have real audiences and purposes. As the teacher, I serve as a leader and facilitator, but leadership is shared and students take responsibility for their learning. During our readers' and writers' workshops, students write about topics of their choice, and read literature they choose. Collaborative learning occurs as students confer with each other to discuss their writing, and engage in readers' roundtables, student-led book clubs in which they read and discuss shared texts. The instructional discourse of our classroom is dialogic and conversational as students learn from and with each other and adults in the classroom (c.f., Cazden, 1988; Gutierrez, 1993; Mehan, 1979; Nystrand et al., 1997 for discussion of instructional discourse). Students are engaged in complex relationships and serve as both experts and novices as they interact with each other. No role is seen as passive. I assess students throughout the day by observing them as they engage in activities. I use my assessment to guide students' participation in the future, and to inform instruction tailored to the students.

Student choice is an inherent component of a workshop approach to teaching reading and writing. I consider myself lucky that I have been able to make genuine choices about literacy learning in my classroom. The choices I make in relation to literacy learning are based on what I know about my students—their likes, dislikes, and interests, as well as their academic and social strengths and areas in need of development. My choices are also based on state standards and local curriculum, my knowledge and experience as a teacher, and my passionate beliefs about teaching, learning, and literacy. My students and I are fortunate that we can make real choices in relation to literacy learning; we have not had a mandated instructional program imposed on us.

AMERICA'S CHOICE

My genealogical analysis begins with a description of America's Choice based on language provided by their own marketing and instructional materials—language that points to roots firmly planted in scientific notions of curriculum and autonomous models of literacy. The roots of the America's Choice family tree uncovered in this genealogy reach from the scientific management and social efficiency movements of the early 1900s to the present day and the No Child Left Behind Act. After a brief description and discussion of America's Choice, I will provide an overview of the scientific management and social efficiency movements, and describe autonomous models of literacy to show how they are reified in America's Choice. Then I will show how the roots of America's Choice intertwine to connect *A Nation at Risk* (1983), the National Business Council, the National Center on Education and the Economy, the McGraw-Hill Corporation, the No Child Left Behind Act, and the Reading First Initiative to America's Choice. This analysis will also show how those involved in policy making for NCLB have directly benefited from its mandates.

According to their marketing materials, America's Choice, Inc. offers a variety of products to help states, districts, and schools meet the requirements of NCLB. America's Choice "is built on the premise that teaching to explicit standards is the best strategy for helping disadvantaged and low-performing students—the same strategy adopted by the authors of NCLB" (NCEE, 2006). America's Choice School Design started its model of standards-driven, whole-school design solutions in the areas of literacy and math in 1998 as a nonprofit organization under the umbrella of the National Council on Education and the Economy (NCEE). The program is based on NCEE's New Standards Performance Standards. America's Choice provides standards, assessments, curriculum materials, professional development, and on-site technical assistance to its schools. Components of the program highlighted by America's Choice include evaluations, curriculum that provides "explicit and systematic instruction," a classroom organization system, routines and rituals for students that promote on-task behavior, and a data analysis tool. Adoption of America's Choice School Design costs between $70,000 and $105,000 per school.

The centerpiece of the America's Choice elementary school instructional program is an extended daily literacy block. America's Choice materials (NCEE, 2006) say that the literacy blocks are based on a workshop model that includes one hour of reading instruction, one hour of writing instruction, and a half hour of skills development in phonemic awareness, phonics, diction, spelling, and vocabulary using the Open Court Phonics Kit (1995). Instruction during the workshop includes author and genre studies, 25-day units of instruction that "lead students through a series of assignments" (NCEE, 2006, p. 4). Literacy instruction at the middle and high school levels uses Ramp-Up Literacy, which includes advanced phonics and fluency instruction for students who score two or more years below grade level on reading tests.

Although America's Choice says they use a *workshop* format, their emphasis on skills development through the use of Open Court, isolated phonics instruction, and the notion of leading students through a series of packaged assignments seems incompatible with workshop format. As commonly understood by teachers, workshop models of literacy learning (Atwell, 1998; Calkins, 1994; Graves, 1983) usually focus on student choice, collaboration, and authentic literacy experiences that have personal significance and meaning for students. Authentic literacy experiences do not include the artificial breaking down of reading and writing into sequences of abstract skills out of the context of functional use (Goodman & Goodman, 1990).

In 2004 NCEE announced its decision to make America's Choice, Inc. a for-profit subsidiary. The move was made because NCEE was shifting its focus from developing programs to providing services to help schools comply with No Child Left Behind mandates. Marc Tucker, head of NCEE, indicated that with the switch to for-profit status, America's Choice could serve thousands, instead of hundreds of schools

(Trotter, 2004). In addition, Trotter reported that for-profit status would enable America's Choice to unbundle their products so that schools could select from a variety of materials, programs, and services. With for-profit status, America's Choice could reap the benefits of federal Reading First monies as NCLB mandated adoption of programs like America's Choice for schools determined to be underperforming.

EXPOSING THE ROOTS OF THE AMERICA'S CHOICE
FAMILY TREE: SCIENTIFIC MANAGEMENT
AND SOCIAL EFFICIENCY MOVEMENTS

The technical-rational roots of America's Choice extend back to Frederick Winslow Taylor's (1911) theory of scientific management, which brought economic practices found in factories of the early twentieth century into schools with the use of task analysis through which tasks were broken into their constituent parts. Taylor's scientific management provided a methodology for scientific curriculum development (Pinar, Reynolds, Slattery, & Taubman, 2004) in which tasks were identified and broken down into discrete, measurable parts that were used to set goals and detail instruction. In 1922 Edward Thorndike noted that education is a form of human engineering that benefits from measurement of student achievement. He believed that education itself must be scientific and ushered in an era of behaviorism in which human actions were reduced to their smallest units, thereby allowing comparison and profitability (Pinar et al., 2004). Similarly, Franklin Bobbit (1918) extolled the virtues of scientific methods for measuring and evaluating educational processes, and the development of curriculum that focused on addressing identified deficiencies. He believed that the "nature of the deficiency points to the abilities and dispositions that are to be developed in the child and the way of bringing about the correct forms" (p. 13).

Scientific management and efficiency are overarching themes that emerge from America's Choice's materials. The program emphasizes "systematic instruction" and "well-aligned instructional materials" for "higher rates of implementation and stronger effects" (NCEE, 2002, p. 1) provided through proprietary instructional materials. America's Choice also stresses organization for teachers, and standards-driven instruction for students that takes place within established "rituals and routines." New Standards Reference Examinations, standardized examinations used in America's Choice schools, are an integral part of the program. Leadership teams in America's Choice schools establish student performance targets and focus on coordinating program implementation. Professional development with America's Choice focuses on efficiency. Rather than encouraging teachers to investigate promising practices, innovative or alternative methods, and diverse topics, professional development in America's Choice schools focuses on extensive training to help teachers strengthen their understanding of the model and support its consistent implementation.

A deficit ideology is underscored in curriculum and instruction based on scientific management and efficiency evident in America's Choice, and is rooted in beliefs about perceived deficiencies not just in students, but in teachers as well (Irvine & Larson, this volume). As enacted in America's Choice programs, this focus on deficiency results in the devaluation and deskilling of teachers. Packaged literacy programs like America's Choice assume control of reading materials, goals, methods of instruction, and procedures for evaluation and assessment, leaving teachers with little reason to reflect on their practice, innovate their instruction, or adopt new methods (Shannon, 1987). Teachers are further devalued as their roles in schools that adopt programs like America's Choice shift from an emphasis on designing curriculum and planning instruction to responsibility for technical tasks and management concerns involved in implementing the components of the program (Apple, 1986). In addition, the emphasis on professional development focused on assuring consistent implementation of America's Choice programs cuts teachers off from their own fields, and forces them to rely on America's Choice trainers and coaches as "experts." Knowledge about and control of instruction in the classroom is removed from teachers, and placed in the hands of corporations (Gatto, this volume). NCLB requirements for *highly qualified* teachers seems to be at odds with mandates for the use of scientifically research-based packaged literacy programs that only require teachers to follow predetermined, scripted lessons, and complete the accompanying assessments and paperwork.

INTERTWINING ROOTS: AUTONOMOUS MODELS OF LITERACY

Intertwined with aspects of scientific curriculum making evident in America's Choice are notions of literacy based on an autonomous model and perceptions of "real" literacy being related to school-based practices. Street (1995) discusses the "pedagogization" of literacy in referring to ways in which literacy associated with school-based notions of teaching and learning has come to be accepted as the only literacy at the expense of other literacies practiced in the home, workplace and community. The pedagogization of literacy is based on acceptance of an autonomous model of literacy (Street, 1995) in which literacy is conceptualized as a set of neutral skills autonomous of social context. In an autonomous model, teaching is seen as the scientific management and transmission of skills with little or no social and cultural connection (deCastell & Luke, 1983).

Lankshear and Knobel (2003) explain how pedagogy and school routines that support and maintain an autonomous view of literacy have become part of the "deep grammar" of schools in which learning is seen as a sequenced series of steps derived from predetermined curriculum directed by the teacher. These practices, firmly entrenched in administrative systems, and educational policies that are part of the "deep grammar" of schools, result in the separation of school learning from participation in mature practice that is a part of everyday life, and the privileging of a very limited concept of literacy.

Since a school-based, autonomous model of literacy is accepted as "normal", students whose upbringing and experiences vary from that model are often considered to have deficits in school:

> The languages and experiences of children in affluent schools are resources. The languages and experiences of students in poor and working-class schools are problems. Poor and working-class students learn skills that can be used in the marketplace; students from affluent homes learn the skills to use the marketplace to their own ends. (Dudley-Marling & Paugh, 2005, p. 166)

Rogoff (2003) reminds us that "school-like ways of speaking are valued in some communities but not others, and children become skilled in the narrative style of their community" (p. 22). Gee (this volume, 2004) connects this to literacy learning when he notes that our popularly held notions of literacy reflect specialist varieties of language, academic varieties in particular. He posits that school-based literacy practices grant privilege and advantage to children who come to school with prototypes of the academic language they have learned at home, typically students from more affluent homes. Students from disadvantaged homes who have not acquired a prototype of academic language are at a distinct disadvantage when they enter school, not so much because they lack literacy skills, but because they are not familiar with literacy as an instructed process and the academic language structures that are part of this process—language structures that are valued by schools and measured by high-stakes tests.

The consequences of high-stakes tests on literacy learning are exacerbated when rewards and punishments are doled out in response to test scores. Individual students as well as entire schools determined to be low-performing, for example, are often required to use programs that emphasize phonetically based approaches to reading instruction, and packaged literacy programs—like America's Choice.

BRANCHING OUT: A NATION AT RISK

The voices of scientific curriculum development and autonomous models of literacy coalesced in *A Nation at Risk* in 1983 (National Council on Excellence in Education). Authorized by Congress and authored by the National Commission on Excellence in Education on the heels of recession and double-digit inflation of the 1970s, and amid a perceived crisis brought on by an economic boom in Japan, the report placed the blame for a failing economy squarely on the shoulders of schools and came to serve as a policy statement for the Reagan administration (Sacks, 1999). The warning in the report was clear: "Our once unchallenged preeminence in commerce, industry, science, and technological innovation is being overtaken by competitors throughout the world" (National Council Commission on Excellence in Education, 1983. p. 135).

The report directly linked economic competitiveness to educational achievement. Of thirteen "Indicators of Risk" that "amply documented" the "educational dimensions of the risk," eight were directly related to performance on standardized tests. Three other indicators focused on literacy, decrying the number of "functionally illiterate" people and those who needed "such basic skills as reading, writing, spelling, and computation" (p. 154).

A Nation at Risk made the cause of the crisis clear: diluted curriculum content, the proliferation of electives, too little homework, unmotivated students, and incompetent teachers. The report validated a perceived need to re-form schools and curriculum. In this sense, my notion of re-form can be contrasted with reform. Reform implies change with the intent to improve or make better. Re-form, on the other hand, suggests that something is being returned to a previous shape or form. The proponents of *A Nation at Risk* advocated school re-form, returning schools to some perceived era that had focused on *the basics* through rigorous curriculum and consistent discipline. In response to the crisis, the language of business was brought into schools in the form of standards and accountability. In this business model, test scores were the new capital. All that was needed for America to be competitive and free of the impending risk were more rigorous curricula, instructional materials whose quality was determined by "evidence . . . based on results from field trials and credible evaluation," and accountability measured through standardized tests. The report recommended that:

> Standardized tests of achievement . . . should be administered at major transition points from one level of schooling to another. . . . The purpose of these tests would be to (a) certify the student's credentials; (b) identify the need for remedial intervention; and (c) identify the opportunity for advanced or accelerated work. The tests should be administered as a part of a nationwide system of State and local standardized tests. (p. 153)

We still see evidence of the response to *A Nation at Risk* today especially in NCLB legislation. Not only was there greater emphasis on increased standards and accountability, but more educational laws and regulations were enacted in the few years after *A Nation at Risk* than in the previous twenty (Tyack & Cuban, 1995). The authors of *A Nation at Risk* called on a number of "scholarly, scientific, and learned societies" including the National Academy of Sciences for their help. This call has direct ties to both NCLB and America's Choice. The National Research Council, a division of the National Academy of Sciences, published *Preventing Reading Difficulties in Young Children* (Snow, Burns, & Griffin, 1998), which strongly influenced the National Reading Panel report and was the basis for the Reading First Initiative of NCLB.

GRAFTING BRANCHES TO THE TREE: THE BUSINESS
ROUNDTABLE AND McGRAW-HILL

The Business Roundtable, an association of chief executive officers of leading U.S. companies, was established in 1972 in the belief that the business sector should play an active role in the formation of public policies that ensure vigorous economic growth (Business Roundtable, 2006). In 1989 President George H. W. Bush called on the Business Roundtable to commit to improving elementary and secondary schools. The Roundtable responded with calls for high standards and increased accountability. Through its publication *Using the No Child Left Behind Act to Improve Schools in Your State: A Tool Kit for Business Leaders*, the Business Roundtable encourages members to "testify," "lobby," and "leverage" for implementation of NCLB.

Business Roundtable member, and current chairperson, Harold McGraw III, CEO of McGraw-Hill Publishing, could not only help with the Roundtable's goals, but could profit from them as well. His company's education division produces the Comprehensive Test of Basic Skills and other standardized tests, extensive test preparation materials, and Open Court, a component of America's Choice. In April 2004 Harold McGraw III, a long-time Bush family friend and member of George W. Bush's transition team, reported that the company's reading and test markets were responsible for the company's recent improved performance. He attributed the improvement directly to the No Child Left Behind Act (Edelsky & Bomer, 2005). To tighten their hold on America's schools even more, McGraw-Hill is currently offering school evaluation, analysis, and strategizing through its business and finance division, Standard and Poor's. The Business Roundtable would become connected to the National Center for Education and the Economy when America's Choice adopted Open Court as part of its program.

THE BRANCHES EXTEND: THE NATIONAL
CENTER FOR EDUCATION AND THE ECONOMY

Building upon the rhetoric of *A Nation at Risk* to warn that America's workers were unprepared for future economic demands, Marc Tucker, president of the National Center for Education and the Economy (NCEE), authored *America's Choice: High*

Skills or Low Wages! in 1990. The report discussed American students' poor performance on standardized tests in comparison to European and East Asian students, and recommended an internationally benchmarked educational standard. The National Center on Education and the Economy is a non-profit launched in 1989 to develop instructional systems and standards to prepare students to compete in a world economy. The New Standards Performance Standards, published by the NCEE, provided integrated standards they claim are benchmarked against countries with the highest performance standards in the world. These performance standards served as the catalyst for America's Choice School Design, which became America's Choice, Inc., a for-profit subsidiary of NCEE.

GOING OUT ON A LIMB: THE SHAKY SCIENCE OF THE NATIONAL RESEARCH COUNCIL AND THE NATIONAL READING PANEL

Perhaps heeding the call for help from *A Nation at Risk*, the National Research Council, a division of The National Academy of Sciences, presented *Preventing Reading Difficulties in Young Children* (Snow, Burns, & Griffin, 1998), a review of reading research and recommendations for instructional strategies. The report claimed a strong correlation between phonemic awareness and explicit instruction in phonics, and later success in learning to read (Gee, 1999). Ironically, Gerald Coles (2000) reports that much of the support for an emphasis on phonemic awareness and explicit instruction in phonics was based on one study, authored by two members of the National Academy of Sciences committee, one of whom was a coauthor of Open Court, the phonics program published by McGraw-Hill and adopted by America's Choice.

In 1997 the National Reading Panel was convened by the National Institute of Child Health and Human Development, and charged by Congress with recommending scientific studies that were worthy of consideration in the design of reading instruction. The panel conducted a meta-analysis of scientific studies of reading and used the National Research Council's Report, *Preventing Reading Difficulties in Young Children* (Snow, Burns, & Griffin, 1998) as their primary reference. The National Reading Panel report, *Teaching Children to Read: An Evidence Based Assessment of the Scientific Research Literature and its Implications for Reading Instruction* (2000), limited studies it would consider to those with evidence-based methodological standards similar to efficacy reports for medical interventions. In addition, the panel considered studies in which "reading" was defined as "reading real words in isolation or in context, reading pseudo words that can be pronounced but have no meaning, reading text aloud or silently, and comprehending text that is read silently or orally" (p. 5), a definition clearly rooted in an autonomous model of literacy.

The National Reading Panel report was issued in two different print versions, a thirty-three-page summary and a nearly four hundred page full report. There are significant differences between the summary that was distributed to thousands of teachers and administrators, and the full report. The summary, for example, states that, "systematic phonics instruction produces significant benefits for students in kindergarten through 6th grade and for children having difficulty learning to read" (NRP, 2000a, p. 9). The full report, however, states:

> Because most of the comparisons above 1st grade involved poor readers (78%), the conclusions drawn about the effects of phonics instruction on specific reading outcomes pertain mainly to them. Findings indicate that phonics instruction helps poor readers in 2nd through 6th improve their word reading skills. However, phonics instruction appears to contribute only weakly, if at all, in helping poor readers apply these skills to read text and spell words. There were insufficient data to draw conclusions about the effects of phonics instruction with normally developing readers above first grade. (NRP, 2000b, p. 2–116)

Like the National Academy of Sciences report, the summary version of the National Reading Panel report asserted that teaching children to manipulate phonemes and systematic phonics instruction significantly improves reading. The summary report, not the full report, is the basis for current legislation and mandates found in NCLB and Reading First initiatives (Garan, 2004).

FERTILIZING THE TREE: NO CHILD LEFT BEHIND AND THE READING FIRST INITIATIVE BOOST THE GROWTH OF PACKAGED LITERACY PROGRAMS

The *No Child Left Behind Act of 2001* (NCLB) requires all states to identify academic standards for core subject areas at each grade level, create assessment systems to monitor student progress toward identified standards, and develop systems of accountability that include rewards and sanctions to schools in relation to their performance toward Adequate Yearly Progress. While NCLB has established unprecedented federal control over curriculum and instruction in all areas, due to the Reading First Initiative of the legislation, there are extraordinary consequences for reading instruction, particularly for students and teachers in urban schools, that I discuss later in the chapter (see also Gatto, this volume).

Based on findings the National Reading Panel reported in their summary, NCLB prescribes reading assessment, instruction, and curriculum that provides "explicit and systematic" instruction in essential components of reading defined as: phonemic awareness, phonics, vocabulary development, reading fluency, and reading comprehension strategies. The Reading First Initiative of NCLB is intended:

> To provide assistance to State educational agencies and local educational agencies in establishing reading programs for students in kindergarten through grade 3 that are based on scientifically based reading research, to ensure that every student can read at grade level or above not later than the end of grade level. (Part B, Subpart 1, Sec. 1201)

Reading First funding is targeted at K-3 students reading below grade level and districts and schools with large numbers of low-income students. Reading First funding for 2004 was $1.1 billion (USDOE, 2004), making a substantial amount of money available to publishers of commercial literacy materials, standardized tests, and test preparation materials. In 2002, the National Council for Teachers of English (NCTE) passed a resolution in response to the Reading First Initiative. In part it declared:

> This initiative is the culmination of a recent trend, as the federal government has increasingly attempted to define what reading is, what counts as research in reading, and to dictate how reading should be taught in our classrooms. As a consequence, the government is channeling educational funding to a few corporate purveyors of a limited set of methods for teaching reading. (as cited in Smith, 2003, p. 48)

The most lucrative portion of the market is the primarily urban schools that rely on Title I funds, or which have been sanctioned under NCLB. Altwerger et al. (2004) point out that:

> Commercial reading programs . . . which utilize systematic, explicit teaching of phonics and skills as the dominant approach to early reading instruction are ever more frequently being mandated for use by entire school systems. This is due in part to the widely acknowledged fact that system-wide adoption of these programs greatly facilitates approval of NCLB grant funding. Poorer urban school systems that must rely on federal support for their program are particularly vulnerable to pressure to adopt these one-size-fits-all programs in order to ensure continuing funding. (p. 120)

America's Choice, with its use of Open Court phonics, is an example of a commercial program that fits the Reading First description of scientific research-based reading programs. The United States Department of Education must agree. It suggests America's Choice as a program to help schools meet the requirements of NCLB. In fact, there are 70 references to America's Choice on the Department of Education's website (http://www.ed.gov/index.jhtml, USDOE, 2006), including an article in the DOE newsletter, *Innovators*, and an entire PowerPoint presentation created by America's Choice, Inc. promoting their program.

CONSEQUENCES FOR URBAN SCHOOLS

The pairing of high-stakes accountability through standardized testing and mandated curriculum is problematic, especially for urban schools. For Foucault (1975), testing and measurement were directly related to power. He believed that the "examination" marked the beginning of pedagogy that functioned as science. "The examination introduced a whole mechanism that linked to a certain type of the formation of knowledge a certain form of the exercise of power" (p. 199). Examination, therefore, was directly linked to power, a power that has become such a taken-for-granted part of education, that it often goes unquestioned. When a practice like testing becomes pervasive and has no competing alternative it tends to become invisible and creates hegemony (Eisner, 1992).

Tests, by and large, especially high-stakes standardized tests, privilege certain types of knowledge and value certain ways of thinking and knowing. Since these tests measure performance derived from traditional, scientific models of curriculum, and dole out rewards and punishments based on performance, they serve to further legitimate a scientific approach to curriculum and instruction and further tighten the hegemonic grip of traditional models of curriculum and instruction.

Like Foucault's (1975) conception of the "examination," high-stakes standardized tests provide "a normalizing gaze, a surveillance that makes it possible to qualify, to classify and to punish" (p. 197). Through NCLB, greater levels of surveillance evidenced by ever-increasing levels of accountability, and more stringent insistence on normalization reflected in increasingly standardized curriculum and instruction, however, are applied to some groups while others are exempted. Students who do well on standardized tests, typically middle-class and affluent students, are free to benefit from more child-centered approaches to curriculum and instruction; while students who do not do well, typically minority students and those from lower economic classes, are relegated to "scientific, researched-based" instruction and fragmented curriculum with routine examination for accountability and continued access to federal funding.

If high-stakes standardized tests provide "a normalizing gaze" to surveil, classify, and punish, then mandated and standardized curriculum provides the normalizing voice that accompanies and directs this gaze. The invisible power of this normalizing voice is codified in curriculum and programs like America's Choice, and further reified in a seemingly endless series of textbooks, computer programs, test preparation supplies, and instructional materials that accompany them. Like the normalizing gaze of the examination, the disciplinary power of curriculum is exercised through its invisibility; invisibility achieved through a focus on sameness, and supposed neutrality, which legitimates and may even disguise the exercise of power (see Gutiérrez, this volume).

Notions of power are also found in the language of accountability, and standardized curriculum and instruction. To begin with, the fact that America's Choice is marketed at "low-performing" and "disadvantaged" schools and students is problematic. Beatrice Fennimore (2000) discusses the tendency to attach deficit-based language like "disadvantaged" and "low-performing" to children from economically, racially, culturally, and linguistically diverse backgrounds. She argues that these negative descriptions often result in "parallel tracking or grouping designations that limit access to opportunities" (p. 8). Mandated use of skills-based literacy programs evidence this parallel tracking. In addition, Fennimore recognizes that when generalizations about groups are made with terms like "disadvantaged" and "low-performing," individuals are subsumed into the group, and negative characteristics are attached to individuals.

Harris (1996) reminds us that in the period from Reconstruction until World War II, decisions about selection of curriculum materials were out of the hands of most African Americans. Federally and state mandated curricula and instructional programs reintroduce and perpetuate this phenomenon when their selection is tied to Title I funds and school improvement plans through NCLB. McNeil (2000) argues that:

> The narrowing of curriculum in test-prep schools is creating a new kind of discrimination—one based not on a blatant stratification of access to knowledge through tracking, but one that uses the appearance of sameness to mask persistent inequalities. (p. 279)

McNeil further finds that the incremental dominance of the technical language of accountability silences alternative voices and justifies the normalizing voice of curriculum.

Although America's Choice highlights a workshop approach to reading and writing, this seems strikingly incongruous with the rest of the program. A workshop approach to literacy instruction (Atwell, 1998; Calkins, 1994) uses students' own interests and daily work to guide instruction, not a prepackaged, scripted curriculum. Readers' and writers' workshops are inherently active and interactive. This approach recognizes and celebrates the social nature of reading and writing, and encourages praxis (Freire, 1989), purposeful reflection, and action, by both students and teachers, rather than transmission and acquisition of isolated skills. By adopting a workshop approach, teachers explicitly recognize that reading and writing are not neutral, nor is the way in which they are taught. In discussing her writers' workshop Atwell says, "I nudge students to explore social, political and ethical issues that encircle personal experience" (1998, p. 78).

When urban schools "choose" America's Choice because it will facilitate Reading First grant money, or because they are deemed "low-performing," it presents these schools with a forced choice. The choice dictates a certain kind of instruction that is supposed to be good for "disadvantaged" students and "low-performing" schools. From the perspective of scientific curriculum and autonomous literacy, poor reading results for urban schools aren't related to poverty or culturally irrelevant curriculum; improving reading is just a matter of breaking skills down to more discrete units, and making instruction more systematic and explicit.

Literacy is a much more complex social practice than mandated instructional programs and assessments can address. Rather than recognizing this, adoption of programs like America's Choice perpetuates notions of literacy as autonomous and curriculum materials as neutral. The consequence is continued skills-based instruction, the need for which is reinforced by results on standardized tests. When programs based on an autonomous model of literacy are mandated for some schools and students based on economic factors and wholesale group identifications like "disadvantaged" and "low-performing," there is an inherently unequal distribution of resources. This unequal distribution will not necessarily be measured in dollar amounts spent, but in long-term consequences for students and teachers that we are just beginning to see. Exploration of America's Choice and similar mandated packaged literacy programs helps us understand the power relationships inherent in their origins and implementation. We can see that when planted too close to schools, the branches and trunk of the tree can block the light, and the deep and tangled roots can cause problems with the school's very foundation.

REFERENCES

Altwerger, B., Poonan, A., Lijun, J., Jordan, N., Laster, B., Martens, P., Wilson, G., & Wiltz, N. (2004). When research and mandates collide: The challenges and dilemmas of teacher education in the era of NCLB. *English Education*, 36(2), pp. 119–133.

Apple, M. (1986). *Teachers and texts*. New York: Routledge & Kegan Paul.

Atwell, N. (1998). *In the middle: New understandings about writing, reading and learning*. Portsmouth, NH: Heinemann.

Barton, D. & Hamilton, M. (1998). *Local literacies: Reading and writing in one community*. London and New York: Routledge.

Bobbit, F. (1918). Scientific curriculum making. In D. Flinders & S. Thornton (Eds.) (2004). *The curriculum studies reader* (Second Ed.) (pp. 9–16). New York: RoutledgeFalmer.

Business Roundtable. "About Business Roundtable." Retrieved August 19, 2006 from http://www.businessroundtable.org//aboutUs.history.aspx

Calkins, L. (1994). *The art of teaching reading*. Portsmouth, NH: Heinemann.

Cazden, C. (1988). *Classroom discourse: The language of teaching and learning*. Portsmouth, NH: Heinemann.

Cole, M. & Engeström, Y. (1993). A cultural-historical approach to distributed cognition. In G. Salmon (Ed.), *Distributed cognition: Psychological and educational considerations* (pp. 1–46). New York: Cambridge University Press.

Coles, G. (2000). *Misreading reading: The bad science that hurts children*. Portsmouth, NH: Heinemann.

deCastell, S. & Luke, A. (1983). Defining literacy in North American schools: Social and historical conditions and consequences. *Journal of Curriculum Studies*, 15, pp. 373–389.

Dudley-Marling, C. & Paugh, P. (2005). The rich get richer; the poor get direct instruction. In B. Altwerger (Ed.), *Reading for profit: How the bottom line leaves kids behind* (pp. 156–171). Portsmouth, NH: Heinemann.

Edelsky, C. & Bomer, R. (2005). Heads they win; tails we lose. In B. Altwerger (Ed.), *Reading for profit: How the bottom line leaves kids behind* (pp. 11–20). Portsmouth, NH: Heinemann.

Eisner, E. (1992). Curriculum ideologies. In P. Jackson (Ed.), *Handbook of research on curriculum*, pp. 302–326. New York: MacMillan.

Fennimore, B. (2000). *Talk matters: Refocusing the language of public schooling*. New York: Teachers College Press.

Foucault, M. (1975). The means of correct training. In P. Rabinow (Ed.), *The Foucault reader* (pp. 188–205). New York: Pantheon.

Freire, P. (1989). *Pedagogy of the Oppressed*. New York: Continuum.

Garan, E. (2004). *In defense of our children: When politics, profit, and education collide*. Portsmouth, NH: Heinemann.

Gee, J. (1999). Critical issues: Reading and the new literacy studies: Reframing the National Academy of Sciences Report on Reading. *Journal of Literacy Research*, 31(3), pp. 355–374.

Gee, J.P. (2001a). Reading as situated language: A sociocognitive perspective. *Journal of Adolescent and Adult Literacy*, 44(8), 714–725.

Gee, J.P. (2001b). Reading, language abilities, and semiotic resources. In J. Larson (Ed.), *Literacy as snake oil: Beyond the quick fix* (pp. 7–26). New York: Peter Lang.

Gee, J.P. (2004). *Situated language and learning: A critique of traditional schooling*. New York: Routledge.

Goodman, Y. & Goodman, K. (1990). Vygotsky in a whole-language perspective. In L. Moll (Ed.), *Vygotsky and education: Instructional implications and applications of sociohistorical psychology* (pp. 223–250). Cambridge, UK: Cambridge University Press.

Graves, D. (1983). *Writing: Teachers and Children at Work*. Portsmouth, NH: Heinemann.

Gutierrez, K. (1993). How talk, context, and script shape contexts for learning: A cross-case comparison of journal sharing. *Linguistics and Education*, 5, pp. 335–365.

Harris, V.J. (1996). Historic readers for African-American children (1868–1944): Uncovering and reclaiming a tradition of opposition. In M. Shujaa (Ed.), *Too much schooling, too little education: A paradox of Black life in White societies* (pp. 143–175). Trenton, NJ: Africa World Press.

Irvine, P. & Larson, J. (2001). Literacy packages in practice: Constructing academic disadvantage. In J. Larson (Ed.), *Literacy as snake oil: Beyond the quick fix* (pp. 45–70). New York: Peter Lang.

Lankshear, C. & Knobel, M. (2003). *New literacies: Changing knowledge and classroom learning*. Philadelphia: Open University Press.

Larson, J. & Gatto, L. (2004). Tactical underlife: Understanding students' perceptions. *Journal of Early Childhood Literacy*, 4(1), pp. 11–39.

Larson, J. & Marsh, J. (2005). *Making literacy real: Theories and practices for learning and teaching*. London: Sage Publications.

Lave, J. & Wenger, E. (1991). *Situated learning: Legitimate peripheral participation*. Cambridge: Cambridge University Press.

McNeil, L. (2000). *Contradictions of School Reform: Educational Costs of Standardized Testing*. New York: Routledge/Falmer.

Mehan, H. (1979). *Learning lessons*. Cambridge, MA: Harvard University Press.

National Center on Education and the Economy (1990). *America's choice: High skills or low wages!* Executive Summary. In *Jossey-Bass reader on school reform* (2002). San Francisco, CA: Jossey-Bass.

National Center on Education and the Economy (2002). *America's choice school design: A research-based model* [Brochure]. Washington, DC.

National Center on Education and the Economy (2004). *Great solutions for top student performance*. [Brochure]. Washington, DC.

National Center on Education and the Economy (2006). *Ramp-up literacy: A comprehensive system that accelerates reading and writing performance* [Brochure]. Washington, DC.

National Center on Education and the Economy. *Aligned instructional systems.* Retrieved March 16, 2006 from http://www.ncee.org/acsd/program/elementary/curriculum.jsp

National Commission on Excellence in Education (1983). *A nation at risk: The imperative for excellence in education.* In *Jossey-Bass reader on school reform* (2002). San Francisco, CA: Jossey-Bass.

National Reading Panel (2000a). *Teaching children to read: An evidence based assessment of the scientific research literature and its implications for reading instruction.* Washington, DC: National Institute of Child Health and Human Development.

National Reading Panel (2000b). *Report of the National Reading Panel: Teaching children to read: An evidence based assessment of the scientific research literature and its implications for reading instruction.* Washington, DC: National Institute of Child Health and Human Development.

Nystrand, M., Gamoran, A., Kachur, R., & Pendergrast, C. (1997). *Opening dialogue: Understanding the dynamics of language and learning in English classrooms.* New York: Teachers College Press.

Open Court Reading, (1995). *Collections for young scholars.* Peru, IL: SPA/McGraw-Hill.

Pinar, W., Reynolds, W., Slattery, P., & Taubman, P. (2004). *Understanding Curriculum.* New York: Peter Lang.

Rogoff, B. (1994). Developing understanding of the idea of communities of learners. *Mind, Culture and Activity,* 1(4), pp. 209–227.

Rogoff, B. (2003). *The cultural nature of human development.* Oxford: Oxford University Press.

Sacks, P. (1999). *Standardized minds: The high price of America's testing culture and what we can do to change it.* Cambridge, MA: Perseus Publishing.

Shannon, P. (1987). Commercial reading materials, a technological ideology, and the deskilling of teachers. *The Elementary School Journal,* 87, pp. 307–329.

Sheruich, J. & McKenzie, K. (2005). Foucault's methodologies: Archaeology and genealogy. In N. Denzin & Y. Lincoln (Eds.), *The Sage handbook of qualitative research* (pp. 841–868). Thousand Oaks, CA: Sage.

Smith, F. (2003). *Unspeakable acts, unnatural practices: Flaws in "scientific" reading instruction.* Portsmouth, NH: Heinemann.

Snow, C.E., Burns, M.S., & Griffin P. (Eds.) (1998). *Preventing reading difficulties in young children.* Washington, DC: National Academy Press.

Street, B. (1995). *Social literacies: Critical approaches to literacy in development, ethnography, and education.* New York: Longman.

Taylor, F. (1911). *The principles of scientific management.* New York: Harper.

Thorndike, E. (1922). Measurement in education. In *The twenty-first yearbook of National Society for the Study of Education.* Bloomington, IL: Public School Publishing.

Trotter, A. (2004) America's Choice taps profit motive. *Education Week,* 24(12), pp. 1, 13.

Tyack, D. & Cuban, L. (1995). *Tinkering toward utopia: A century of public school reform.* Cambridge, MA: Harvard University Press.

United States Department of Education (2004). *A guide to education and no child left behind* [Brochure]. Washington, DC.

United States Department of Education. Search results for: "America's Choice", retrieved August 28, 2006 from: http://www.ed.gov/index.jhtml

Contributors

Nancy Ares is Assistant Professor at the University of Rochester's Warner Graduate School of Education and Human Development. Ares conducts research using sociocultural, situated social practice, and critical theories as the framework for investigating classroom processes and practices. This research focuses on structures within the classroom that shape participation, how structures and activity are mutually constituted, and how power and roles are negotiated through social interaction. Her most recent research project, WideNet, explores mathematics as social and spatial practice. A second line of work examines local translations of historical discourses of race into schooling and teaching practices, in light of the influence of cultural geographical arrangements of people based on race and class. She recently published a co-authored book, The Geographies of Difference: The Production of the West Side, East Side and Central City School, with Edward Buendía.

Edward Buendía is an Associate Professor in the Department of Education, Culture, and Society at the University of Utah. He has taught in racially, ethnically, and linguistically diverse K-12 schools. His research interests are the production of school knowledge and practice as well as curriculum studies. He has co-authored a book with Nancy Ares entitled *The Geographies of Difference: The Production of the West Side, East Side and Central City School.*

Gerald Coles lives in Ithaca, New York, and writes on literacy and learning. He has published several books and numerous articles in education, psychology, and neuropsychology journals. His most recent book is *Reading the Naked Truth: Literacy, Legislation, and Lies.* He is currently finishing a book on how brain research informs the debate over reading. He has taught in the Department of Psychiatry at Robert Wood Johnson Medical School and the Warner Graduate School of Education and Human Development at the University of Rochester. As a political activist, he is on the steering committee of the Tompkins County Workers Center and is chair of the Social Action Committee of Congregation Tikkun v'Or/Ithaca Reform Temple.

Lynn Astarita Gatto, an urban educator for over thirty years, has taught all grades at the elementary level, as well as special education. Her classroom has been a demonstration site for hundreds of teachers, and she currently serves as a district mentor teacher. She is a recipient of the Presidential Award for Excellence in Mathematics and Science Teaching, the 2004 New York State Teacher of the Year, and a 2006 Disney Teacher award winner. She is the subject of a documentary film, *A Life Outside* (2006). Ms. Gatto is a doctoral candidate at the University of Rochester's Warner Graduate School of Education and Human Development.

James Paul Gee received his Ph.D. in linguistics from Stanford University. In 1998, he became the Tashia Morgridge Professor of Reading in the Department of Curriculum and Instruction at the University of Wisconsin at Madison, the first endowed chair in reading in the United States. His books include *Sociolinguistics and Literacies* (1990/1996); *The Social Mind* (1992); *Introduction to Human Language* (1993); *The New Work Order: Behind the Language of the New Capitalism* (1996, with Glynda Hull and Colin Lankshear); and *An Introduction to Discourse Analysis: Theory and Method* (1999). Recent books include *What Video Games Have to Teach Us about Learning and Literacy* (2003) and *Situated Language and Learning: A Critique of Traditional Schooling* (2004).

Kris D. Gutiérrez is Professor of Education at UCLA's Graduate School of Education and Information Studies. Her research focuses on language, culture and learning, and the sociohistorical traditions in which language and literacy practices are embedded.

Patricia D. Irvine, Associate Professor at San Francisco State University, has researched literacy in Native American communities and the Eastern Caribbean. Her research focuses on understanding the impact of sociohistorical context on language learning among language minority students. She has published in the *Harvard Educational Review, Language Arts,* and *Journal of Education.*

Joanne Larson is the Michael W. Scandling Professor of Education and Chair of the Teaching and Curriculum program at the University of Rochester's Warner Graduate School of Education and Human Development. Her ethnographic research examines how language and literacy practices mediate social and power relations in literacy events. Her recent book, *Making Literacy Real: Theories and Practices in Learning and Teaching* (2005) co-authored with Jackie Marsh, explores the breadth of the complex field of literacy studies, orientating literacy as a social practice grounded in social, cultural, historical, and political contexts. She is co-editor of the *Handbook of Early Childhood Literacy* (Sage, 2003), which provides an overview of contemporary research into early childhood literacy. Larson has recently branched out from traditional publication venues to collaboratively produce a documentary with filmmaker David Smith. This film, *A Life Outside*, documents the teaching life of Lynn Astarita Gatto.

Adam Lefstein is an Academic Fellow in Pedagogy and Classroom Interaction at Oxford University Department of Educational Studies. His research interests include classroom interaction and the problem of change, dialogue in schools, teacher enactment of curricular materials, reading comprehension, grammar teaching, and media coverage of literacy education. Recent publications include: "Literacy makeover: educational research and the public interest on prime time" (*Teachers College Record*), and "Thinking about the technical and the personal in teaching" (*Cambridge Journal of Education*).

Dan Osborn collaboratively teaches in a multiage class at the elementary level. He has also taught special education at all levels, and has been a K-12 inclusion facilitator, and special education consultant. Dan is an adjunct instructor and doctoral candidate at the University of Rochester's Warner Graduate School of Education and Human Development.

Kate Pahl's research interests focus on the New Literacy Studies and ways in which that theoretical framework can be applied in home, school and community settings. Publications include *Literacy and Education: The New Literacy Studies in the Classroom* (2005) with Jennifer Rowsell, and an edited book, *Travel Notes from the New Literacy Studies* (2006), also with Jennifer Rowsell. She is currently involved in a research project funded by Creative Partnerships on the work of visual artists in schools and museums, as well as an AHRC-funded project on narratives of migration and artifacts in the homes of the Pakistani community in Rotherham, South Yorkshire. She is a Lecturer in Education at the University of Sheffield.

Patrick Shannon is a Professor of Education at Penn State University. His most recent books are *text, lies & videotape* (1995), *Reading Poverty* (1998), *You'd Better Shop Around: Selling Literacy* (2000) and *Becoming Political Too* (2000). Currently, he is studying adolescents' understanding of history and social movements.

Brian Street is Professor of Language in Education at King's College, London University and Visiting Professor of Education in both the Graduate School of Education, University of Pennsylvania and in the School of Education and Professional Development, University of East Anglia. Professor Street undertook anthropological fieldwork on literacy in Iran during the 1970s and taught social and cultural anthropology for over twenty years at the University of Sussex before taking up the Chair of Language in Education at King's College London. He has written and lectured extensively on literacy practices from both a theoretical and an applied perspective. He has a longstanding commitment to linking ethnographic-style research on the cultural dimension of language and literacy with contemporary practice in education and in development, and has recently extended this to research on social dimensions of numeracy practices. He has been involved in Technical Support teams, lecture tours, workshops, training programmes, and research on these areas in a number of countries—the United States, South Africa, Nepal, India, etc. His publications include: *Literacy: A resource Handbook* (forthcoming); *Navigating Numeracies: Home/School Numeracy Practices* (2006); *Literacies across Educational Contexts: Mediating Learning and Teaching* (2005); *Literacy and Development: Ethnographic Perspectives* (2001); *Student Writing in the University: Cultural and Epistemological Issues* (2000); *Social Literacies* (1995); *Cross-Cultural Approaches to Literacy* (1993); and *Literacy in Theory and Practice* (1985).

Index

Colin Lankshear, Michele Knobel,
Chris Bigum, & Michael Peters
*General Editor*s

New literacies and new knowledges are being invented "in the streets" as people from all walks of life wrestle with new technologies, shifting values, changing institutions, and new structures of personality and temperament emerging in a global informational age. These new literacies and ways of knowing remain absent from classrooms. Many education administrators, teachers, teacher educators, and academics seem largely unaware of them. Others actively oppose them. Yet, they increasingly shape the engagements and worlds of young people in societies like our own. The *New Literacies and Digital Epistemologies* series will explore this terrain with a view to informing educational theory and practice in constructively critical ways.

For further information about the series and submitting manuscripts, please contact:

> Michele Knobel & Colin Lankshear
> Montclair State University
> Dept. of Education and Human Services
> 3173 University Hall
> Montclair, NJ 07043
> michele@coatepec.net

To order other books in this series, please contact our Customer Service Department at:

> (800) 770-LANG (within the U.S.)
> (212) 647-7706 (outside the U.S.)
> (212) 647-7707 FAX

Or browse online by series at:

> www.peterlang.com